AWAITING THE SUN

WWII Veterans Remember the ALEUTIANS

Bil Paul

SCHIFFER MILITARY

4880 Lower Valley Road   Atglen, PA 19310

Designed by Christopher Bower
Cover design by Brenda McCallum
Type set in Proxima Nova/Minion Pro

ISBN: 978-0-7643-6518-8
Printed in India

Published by Schiffer Publishing, Ltd.
4880 Lower Valley Road
Atglen, PA 19310
Phone: (610) 593-1777; Fax: (610) 593-2002
Email: Info@schifferbooks.com
Web: www.schifferbooks.com

For our complete selection of fine books on this and related subjects, please visit our website at www.schifferbooks.com. You may also write for a free catalog.

Schiffer Publishing's titles are available at special discounts for bulk purchases for sales promotions or premiums. Special editions, including personalized covers, corporate imprints, and excerpts, can be created in large quantities for special needs. For more information, contact the publisher.

We are always looking for people to write books on new and related subjects. If you have an idea for a book, please contact us at proposals@schifferbooks.com.

Dedication

This book is dedicated to my father, Harry B. Paul Jr., a navy officer who served on Adak during the war, and to my mother, Roberta Paul, who raised my brother and me while he was away.

Epigraph

Keep in mind, this was the first time I had ever been away from home more than overnight … But somehow I got through it.
—Don Brydon, Army Air Force on Shemya

Contents

Introduction:
An Aleutian Odyssey

At one point while researching this book, I was reading and taking notes from a dog-eared paperback titled *The Capture of Attu, As Told by the Men Who Fought There*. Published while the war with Japan was still in progress, the pages were very thin, turning yellow, with brown and flaking edges. Some pages were falling out of the binding. I handled it with kid gloves because it was a rich source of battle experiences. It was also musty, and my system reacted quickly to the spores the pages released—I began sneezing and my eyes watered.

I found this interesting, because there's the distinct possibility that I was breathing some spores that had lain dormant in the book since the 1940s. It's as though these spores had been waiting all these years to reestablish themselves in a new host.

It's a stretch, but in the same way, the voices of some of the thousands of Aleutian war veterans wanted to tell "how it was," seventy-five years later. I decided to be their conduit.

Even though almost all of these Aleutian vets have passed on, I heard many of their voices via written memoirs, and audio and video interviews conducted by interviewers ranging from high school students to professional historians. I appreciate their efforts.

Stories I heard from my Aleutian-vet father, Harry Paul Jr., planted the seed that started this project, although I didn't get started on the book until after his death. He was a rural letter carrier and former national guardsman with two children when he was either drafted or enlisted in 1943, trained as a communications officer by the navy and sent to the island of Adak. Some of his memorabilia and excerpts from his letters appear here.

Several years ago, I connected with veteran James Doyle, who'd worked in the same unit as my dad (intercepting Japanese Morse code), and wrote a magazine article about him. That got the ball rolling for a book-length project.

As I began this project, I had a clear vision of what I wanted: not a history-heavy book with tons of footnotes and references, but a simple book of stories and anecdotes about men (and, yes, even teenagers) sent to the Aleutians who were expected to keep the Japanese at bay. A book with stories and anecdotes about often-primitive living conditions and the ins and outs of military life.

I decided to organize the book not in a chronological fashion and by location, but rather by subject matter. For some readers, some of the details may seem mundane, but for others—especially the families of vets who served there—glimpsing the reality of being stationed there in the 1940s may be fascinating. Some of the details are unique to World War II and to the Aleutians, while others speak to soldiers' and sailors' lives universally—whichever war one looks at.

This book draws from approximately 290 sources—many only available following the creation of the internet. I decided to use the men's own voices as much as possible, and strove to make their stories as comprehensible as possible. I decided, in most cases, to not correct men's grammar or spelling or add the traditional "sic" to indicate that a grammatical error was not mine. There would have been too many "sics."

Where quotes are attributed to men's names only, assume that I drew the quotes from online interviews.

Thanks to writer Pete Fineo of Anchorage, who pointed me in the direction of the National Archives in Seattle. Thanks also to Paul Carrigan, Charles Fitzpatrick, and Eliot Asinof (all who have passed on) for their well-written and extensive Aleutian memoirs which contributed heavily to this project. Rachel Mason and Barbara James at the National Park Service in Alaska provided many excellent photos from their archive. I also appreciate access to the Brian Garfield (author of *The Thousand-Mile War*) archive at the University of Oregon library in Eugene.

All of the excellent cartoons in this book are from *The Adakian* military newsletter on Adak, and I'm thankful my father saved so many of them.

Finally, a hearty thanks to my biking and kayaking partner Jeff Brook, who politely listened as I relentlessly told him story after story from my evolving manuscript. He and his wife Libby (both teachers) also proofread the book.

I hope you enjoy the read.

Bil Paul
Dixon, California

Note: I have tried to be accurate, but there are bound to be errors in this book. I would like to correct them in later editions. Contact me at naturalbornwriter@hotmail.com.

Chapter 1
Why the Aleutians?

If the Japanese established air bases on the easternmost Aleutian Islands or on mainland Alaska, they would be within bomber striking distance of Seattle.

As war with Japan approached in 1940, Alaska was a backwater place with a small American military presence. The then-territory's population was a mere 72,000. Military planners had seen the need for a buildup, but not much was done until after the devastating Japanese attack on Pearl Harbor in the Hawaiian Islands on December 7, 1941.

Six months later, when a Japanese naval task force's planes bombed the American base at Dutch Harbor in Alaska's Aleutian Islands and then invaded and occupied two of the outermost islands (Attu and Kiska), the island chain assumed a more important part in the Pacific war. They had to be better defended, and the Japanese had to be ousted. Slowly at first, and then at an accelerated pace, more and more men, materiel, and weapons of war were shipped north to the Aleutians. Bases and airfields were added at a frenetic pace.

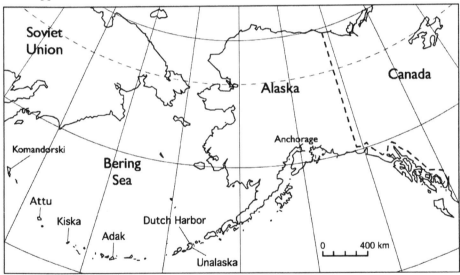

The Aleutian chain of volcanically formed islands, stretching over 1,000 miles, includes some of the most remote areas of the United States. The larger islands are labeled. During World War II, the furthest-out American island, Attu, was only 800 miles from the northernmost Japanese islands. The Komandorski Islands belong to Russia. South of the chain lies the Pacific Ocean. *Wikimedia Commons*

The strategic location of the fourteen large and fifty-five small Aleutian Islands isn't immediately apparent, but if you own a globe and use a measuring tape to measure the shortest routes between two points on the globe, you're in for a surprise. It turns out that the shortest flying and nautical routes between Tokyo, Japan, and Seattle (or San Francisco) pass very near the Aleutian Islands.

This meant that if the Japanese established air bases on the easternmost Aleutian Islands or on mainland Alaska, they would be within bomber striking distance of Seattle. Also, if the Japanese enjoyed naval supremacy in Alaskan waters, that would constitute a grave threat. These possibilities, along with the Japanese occupation of Attu and Kiska, explains the huge American military buildup in the Aleutians. The war changed everything in Alaska, so much so that the population nearly doubled between 1940 and 1950.

Sending young soldiers and sailors—many just out of high school or in their early twenties (who often still lived at home and hadn't traveled much)—to the islands was a demanding transition. For many, it was like being sent to purgatory. The country asked a lot of them.

War can bring out the best or worst in men, and oftentimes men remember most vividly the times in their lives when life was the most difficult—when they were stretched to their limits—as often happened in the Aleutians.

And many never returned home.

Chapter 2
The Japanese Draw First Blood at Dutch Harbor

We was waiting for them to come.

Six months after the infamous Pearl Harbor attack, Japan was on the move again in the northern Pacific. Japanese strategists decided to draw much of what was left of America's Pacific fleet into a grand naval battle which they expected to win decisively, giving them even more control over the Pacific region. What they didn't know was that after Pearl Harbor, an American intelligence group in Hawaii had broken Japan's most secretive naval messaging code. As a result, the American navy learned the outlines of the Japanese plan and thwarted it decisively at the Battle of Midway, which began on June 4, 1942. They also learned that a small portion of the Japanese fleet would attack and possibly occupy an Aleutian island or islands at about the same time.

Some military men thought the target would be the only large American base in the Aleutian Islands at that time: Dutch Harbor, on Amaknak Island near the town of Unalaska. The American army and navy prepared for an attack there, and even the possibility of an invasion, without knowing its timing.

The small contingent of military personnel there were saddled with old weaponry and limited ammunition and training. They were half-prepared to die should the Japanese invade.

Army soldier Ramon Rivas helped get ready for a Japanese attack. "We had tunnels underneath [the ground]," he related. "Everything was camouflaged. We sleep under the ground and live there and we had to walk about a mile down to the base to eat. They [had] sent thirty-five of us … to the other end of [Amaknak Island] with nothing but our rifles and two .30-caliber machine guns—and that was it—to hold [that] end of the island."

GIs described digging and building covered dugouts for gun emplacements around Dutch Harbor, using whatever materials they could scrounge. As with Rivas, many lived there underground, where a big problem was rats.

Lowell Thorsness, a civilian twenty-four-year-old Caterpillar driver, was in Dutch Harbor to help build roads, barracks, and warehouses. "My foreman told us that they'd gotten word the Japanese had sent carriers … with orders to bomb Dutch Harbor, so we were told to get ready for it," he said. "He told us to dig a foxhole 'cause they were coming. Typical of construction stiffs, someone said, 'Let's get up a pool' and we made bets [about] the day of the attack. Little did I know I'd be helping dig out bodies a few days later."

Despite navy patrol planes' flights and other attempts to detect an oncoming Japanese task force (which included two small aircraft carriers), the ships escaped detection due to fog and cloud cover, launching aircraft toward Dutch Harbor on June 3, 1942. When the planes—"Zero" fighters and light bombers—arrived over the harbor and facilities at 4:00 a.m., around dawn, they were unopposed by American aircraft. The Zeros came in fast and low, raking military targets with gunfire.

Rivas said, "[Later,] I was on boat detail [at Dutch Harbor when the attack happened]. We was unloading the boat, when we see the bunch of planes coming over. We was waiting for them to come.

"Anybody who says that 'I didn't cry' and things like that, I say they have to be crazy … because when you see those bombs coming down … you cry and you pray for your life."

Harrel Chancellor wrote, "My outfit arrived at Dutch Harbor about midnight on June 2 … I got my platoon up at 3:30 the next morning to go to the dock to unload our equipment. The Japanese attacked at daylight … Japanese planes were bombing and strafing Fort Mears and the naval air station for about two or three hours. I saw one fighter plane cripple the PBY mail plane as it was taking off across the harbor.

"I worked my platoon back to our barracks at Fort Mears after taking cover under the navy theater for thirty minutes. We took cover in foxholes and hillsides near our barracks. The enemy planes were bombing Fort Mears. They hit just about every other building. Luckily my barracks was skipped … We had a lot of dead and injured. My platoon was covered in their foxholes. I lost only one man who was cut by shrapnel. He was not deep enough in the foxhole."

Army enlisted man Roald Forseth remembered:

When the alarm sounded I ran down the hill to the battery office to get orders. One foot caught in the muck and the other one slid. My left knee jammed up and split the cartilage under the kneecap. I didn't have time to worry about that, so I kept going.

There wasn't much we could do except get into our foxholes. A 155 howitzer can't fire at planes. We watched the Japanese bombers and fighters attack the ships and the base at Dutch Harbor. One of our scout planes took off from the bay and headed our way. It was a biplane with a gunner in the back. He fired his puny .30-caliber machine gun at the nearest planes, and the pilot did his best to hug the ground and zig-zag up the mountain. We thought it was funny and laughed about it for days. The plane looked like a scared rabbit.

We got off a few shots with our rifles. The Japanese pilots were also scrambling for the mountains after they pulled out of their dives. As they passed by they were only a few hundred feet over our head. The attack only lasted twenty minutes.[1]

According to another account, an officer came on the radio saying the planes were "friendlies" and to stop firing. That was easily disregarded; the bombs and strafing were real enough.

Neil Fugate wrote, "I watched one bomb come down; it fell. I watched that thing from the time they kicked it out [of the plane] until it hit the ground. It hit down there toward a foxhole. I tore down there; a couple of other guys came down too. We estimated it hit about four feet from the foxhole; there were three guys [there]. That bomb just lifted the dirt and dropped it right in that hole. Except for shell shock and one guy with a piece of shrapnel in the back of his helmet, they were OK."

Some felt they shot down several fighters. Others said their guns and ammunition were woefully inadequate to shoot down aircraft.

"The Japanese came back the next afternoon," wrote Roald Forseth. "We had been ready all day. They bombed an old ship which had been beached at Dutch Harbor. Then the fuel tanks got hit, first one, and then four at once. The blast echoed for a long time. There was smoke everywhere. Everyone blazed away [with guns], but none of the Japanese planes were shot down. I guess it all lasted for a half hour or less."

In total, thirty-two Japanese planes attacked on the second day.

Lowell Thorsness, the civilian worker, added: "On the second day, I was in a bomb shelter with about eight other guys. Most were infantry, firing .30-06 [Springfield rifles]. One guy, I'll never forget it, fired two rounds and had his rifle jam. In the middle of the bombing, here he sits, talking to his rifle. He said, 'I had you in Fort Ord [in California] and you never failed me. I had you in the desert on maneuvers and you never failed me. The first Jap I see, you fail me … '"

Harrel Chancellor wrote, "My company was dug in on Hill 400, where I had machine guns on the rim of a fifty-foot cliff. One [Japanese plane] made two passes by our position, spraying sand over myself and four of my men. We waited for more attacks, but none came."

Over at Umnak Island, about 70 miles from Dutch Harbor, an American airfield had been secretly built, unknown to the Japanese. On the first day of attacks, American P-40 fighter aircraft there didn't fly to the assistance of Dutch Harbor due to a communications failure. On the second day of attacks, they were in the thick of things, since the enemy planes' flight path that day brought them nearby.

Army infantryman Mac Eads remembered:

They immediately sent up these P-40s after [the Japanese planes]. They were eager to get after them. They were flying around there firing at each other. Of course, we were infantry men. We didn't know one airplane from another … Our pilots soon found out that they were outflown, outgunned and outmaneuvered by these Zeros and they couldn't do anything with them except get them on [the P-40s'] tail and bring them down over the runway where we could shoot at them. We thought the Americans were chasing the Japanese. We didn't have any idea that an American would be running away from a Japanese.

So here they come down over the runway one right after another and we're shooting at this first airplane out there … but we're hitting [the one behind it]—we were hitting the Zero … We had tracers and I could see [them] curving off … and going toward the back airplane. Then I thought, well, I'd better take a lead on these guys, but then I thought, well, maybe we'd better find out which airplane's which.[2]

Army air force mechanic Mac McGalliard saw it differently from Umnak:

The [dogfights] took place very low, I would say between 100 feet and 2,000 feet altitude. Each P-40 had his own Jap aircraft to himself … Well, one Jap came barreling by at about 200 feet, a P-40 in pursuit [when] from a 90-degree angle comes [a second P-40] at about 500 feet. The P-40 following [the] Jap pulled up sharply … under his buddy. The lower P-40 prop cut the top P-40 absolutely in two. The astonishing part was that they were so low to the ground we could see the pilot twist around in his chair, because that's where the prop chewed thru the ship, inches behind the pilot. He had the strangest look on his face, then the craft nosed over and went into the water. The pilot was killed, not by the crash but by drowning … The [other] P-40 spewed steam from antifreeze and smoke from oil lines that were crushed, and [he fluttered down] like a leaf and settled down to the water. He came out OK.[3]

Infantryman Harold Johnston said, "They really mixed it up and we saw about six planes go down; all of them … into the water. One pilot bailed out and landed on this next island over."

A slow Navy PBY seaplane 200 miles southwest of Dutch Harbor searching for the Japanese carrier task force on the second day of attacks was jumped by Zeros. The aircraft was disabled and landed on the ocean, where it sank. Three of the crew managed to survive five hours in a life raft before being picked up by the Japanese heavy cruiser *Takao*, part of the carrier task force. Ensign Wylie Hunt, the senior airman, was the first to be interrogated, and later related:

> A Japanese lieutenant commander began asking me questions. He told me that he was from one of the aircraft carriers that had participated in the attacks on Dutch Harbor. I gathered that he had been on the flight which was jumped by army fighters over Umnak [Island]. He appeared enraged over this. He started out by cuffing me about the head several times and striking me with a stick he carried.[4]

Hunt didn't reveal the existence of the secret Umnak airfield even when threatened with drowning, and later survived internment in Japan (from the *Aleutian World War II National Historic Area Calendar*).

Another patrolling PBY seaplane piloted by Lt. L. D. Campbell located Japanese ships 80 miles from Umnak, but was also shot up by a Zero. "It only lasted a minute," Campbell recalled. "We heard the roar of his guns as he zoomed down on us, then he was gone. But in that brief moment he'd given us everything he had." One of the bullets pierced their gas tank, and they were low on gas anyway, so they also had to ditch in the frigid ocean. But they were able to keep the plane afloat until a coast guard cutter rescued them.

The aftermath of the Japanese bombing of Dutch Harbor. Men died, buildings were destroyed, oil tanks were on fire. *Alaska State Library, Aleutian/Pribilof Project Photo Collection. ASL-P233-V114*

In the aftermath of the air attacks, the resulting fires at Dutch Harbor burned for three days. Forty-three Americans were killed on the ground, many in an incident described by Neil Fugate: "When they got notice that the Japs were coming in … some officer … got everybody out in the street [next to their barracks] and got them in formation … [A Japanese bomb] hit dead center in the guys."

Robert Johnson, an army band musician at Dutch Harbor, said, "Part of the Officer's Club, [an] area used to store liquor, was hit [and] the wall that enclosed the liquor stores [was damaged]. Some of the [enlisted] men made off with the good bourbon and scotch before a guard could be posted."

The Japanese lost nine planes and the Americans ten, with twenty-five American pilots and crewmen lost. The Japanese had ships carrying an estimated 2,500 troops as part of their task force, and if they'd planned to, they could have invaded Dutch Harbor and the surrounding area. But the Japanese had other plans. Not knowing this, Dutch Harbor personnel braced for even further attacks which failed to materialize.

The Japanese fleet then turned around and had the opportunity to occupy Adak Island, but instead chose to attack and occupy the westernmost islands of Attu and Kiska. As the Japanese fleet approached Kiska, the only Americans there were manning a naval weather station. They were led by Charles House, who later described their ordeal:

Just after 0200 hours … Winfrey … shouted ATTACK ATTACK. I told him to go back to bed … Wimpy then turned on the lights and showed me a bullet hole in his leg. About that time I observed window glass in our bunk room being broken by bullets … As I ran from the building the first light permitted the observation of many Japanese landing craft moving up the inner harbor with machine guns blasting away from their bows … In this early morning light, the tracer bullets looked like baseballs curving toward us.

I scrambled madly up the hill until overcome by exhaustion and lay on the ground for a rest … I analyzed my situation. I was alone, not warmly dressed, but had grabbed a couple of gray blankets as I ran outside. The Japanese were landing in force and I would assume that they would knock out our facilities and leave.[5]

House moved farther away from the harbor area, but still kept an eye on it. He soon determined that the Japanese intended to stay, so he moved to a more distant part of the island where he concentrated on survival:

A couple of days had passed since I had last eaten [so] my thoughts turned to food. The only thing available for food was limited vegetation: tundra grass, wild celery, and lupine bulbs … The wild celery was bitter, so I eliminated that, and concentrated on lupine bulbs and tundra. On the eighth day I realized that I had not had a bowel movement, so decided to concentrate on filling up with tundra. The tundra didn't seem to agree with me, as I became very sick and nauseated, then [had] an urge for a bowel movement. The stool was mostly undigested tundra mixed with clotted blood.[6]

House found a cave in a steep bank above a small creek that became his home:

I was able to subsist at that location for another forty days. There was a plentiful supply of new tundra for food. By this time I discovered that I could eat the inside, tender part of the stem. It was tasty, something like fresh corn … Angleworms from the nearby stream provided some protein even though they were a little bitter.[7]

In his Robinson Crusoe-like existence:

I had a pencil but nothing to write on, so I kept track of time by making a mark on the pencil every day ... [I thought] of my wife and young daughter ... [and wondered] if I might ever see them again ... thinking with some satisfaction that I had taken out the maximum amount of government life insurance ...

On the forty-eighth day I was on my way to the creek for some water when I fainted. This called for some soul searching; if I remained there I would surely die.[8]

He then headed toward the harbor to surrender.

I got right close to [a Japanese antiaircraft gun emplacement] and was then faced with the surrender act, as it was humiliating and scary. Traditionally a white flag is used, so I ripped off a piece from my undershorts and waved it as I marched in. Some of the Japanese marines ran toward me and assisted me as I was pretty lean and gaunt at that time. They would indicate which persons I should salute. They poured some tea and gave me some biscuits.[9]

After being brought to the Japanese headquarters:

They had me [sit] on a grass sack. A large ring of Japanese formed ... around me and just stared. I had the feeling of a monkey in a zoo ... The ring remained constant for several hours with some dropping out and others taking their place. Late in the afternoon, I was put into our old power station ... The Japanese curiosity did not stop as a long line formed at the window and they would have a minute or so to look at me then move off ... [Later, every time] a ship arrived ... there [would] be a new line at the window. Japanese reporters and photographers came by frequently for pictures and stories. Several of the Japanese would come in for a friendly visit.

[A] frequent caller was an enlisted pilot that flew one of the Zeros on floats. He was also a very good artist and made portraits of me ... He was intent on teaching me Japanese ... One evening he came in and sketched some destroyers, and said, "Your country's warships [are] right out there." He was correct, for the next day [American ships fired salvoes, and] the path of shell explosions ran right through the middle of the camp.[10]

As time went on, there were more and more American air attacks, and there were Japanese funerals. House noted, "The Japanese seem to have more respect for the dead than the living. We stood at attention most of the day as the coffins were carried by."

After about two months as a prisoner, Charles House was shipped to a POW camp in Japan, to remain there until the end of the war.

Chapter 3
Weathering the Weather

A williwaw is very impressive; you'll remember it to your dying day. It blows up, down, and backwards. One time our lumber yard just disappeared.

GIs will bitch and moan about a lot of things, but in the Aleutians they had every right to despise the weather, some of the worst in any theater of World War II.

For starters, Earl Long (a "Seabee" or "CB"—a sailor working in the navy's construction branch) wrote:

> We disembarked at what was then called Navy Town on Adak Island. This was, it would turn out to be, our home for the next eleven months. Adak is a barren, treeless, dismal place. I could probably count on my fingers the days during our stay there that it did not rain or snow to some degree.
>
> At the risk of belaboring my point about the weather, let me … give you a sense of what we were up against. The weather was one of our main and constant concerns. After [the] eleven months, I don't believe it would be an exaggeration to state that in all that time, there were but a handful of really nice, balmy, warm days, even in the summer season. A typical day was gray [with] rain, snow, or sleet, and wind at a velocity that very often knocked you off your feet.[1]

It isn't that the Aleutians are that far north. They're only as far north as England and Germany, or British Columbia in Canada. Temperatures at Adak, midway out on the chain, range from an average daily high of 36 degrees Fahrenheit in February to an average high of 55 degrees in August. Temperatures rarely go below zero.

The weather factors that can really make Aleutian living challenging (to use a kind word) are wind, rain, sleet, snow, fog, and clouds. St. Paul Island, just north of the chain, has a mean year-round wind speed of 17 miles per hour, which means that half the time, the winds are stronger. Gale-force winds are common all along the chain. These winds in turn can whip up mammoth, menacing ocean waves.

Rain, snow, or sleet, or combinations of these, can be expected to hit any particular Aleutian Island at least 200 days per year. The westernmost island, Attu, can expect five to six days with rain, sleet, or snow per week.

Fog or overcast conditions predominate, and come and go with rapidity—and there are only about nine completely clear, sunny days on Attu per year. A rule of thumb is that the farther west one goes in the Aleutians, the worse the weather.

Finally, the Aleutians area has been called "the cradle of storms" because the Aleutian Low (or low-pressure area) forms there every winter. According to Wikipedia, "The low … can generate strong storms that impact Alaska and Canada."

A lad from any of the southern states might have had a hard time adjusting to the unfamiliar and often miserable weather in the Aleutians. It played a part, I'm sure, in pushing some men over the edge. Other men, such as my father, from the northern states where cold, rainy weather, or snow is seen more often, might've had an easier time adjusting. However, one stark fact affected nearly everyone serving in the Aleutians: Because of the high winds and other environmental factors, there are virtually no trees on the islands.

In the final analysis, Aleutian weather was a more formidable enemy than the Japanese.

Every GI who returned from Aleutian duty likely had a story to tell about the islands' famed williwaws. Novelist Gore Vidal, who served on a ship in the Aleutians during the war, named his first book *Williwaw*. Tom Bodett, of Motel 6 fame, had his teen novel of the same title published in 1999.

Basically, a williwaw is a strong, freakish blast of colder air pouring downhill off an Aleutian volcano (some rising as high as 9,000 feet). It seems the term is overused, often referring to any gale- or hurricane-force wind (which can blow for days). But true williwaws were characterized by quickly-shifting wind directions, and sudden onset and end.

As Ray Galloway observed, "'Willie-waughs' were winds blowing close to a 100 miles per hour that in a split second reversed … 180 degrees. What was so unreal was that the area affected could be very, very small, maybe a hundred feet in diameter, or even less."

From an unidentified source in the Brian Garfield archive: "A williwaw is very impressive; you'll remember it to your dying day. It blows up, down, and backwards. One time our lumber yard just disappeared."

Murray Hanson wrote in the *Military Journal Online* that "Periodically a dreaded 'williwaw' moved through [our] area … Wind shear … became horrific. Every once in a while a williwaw would invade Dutch Harbor, the force of the wind [rising] … to as much as 150 miles an hour, and damage invariably resulted. After one such passage, one of [our large PBY seaplanes] was completely inverted on the parking apron, resting on its back … [looking] for all the world like a huge roast turkey laid out on a platter for Thanksgiving dinner."

Men attempt to secure an aircraft to a caterpillar due to high winds in November 1942. Aleutian windstorms and williwaws were capable of flipping aircraft over on their backs. *Courtesy of Bill Maris via National Park Service*

Found in a National Park Service archive, a Bill Maris note: "Had a bad willie-waw … and lost all of our squadron [aircraft] due to storm damage while the planes were sitting on the ramp in tie-downs, with dump trucks parked around the planes to break the force of the wind. Seabees built wooden cradles to slide under the hulls to keep the beaching gear from collapsing and damaging the hulls. A willie-waw stood [a PBY seaplane] up on her nose and she fell … upside down, breaking her back."

Cal Olson was trying to tie down a fighter plane when a williwaw hit: "We … lay down flat on the runway [and] watched as the plane was lifted into the air, turned upside down and dropped on the deck. One of the chiefs waited too long to lie flat and the williwaw blew him into the hanger wall."

And then there were run-of-the-mill windstorms. Roy Dover wrote, "I watched stacks of half-inch plywood peel off like a deck of cards and scatter all over Massacre Bay [at Attu Island]."

Mel Plate remembered winds at Dutch Harbor so bad that he and his pals had to crawl to get to their mess hall.

In Billy Wheeler's 36th Squadron war diary, he noted, "During the first four days of November rain fell in torrents day and night … [often] accompanied by winds of velocities in excess of sixty miles per hour. [To be walking] in this weather meant to be soaked to the skin within ten minutes … [so] many men preferred to remain in their tents rather than face the elements during a dash to the mess hall … [Anyway,] the mess had little to offer except type 'C' rations."

Weatherman Paul Carrigan said that on Attu, "Off-watch people in the barracks hut sometimes trudged down off the mountain to [eat]. To leave the warm confines of the hut and dress against rain, snow, sleet and winds for the long round trip … usually wasn't worth the effort."

Veteran Johnnie Cobb said winds could even uproot Quonset huts despite their low profile and rounded shape.

A hint of the powerful wind currents moving over a volcanic peak on Adak, with a tent city below. *Courtesy of James Weatherstone via National Park Service*

Navy meteorologist Paul Carrigan wrote in his memoir that the worst windstorm during his Aleutian tour arrived in April 1943 on Adak Island:

Sustained winds estimated at 140 knots with gusts to 180 knots (208 mph) were damaging … It was downright frightening to be in a shaking, trembling weather shack while staring wide-eyed at the anemometer [which measures wind speed] … One of the three anemometer cups was carried away … A REEK, SCREEE-EEEK … sound … meant another section of corrugated tin roofing was ripping off.

During the height of this storm we worked desperately to keep from being blown bodily out of our barracks hut. The wind … was so strong it started to cave in the south end of our Quonset … Eight … braces [at] that end of the hut … saved us. If the end had collapsed under wind pressure our hut would have been transformed into a … wind tunnel … Like dry peas propelled through a blow gun, all in the hut would have been hurtled out.

Just prior to this storm, [the] Army Communication System (ACS) completed construction of a wooden-framed and plywood building [which] was glassed [in] on four sides [by] several hundred foot-square window panes … Wise to the winds, weathermen had questioned the use of so much glass. Five-eighths-inch steel guy wires were installed at each of the building's corners … and cement poured … to anchor these cables.

During the storm, Don Livingston and I decided to go outside and view the destructive winds in action. Debris of all sizes, shapes and forms, much of it quite lethal, was flying through the air … The ACS building was trembling and jerking against its guys when an exceptionally violent gust blew in one of the panes, [creating] a sudden and tremendous increase in pressure inside the building. This blew the roof off. Intact, it went up thirty feet like a two-ton kite, then out to sea. Four walls followed suit amid sounds of shattering glass and splintering wood … In seconds, all that remained of the building were the four [loose guy wires].

Elsewhere on the base, a Seabee was reportedly struck and killed by a flying object. A soldier found dead was believed to have been decapitated by either a whirling piece of metal or plywood.

Mother Nature's absolute power at times like these does not well lend itself to description.[2]

Bill Maris said that "sheet metal, barrels and plywood got more flight time than anything else other than the blowing snow. If it wasn't secured, it disappeared … The only thing we lacked were dancing girls to go with the music from the wind as it whistled thru the area."

During one strong gale, Private Edward Thomas went to the movies dressed "like a mummy … The hood of my parka covered up my head, mouth and nose. Goggles covered up the remaining part of my face. I forced myself [into the wind] at a 45-degree angle."

My father, Lt. Harry Paul Jr., wrote in a letter, "It's a standing joke here [on Adak] that you can tell a newcomer from an old timer by the way he walks. The old timer (from experience) leans over when he walks into the wind, while the newcomer tries to walk standing up straight. It really is true. If you don't lean way over, the wind will blow you over."

The strong winds could also carry fine volcanic particles that sandblasted one's skin and became embedded in one's clothing. Roald Forseth related in the *Baltimore Post-Examiner* (at baltimorepostexaminer.com) that volcanic "Grit stung your skin and coated everybody and everything. You couldn't even look at the wind when it was blowing bad."

If the winds didn't get them, the fog might have.

My father noted in a letter: "This is the only place where I've seen the wind blowing like sixty and be foggy."

Lt. Herman Miller wrote, "When driving in dense fog, it was necessary to know the exact distance to drive in each direction and watch the odometer so one could turn at about the right place."

Navy man James Doyle remembered that roads on Adak could get quite muddy due to the rain and snow.

Paul Carrigan mentioned:

Adak was hit by monsoon-proportion rains that continued unabated for a week … Muddy creeks, rivulets and draws … overflowed, sending torrents of water cascading down [to] cover the airstrip.

Not a single plane could land or take off at Adak's new airfield which, by then, was flooded to a depth of several feet … Squadrons of PBYs, B-17s, B-24s, B-25s, P-38s, P-39s and P-40s sat immobilized in neat rows or in revetments. Muddy waters swirled over the tops of bomber wheels. Bellies and tail surfaces of some P-40s were partially immersed … If the water level on the airfield had risen another couple of feet … I believe a PBY-5A might have been able to retract its landing gear, taxi out, and make a water takeoff.[3]

"I BEEN HERE TWO YEARS —
I'M WATERPROOF"

From *The Adakian* army newsletter on Adak. Considering that the newsletters were printed using a simple mimeograph machine, the quality of the art was surprisingly good. *Artist: Oliver Pedigo*

Herb Gedney of the army air force said it could rain and snow at the same time. In addition, "There would be mud and then it would freeze … The runways were always either frozen or [full of] mud puddles—[there was] no happy medium … The weather … always … went from bad to worse."

During Aleutian winters, snow—always present at the tops of the higher Aleutian volcanoes—worked its way down their slopes until reaching sea level.

In an article in the *Anchorage Daily News*, former army combat engineer Roy Dover mentioned that on Attu, "D Company had their mess hall on the side of a hill. One day there was a blizzard that covered the whole building. We had to bulldoze 'em out."

Wilkins Dixon told the story of heading to a dentist on Umnak Island with a buddy when they got lost in a blinding snowstorm. They came upon and followed a ditch that eventually led them to their barracks, knowing that if they'd given up trying, they would've died. Another time, Dixon walked outside to a shower building late at night and fell into a mudhole from which he couldn't escape. Fortunately, another guy heading for the shower heard his yells.

Another man wasn't so lucky. A fellow in Paul Worley's unit got lost in a snowstorm on his way to a mess tent. His corpse wasn't located until spring when the snow melted at the bottom of a gully. He was still holding a cigarette lighter, so the story went.

In an oral history interview, an army radar station officer, Robert Dougal, said he told his men on Kiska that during heavy snowstorms, "If you ever have to go out to the toilet, I want you to go in pairs; hold hands and go out to where the [latrine is] and then come back [together]."

"But," said Dougal, "I had one person who did not adhere to that request. And he went out to go to the latrine, and he got lost. And he hid behind a rock trying to keep warm … The next morning, we didn't know where he was; we couldn't find him. And the snow was all over … The Canadians came out with sticks … and they formed a line. And they would go on, one foot at a time, poking [through the snow] until they finally found this one fellow … He froze to death."

Frederick Rust in the 18th Engineers regimental diary told of a high-velocity wind and snowstorm where truckers,

unable to see, had to let their trucks stand wherever they happened to be. At the noon meal it was hard to locate mess tents and harder to keep food in your mess kit … In mid-afternoon the wind was reported averaging 50 mph and the air was so filled with horizontal moving snow that it was hard to see a tent at twenty-five yards. The sleet driving against your eyeballs was extremely painful; you involuntarily turned your back … Some men were lost for considerable periods. Going to bed was an unsatisfactory process because almost every tent contained a whirlpool of snow forced in through the openings, however slight. Beds, rifles, all personal equipment and possessions were snow-covered.

The most important thing about the storm is the way the men took it, with the biggest laughs they've had in weeks.[4]

Joe Baldeschi told, in an oral history recording, about his Quonset hut being buried in snow: "We were smart enough to keep a couple of shovels inside. So we'd dig a tunnel and [get] out." Walter Kellog mentioned being buried in a Quonset hut alone: "The hut got buried 100 percent, and I had to shut off the heat to conserve air to breathe. It took hours to be shoveled out. We had to crawl on our stomachs along a field wire to get to the chow hall."

As it turned out, the winter of 1942–43 in the Aleutians was the worst in thirty-four years.

Diarist Frederick Rust described one day where "at noon we had a sunny spring sky [and an] hour later it was snowing." Hal Goodyear, a navy Seabee ensign, said the whole time he and his crew were based in the islands, they only wore waterproof boots.

There were the very rare, clear days when the sun actually showed its face. The feeling of seeing it and feeling its warmth on one's skin must've been akin to a religious experience. My father wrote, "We had one full day of sunshine here a while ago. It's the first [clear] day since I've been here. I got through working at 4:00 p.m. that day and went for a good two-hour hike along the bay ... Also saw the full moon. That makes four times I have seen the moon in three months."

The long hours of daylight at the height of summer and the short daylight hours of deep winter could interfere with sleep patterns. My father wrote in June 1945, "It stays light here till about midnight. I mean light enough to see without a flashlight. It gets light again about 3:00 or 4:00 a.m. Short night, don't you think?"

Men thought the weather was conspiring against them when important visitors arrived to check on things. Clinton Dutcher wrote, "Senator Chandler, a member of a senatorial investigation party, visiting the Aleutians ... remained there all of three hours. Naturally [while he was here] ... it remained quite clear of fog; disproving [for the senator] the Aleutian [reputation for bad weather]."

My father wrote, "We had about twenty war correspondents here for two days last week and all the two days we had pretty good weather. The day after they left we had the bad storm. I wish some time when we have important visitors they would get to see some of the real weather we have."

There were respites, little windows of weather pleasure that were thoroughly appreciated. Weatherman Paul Carrigan wrote, "During mid-October 1942 there was a stretch of the best weather I'd experienced in the Aleutians. Many days were cloudless. On clear nights shooting stars streaked across the heavens. The fogs and drizzles of summer and early fall had ended. Our ... winter season was still some weeks away."

A chapter about environmental conditions on the islands would be remiss if it didn't mention the active volcanoes there—for example, Mount Cleveland on 65-square-mile Chuginadak Island. In *Yank* magazine, Cpl. John Haverstick wrote about the only outpost on the island, a weather station staffed by five men (after the previous garrison had lost three men during a winter storm). Resupply was infrequent, and their only regular contact with the outside world was by radio.

Often cooped up in their small shack by snow during the winter, they found a little whimsy went a long way. Wrote Haverstick, "They ... agreed upon names for the fox trails on the island ... [There was] Miramar Drive ... along the cliffs beside the Pacific; [and] Pompton Turnpike ... up [in] the mountains behind them ... Their quarters were [called], naturally enough, Spam Shack."

Their efforts at growing a garden in the warmer months predictably failed, so they turned to shooting or catching and cooking the wild ducks, geese, and fish found nearby.

Two of the men, sergeants Alec Alcantara and Fred Purchase, planned to climb the island's volcanic peak during the first good, clear day. One morning Alcantara noticed during a break in the fog that the volcano was belching darker smoke than usual. Later, someone noticed that smoke and steam were rising from the southern slope of the mountain.

Unfortunately, Purchase had already set out on a hike. Alcantara and another man tried to catch up with the sergeant to warn him, trailing him about 2 miles down the beach to the foot of the peak, past steaming-hot, broken rocks. They finally gave up reaching him and turned back.

Haverstick wrote: "The two had retraced their steps only about a quarter of a mile when a fifty-foot wall of lava and mud rushed over the spot where they had stood a few minutes before [and] … splashed into the sea. When they finally reached Spam Shack, they found it had been badly shaken.

"By midnight, the whole mountaintop was ringed in flame like a brush fire."

After the remaining men radioed for help, a crash boat arrived and cruised around the island, unsuccessfully looking for Purchase. The boat and its crew then departed the island with the four survivors. Food was left in Spam Shack for Purchase, but it was untouched when a search resumed two weeks later.

This was one of the few times during the war a life was lost due to hot, rather than cold, conditions in the Aleutians.

Another danger was earthquakes along the islands. As an indication of how strong quakes can be in the area, the world's second most powerful earthquake on record hit south of nearby Anchorage in 1964, killing about 139 people, with one tsunami wave measuring 220 feet in height washing ashore.

Chapter 4
Ten Ways of Preparing Spam

After a delicious entrée of lukewarm C-ration hash and watery navy beans … the dessert of canned fruit salad was embellished with … "C-biscuits," *[spread] with canned [salve-like] butter and jam.*

In rough or challenging times for the military, decent food has helped improve morale. But such food in the Aleutians, in many locations, was hard to come by.

After the Japanese were kicked out of the islands, most of the area became a bit of a backwater zone, while the dramatic, attention-grabbing operations were in Africa, Europe, and the south Pacific. So perhaps the Aleutian area didn't get as much food attention as it should've. What food was shipped up was usually in cans. Sometimes, frozen victuals made the trip.

In some spots, food service was crude. Sgt. Roger Vance wrote about his first day in the Aleutians: "That night we slept in tents that had been pitched on the tundra … At 4:15, we got up and had breakfast … We ate standing or kneeling on the wet grass, in the dark."

Charles Pinney wrote about serving at Cold Bay in 1942 in *Aerospace Historian Magazine*: "We usually passed up the long, wet trek to breakfast and stayed in the sack. The mess hall was small and crowded with picnic-type tables built from packing boxes. Our cups were salvaged vegetable cans."

In one instance in the Chernofski area on the other end of Unalaska Island from Dutch Harbor, men from various outfits landed to build a base. Not all the units were well provisioned and the temperature dropped to 15 degrees overnight. Men complained of freezing. While one unit was blessed with an all-American breakfast of scrambled eggs, ham, oatmeal, and milk, some poorly supplied and hungry men from another outfit tried to join them, but were turned away. They were reduced to standing next to garbage cans, asking for uneaten scraps.

Van Vechten arrived at a primitive location where the commanding officer told them they were in for a treat, as some fresh meat had just arrived. He vividly remembered "that first meal … The draughty old mess tent had no flooring, and … we slogged through ankle-deep muck, past four field kitchens where the anticipated fresh meat was cooked. Somehow the word 'fresh' did not seem the right one … the whole thing stank. So, this was my induction to a very primitive life style, and that night I had some wild dreams."

Army infantryman Frank Bosak said he was never served fresh meat while based in the Aleutians, and wasn't given any until he was later involved in the battle for Okinawa. "Other than that," he said, "we were on C- and A-rations all the time." According to *Wikipedia*, C-rations offered "three variations of the main course [in cans]: meat and beans, meat and potato hash, or meat and vegetable stew. Also issued was one bread-and-dessert can."

Food to survive on, yes, but not quite equal to mom's cooking.

Army air force pilot John Pletcher on Adak recollected, "You took your mess kit … and you went in … and got your tray filled up with whatever was being served. [The] morning breakfast was hotcakes and [scrambled eggs made from a powder] … But anyway, you get your mess kit filled and walk out and stand in the rain or whatever's happening and eat your breakfast. It was food, you were hungry, and you'd eat it! You know these young people were always hungry."

What liquids did men miss the most, other than alcoholic drinks? Coca-Cola—and fresh milk.

There are two stories to be told about milk, the first from the Garfield archive:

Commodore Leslie Gehres was the boss of Patwing Four … While visiting Attu the commodore found that fresh milk was not available so he ordered a barn to be built and while he was at it, he ordered the navy procurement center in Seattle to purchase a milk cow and ship it to the Aleutians by boat, ASAP … [A] barn … was completed on Gehres Point, Attu, in Spring, 1944.[1]

And then, from an interview with army air pilot Hale Burge:

Before I left Shemya to go to the mainland on rest and recreation leave, one of the guys asked me [to] "bring us back some milk, real milk." … The day before I [returned] I picked up some milk in paper cartons, Carnation it was … So I took … it on the [Navy ship on the return trip, and] … kept it in a life boat to keep it cold, and when we got down to Attu, we unloaded there … So the next day, I saw the first sergeant and I said, "There's a B-24 landed down there … You suppose there's a mail driver to take me down [to the plane] and see if I can get out of here? I'm tired of sitting around."[2]

So Burge was finally able to fly the milk to Shemya to his buddies. He didn't note if the milk made it without spoiling.

Men who were not big salad-eaters back in the States began to really miss fresh greens in the islands.

In the Brian Garfield archive, an unnamed GI groused that if a ship came in with a lot of canned spinach, they inevitably ate a lot of spinach for a while.

Clint Goodwin, an army engineer on Umnak, remembered going through the chow line one time and "getting … two big slices of bread over my [coffee cup, and that was the meal]." At least the bread was fresh-baked. On the other hand, noted in Brian Garfield's interview with Lucian Wernick, "The 36th's officers and men got bread for the first time in three months. They ate sandwiches for a week solid."

Frank Davis' take on a meal hit a satiric note: "After a delicious entrée of lukewarm C-ration hash and watery navy beans a la mess kit, the dessert of canned fruit salad was embellished with what were then known as 'C-biscuits,' [spread] with canned [salve-like] butter and jam."

On the mainland at Naknek—near the Aleutian chain—weatherman Sgt. George McBride related, "Our diet was constant—soggy corn-willy [i.e., fried corned beef with added veggies], Vienna sausage, coffee. Our so-called pancakes were popularly referred to as manhole covers. How is it possible to describe the misery of that mess hall? The hunger was maddening, taunted by the mental image of a candy bar."

Also at Naknek, one GI remembered: "The food was terrible, and when we weren't eating salmon, it was Spam. Spam was big. You made Spam meatballs, Spam fettuccini, Spam sandwiches."

An unknown poet wrote an *Ode to Spam*, which appeared in the book *Cheechako Don in Alaska and Aleutians: Collections of a GI*:

> *All armies on their stomachs move—and this one moves on Spam.*
> *For breakfast they will fry it, at dinner it is baked;*
> *For supper—what a delicacy—they have it paddy-caked!*
> *Next morning it's with flapjacks—or maybe with powdered eggs.*[3]

The poet goes on to list other dishes Spam appeared in: with a dough crust, in hash, as croquettes, in a casserole or stew, in a pie, deep-fat fried, in salads, with cabbage instead of corned beef, with spaghetti, and with chili or rice. He fondly recalled a day when they only had it twice.

Charles Donovan, a navy man on Umnak, complained that, besides sometimes being served Spam three times a day, "We had mutton every way you could think of … We had mutton stew, and mutton sandwiches, and mutton, mutton, mutton. So, to this day, I won't eat any mutton."

Elsewhere, some men suspected they were being fed horse meat, according to Navy officer Al Gentle.

Kenneth Skinner was on the crew of a PBY seaplane and expressed that after a flight:

> We were taken aboard the [seaplane tender ship] *Casco*, debriefed and were told to get some food. We got to the galley and the cooks dumped two spoons of pork and beans and one slice of bread on [each] mess tray. Our pilot looked at the tray and asked the cook if that was the best he could do. The cook said, "Yes." And our pilot would not take that for an answer. He told us to take those trays and dump all of that over the side of the ship—which we did.
>
> He then told the officer of the deck, "I want to see the captain." He was told he was asleep. The pilot said, "You wake him up, now." The pilot saved his tray so he could show the captain what we were served. The captain got red in the face when he saw the tray and went down to the galley and the whole galley crew really got a balling out. We wound up with all the canned ham we could eat, some canned pineapple, and cake for dessert. And the captain made the cooks get us some fresh coffee, which sure tasted good.

A chief machinist's mate on the USS *Case*, Joseph Goffeney, said the navy was ill-prepared to supply ships with enough food in remote areas. "We were living, at times," he said, "literally on hardtack [that is, simple biscuits or crackers]." They resorted to fishing from the ship and sometimes caught enough to feed the crew.

Ashore, native caribou were sometimes shot and butchered for their meat. In an article in *Air Force Magazine*, the writer mentioned, "One airbase I visited served up barbecued bear meat. It was delicious. Another outfit caught 600 pounds of trout in one afternoon."

An online article about Ken Kimes mentioned his "trading guns with the indigenous population for fresh fish and caribou, a talent which made him virtually revered during his mess hall's dinner hour—anything was better than canned C-rations."

Some GIs were sent to a remote part of an island to build a radar station, and ended up being stranded there for three or four months, according to Roy Dover. To get sufficient protein in their diet, and without any fishing gear, the men "threw concussion grenades into [a trout-laden] stream and it was fish for dinner."

Army barge crewman Harry Bailey didn't mind scrounging for food. "I was a party to [a] sardine theft," he said. "Actually, I did not care for them that much, but what desire I did have for them evaporated upon opening the first tin. Much to my horror they were not sardines but anchovies. [Fortunately,] a fellow … from Massachusetts came by and was asked if he cared for anchovies. His response was, 'I love them.' Needless to say he walked off the boat overwhelmed by our generosity."

Men who unloaded food from ships knew exactly what food other outfits and officers were getting, and liberated some of it for their own mess halls—especially meat. There's one story of a popular mess sergeant who fed his troops exceedingly well. Officers suspected him of using stolen food, and reassigned him. That didn't go over well, and he was soon back in his old job.

Navy Seabee Thomas Needham said in an oral interview that his outfit "had better food than most people because we were doing heavy work."

Thomas Erickson on Attu and Amchitka thought the food was "passable," especially when he considered he wasn't trading bullets with an enemy elsewhere in the world. Some men actually professed to liking Spam or Vienna sausages.

Seen in the Brian Garfield archive: "A mate on the way out of the mess hall [on Kiska] saw a piece of pie left on one of the tables. He remarked, 'That's the first time I've ever seen a piece of pie left on the table since I've been around here.'"

In an oral interview, army cook Albert King recalled that the most popular foods were meat loaf, stew, and roast beef. "We had good food, you know … We had a good kitchen and even the officers liked the food better at our kitchen. They used to come and eat in our

Some mess halls in the Aleutians were much more primitive. *Artist: Oliver Pedigo*

"SMELLS GOOD, BUT IT CAN'T BE."

place instead of their spot ... And I always gave anybody who wanted seconds, I'd give it to them, you know. Because I figured, the heck, these guys are here, they're doing their job and they should be [eating] whatever they want."

Navy air crewman Joe Baldeschi on Attu said, "Everybody that had a mission scheduled [got] real eggs ... with bacon or ham."

Men began to suffer from bad teeth in the Aleutians either due to poor nutrition or neglecting to brush, or both. The Garfield archive has Dr. Benjamin Davis telling this story: "We had a lot of dental trouble. The chief surgeon visited my base and I told him 'I need a dentist ...' Colonel Moore said, 'But we just got a dentist in.' I said, 'Wonderful, where is he?' He said, 'Right here. It's you.' He sent me pliers and Novocain and I went to work."

One GI blamed bad food for some of his teeth that had to be pulled. The tooth extractions were extremely painful due to a dentist who didn't use a painkiller. With three holes in his mouth, the GI was later offered a partial plate if he would pass on a promotion he was due. He took the plate.

In the Garfield archive, the story was told that "one man, in desperation, made for himself a set of false teeth out of the jawbones of a bear he shot."

Quite a few men remembered the so-so way that mess kits, dishes, or trays were washed after eating on them in some locations. Army pilot John Pletcher described the system:

They had a pit [where] you scraped off whatever you didn't eat ... [Then,] they had two barrels ... both filled with hot water ... Then you rinsed your dishes ... in this first barrel that I suppose had some detergent or soap of some kind in there, and then the last barrel was a sterilizing barrel that you dipped [your mess kit in] ... Then you took your mess kit back to wherever you had your bedroll.[4]

Clint Goodwin mentioned one of those barrels of water in an oral interview: "Of course, it was the same water you used a couple of days before ... So, it kind of looked like soup. And sometimes it'd be so cold and snowing or raining or blowing that the fire was out. So, you just dip your mess kit in cold soup and get on your way."

Then there was Roald Forseth's revulsion: "You dipped your mess kit in the first barrel to knock off the food and grease. That barrel was usually half full of garbage by the time you got to it. The second barrel was the rinse barrel, but it was just as disgusting. Guys were always getting sick."

It was a common belief among GIs that the water, supposedly because of a lack of minerals, would lead to softening of the bones and dental decay.

Perhaps due to the greasy and starchy nature of much of their food—and if their work wasn't very physical—men tended to put on weight. Pvt. Edward Thomas went from 150 to 168, and he was apprehensive about getting to 170. My father wrote in a letter home, "The cool weather gives one a big appetite. Nearly everyone puts on weight. I think I must [have]. We just can't get enough exercise."

Cooks tried to put extra effort into providing holiday meals. Pvt. Edward Thomas wrote that for a Thanksgiving dinner, he was served turkey with dressing, gravy, sweet potatoes, carrots, ice cream, and pumpkin pie. On the side were chocolate and bread and jam.

Rinsing eating trays after chow in the Aleutians: sanitation was often lacking. *From the Alaska State Library, James Simpson MacKinnon Collection. ASL-P80-05*

MSgt. Walter Kellog of the 58th Fighter Control Squadron saved a 1943 Christmas dinner menu from Attu. On it were listed shrimp cocktails, followed by lettuce salad (hard to come by in the Aleutians) and turkey with cranberry sauce. Veggies included whipped potatoes, creamed peas, and asparagus. Topping it all off was pie. Kellog wrote on the bottom of the menu, "We were disappointed with the meal because we ate [at] 9:00 p.m. after a hard day setting poles … My first Christmas away from home."

My father saved the Christmas menu from his navy officers' mess on Adak. For hors d'oeuvres there were three varieties of olives, followed by the traditional turkey and ham, and fresh-frozen peas. Next to the "fresh milk" on the menu he wrote, "First time in months," and next to "assorted hard candy," he wrote "None."

One Thanksgiving on Attu was a disaster, according to Roy Dover: "The Army sent up a bunch of turkeys … but they weren't very careful about how they shipped them and the turkey had all spoiled by the time they served it. The whole company was sick and we only had an eight-hole latrine. You couldn't get a seat."

Finally, the food served for President Roosevelt's visit to an Adak mess hall was modest: boiled ham, stewed tomatoes, mashed potatoes, string beans, and chocolate pudding.

Chapter 5
Tent Living in the Great Outdoors

Anything we could get our hands on that we … could use, we stole it and used it in the tent to make life more comfortable.

Men sent to the Aleutians who had some experience with camping, especially in cold weather, had a huge advantage over others. When camping, one gets used to living in tents and sleeping bags, and cooking with rudimentary utensils. Bathrooms can be latrines.

The first men arriving in the Aleutians as part of the buildup there—especially on the farther-out islands where there had been little civilization and no military presence—had it rough.

In the Brian Garfield archive, Garfield noted that "On leave at Anchorage and Fairbanks [on the Alaskan mainland], men had good quarters [and] dated women; [while] at intermediate Aleutian bases there were [Quonset] huts to live in, hot water and cots, [and] actress photos; [but] at Amchitka, [toward the] end of the line [they] had one frayed nudie mag, … sleeping bags in mud-floor tents [and] ate rations [while standing]."

Sgt. James Liccione Sr. was part of the first party of GIs landing on Adak to establish a base there. Their clothing didn't protect them well enough against the cold, wind, and rain. They lived off K-rations, and tents hadn't yet arrived. So, to get away from the low temperatures and get some shuteye, they were reduced to digging trenches under the muskeg, and then crawling in. This was their home for two or three weeks.

Billy Wheeler wrote in his squadron's war diary, "Where motor vehicles have moved for any length of time, there is a quagmire of [mud of] indeterminate depth" and "tents have been pitched on low hills of grass about two feet in height." Another passage mentioned the rugged life of the first GIs on Amchitka: "Our tents are dug in, but tent pegs can't be driven securely into volcanic rock. We're eating field rations in our tent mess hall … The generator runs by fits and starts [and its] mechanic is a hunted creature these days."

In the early days in the Dutch Harbor area (about the time of the Japanese attack), army gun crews built underground living quarters, dug out with jackhammers or picks and shovels, and they lined and floored their abodes with wood they would find, beg, or steal. The wooden roofs were often covered with sod for insulation.

Harold Johnston was sent to a far corner of Umnak Island. "It was just barren," said Johnston, "and they put us [in small, one- or two-person] pup tents the first night. That was in January, and it snowed the first night. When I woke up the next morning, snow was in the pup tent … " Fortunately, they were able to erect larger tents the next day. "I mean, it was just a bare island," said Johnston.

Sent to Adak, Floyd Erickson mentioned setting up

a pup tent … and [we] left our sleeping bags in there and we went to the canteen … And we came back; it was around midnight and we finally found our place. We got in that little bedroom … and it was [sopping] wet … and the water was coming in all over the place and it was coming down from up above also. We looked at each other on our hands and knees and we started laughing, and I swear we laughed for two hours. Oh, I'm telling you, we just were absolutely so miserable [because] we couldn't get into our sleeping bags [on account of them being] wet … And we were there for a week, and we improved; we made better sleeping quarters. But boy, that was terrible … You got to learn to laugh when you're miserable.[1]

Pilot John Pletcher—in an oral history interview—recounted landing at an Aleutian airfield and spending "the first night sleeping in the airplane, and so did my crew because that was the warmest place just to roll out our sleeping bags … and do the best you could to try to sleep. And then the second night, I had a pup tent that I put up alongside the runway. Next morning I woke up and [the tent] was in a puddle of water … So here I was in this pup tent getting my boots and stuff on, getting dressed, … trying to keep from getting drowned."

Canvas tents never provided good housing in the Aleutians, but if they had to be used, the next step up from a pup tent was square, pyramid-shaped (pyramidal) tents measuring about 16 feet on each side. They could be heated and were high enough to stand up in. There were whole neighborhoods of them.

Billy Wheeler had these droll observations in the 36th Squadron war diary:

Our pyramidal tents are pitched on excavations cut into embankments [that] overlook the perpetual marsh … The construction engineer forgot to include drainage in his plans and as a consequence the tents were erected in an excellent reservoir some four or five feet deep. There is no flooring except a few pieces of heavy paper that the officers had scavenged and placed near our canvas cots … When the rain came, in the first few hours of downpour, the floors became damp and [now] there is nothing but mud. The rolled flaps between the tents have proved to be excellent traps for collecting gallons of water that drain in a steady stream into the tent … The need for drainage became acute and out into the rain went the hardy souls, armed with shovels to dig trenches.[2]

"I always did prefer livin' in the suburbs." The tents, although widely used, offered limited protection against harsh Aleutian weather. *Artist: Oliver Pedigo*

"Our crew," wrote navy flight mechanic Bill Maris, "got flooded out of our tent about 0230 one morning … Snow water was running down the steps in to the … tent and was almost deep enough to run into the crews' sleeping bags. Chief Bill Dunn put his feet over the side [of his cot] to go to the 'head' and let out a scream as he went knee keep in snow water, waking the rest of us up. I turned on the light and was the only one dry as I was sleeping on the food locker. Clothes were floating and wet. So I was detailed to stop the flow of water since I was the only one dry. Water receded finally, [but] we missed our flight that morning."

In a letter home, SSgt. Roger Vance wrote, "I'd lie in bed at night listening to the wind and saying every minute, 'The tent will surely go [soon],' but somehow it came through. The snow works its way into tents through little openings."

Having been stationed on the furthest-out island of Attu, Mack Collings said the following in an oral interview:

We would dig down four feet or so into the soil of the island and put our tents up, but still the winds at night would pick that tent up no matter what we did. We spiked it down, put heavy rocks on it … The wind would come along [anyway] … and take [the tents] off of us and then we would be sitting there freezing in our sleeping bags.[3]

Bill Maris remembered, "It didn't seem to matter which way we tied [our] tent entrance flaps, the wind always changed during the night and we always had fresh snow in our tent in the morning."

From the Brian Garfield archive: At Cold Bay, a GI named Webster related, "We slept in tents, in cots that sank slowly into the mud until we had to get up and move them to keep ourselves from sinking under." At Dutch Harbor, even the army band lived in tents for a time.

An Army officer on Kiska, Robert Dougal, from balmy Florida, called living in canvas tents "real, real rough living … It would snow at night, and the tent would get heavy, and it'd fall down on top of the men."

Ray Galloway on Umnak Island wrote: "For living quarters, we were issued one canvas tent to every six men. Each man received a canvas cot and a sleeping bag … Eventually all tents sported wooden doors, some primitive and some very elaborate … The men in one tent had unfortunately hung their door to swing outward and the first snow filled the approach so full that the door wouldn't open … No one dug them out for three days!"

In a letter home, Dr. Will Eubank wrote about having a rubber air mattress and "a fancy warm sleeping bag" in a tent. "I'm writing by light of a candle," he penned, "mounted on the end of a stake, with a tin can improvised as a reflector. The other fellows are sitting around on their bunks reading or writing … One of the fellows has a radio which gets the West Coast short wave stations OK."

An army engineer on Umnak, Clint Goodwin, recalled in an oral history interview, "Anything we could get our hands on that … we could use, we stole it and used it in the tent to make life more comfortable … lumber, plywood, two by fours, nails, hammers, saws, wire, rope … We had to build floors to make it livable."

Lt. Col. Elmer Rafiner noted that on Kiska between eight and ten men slept in each square tent, and that he used a tent within a tent for two layers of insulation and protection.

Tents served purposes other than living quarters, as well. Frank Davis wrote about working in a control center in a tent on a bare ridge where they kept their feet warm in boxes of shredded paper.

Men went to great lengths to get electricity in their tents. PBY crewmember Bill Maris mentioned setting up lights in his tent after someone shinnied up a nearby power pole to jury-rig a connection.

A big step up from tents in the wartime Aleutians was living in a Quonset hut. "Quonset" was not the name of the inventor or manufacturer, but was rather the location where the first American ones were built in Rhode Island. The plain, semitubular Quonset huts were popular because they were relatively easy to manufacture and ship, could be put together by regular GIs, and they resisted the elements. During the war, over 150,000 were produced. The Aleutians got a lot of them. If you look at 1940s photos of military bases in the Aleutians, the predominant buildings were Quonsets.

When configured as living quarters, they were about 10 feet high in the center.

Paul Carrigan in his memoir tells about erecting some huts for a weather complex on Adak:

Five prefabricated Quonsets were duly delivered ... and unloaded. It was at this time that Tatom mustered us and told us we would erect the Quonsets ourselves. "Nothing to it," he said, "just a hammer, nails, screwdriver, wrenches, nuts and bolts. Any simpleton can put one of these up."

Tatom then turned to Chief Hudson and there followed a classic conversation. "What do you know about electricity?" asked Tatom. "We'll have to wire the huts."

"All I know, sir," replied Hudson, "is that if you grab hold of one wire it's OK, but if you grab both you get knocked flat on your butt!"

"Fine," Tatom beamed. "You're in charge of it then."

With corner stakes driven and string stretched, we began to assemble the first Quonset, the weather office.

During one stretch of this early construction we went 72 hours without sleep. A portable generator supplied light at night so the roofing phase could be completed before the onslaught of a storm. The last of our unopened crates [of weather equipment] ... was unloaded at our new location late one night in shrieking winds and slashing sleet ... When this had been lifted off the truck and carried inside I was so exhausted that I fell sound asleep standing against a crate in our storeroom.[4]

The huts were often placed so they were partially below ground level, to reduce the possibility of Japanese bomb damage and to help prevent damage from high winds. During one spring thaw, Sgt. George McBride remembered that "the muskeg softened, and we anxiously watched the surface water drain into the hollow under our hut ... After a day or so we could see the level of the rising water through the cracks in our floor. After four days the floor was inches deep in water. Everything became clammy. The smell of rotting muskeg and waste fuel oil permeated the air."

Army man Wilkins Dixon remembered stepping on hut floorboards and seeing mud oozing up. He said that in his enlisted men's hut, the beds or cots were close together in staggered fashion, so that one man's head would be next to other men's feet.

MSgt. Frank Carnes of the signal corps wrote:

We lived in Quonset huts that were located in a huge gully, situated so that the tops were even [with] or lower than ground level. One night with an Adak snowstorm in full fury and while we were all asleep, a soldier loudly announced that we were to grab personal items and leave immediately to a hut near the headquarters building. Farther down the gully, some huts were flattened by the weight of the snow and we heard of a death by suffocation.[5]

He added that they slept on cots with sleeping bags that [resulted in] a dank, smelly hut. On a rare day without rain, he ordered a house cleaning with sleeping bags aired outside, and remembered how nice it was to enter a clean environment. Charles Pinney at Cold Bay said their sleeping bags had to be replaced about every three months.

Wooden boardwalks with rope handrails to grab onto during high winds connected the Quonset huts at the navy's Radio City on Adak, according to James Doyle. These ubiquitous walkways, found throughout the Aleutians, eliminated having to walk through muskeg and mud, and were also set up between tents.

Navy air navigator and officer Charles Fitzpatrick, in his book *From Then 'Til Now, My Journal,* remembered that on Attu:

I drew the best bed of the six in our Quonset … The previous occupant had made a very nice table … Truly, it was a dandy … He even had one of the three best dressers in the [officers'] hut. Topping it off, he left his down comforter. Though a bit soiled, it didn't take long for the value of its warmth to make it acceptable [and] its soiled condition and spots of dirt … unnoticed. A few more cool nights on Attu and you were sure the dirt added to the comforter's warmth. An additional such night or two [and I asked] myself, "What dirt—why, it isn't even noticeable"

   My bunk … sagged so far down that when my covers and comforter were pulled up to my ears the bed very nearly appeared to be unoccupied … Sleep came easy. There were always three or four of the hut's six windows opened. The cold air wasn't a bother. My drinking neighbors assured me it was for their best interest and mine to leave them open.[6]

Back then, cigarette smoking was commonplace, and according to James Doyle, a pack cost two cents in the Aleutians. Such low prices may have been a calculated plan by the cigarette companies to get men hooked on nicotine. Even if only one man was smoking in a hut, it would quickly fill with the odor. Said Doyle, "Couldn't do much about that. It was their home too."

Improvisation was the order of the day. Flight mechanic Bill Maris on Kiska and his hut mates started scavenging lumber, doors, windows, roofing and concrete blocks, and built a lean-to addition on the end of their hut so they could have a place to play cards, and installed a stove so they could cook or heat their leftover flight rations.

Weatherman and officer Bernard Mehren recalled that on one of the outermost islands, Shemya:

[Our officers'] hut was set hurriedly on the south side [of a large sand dune], presumably to afford some protection from the strong winds … There was always some question as to whether the hill sheltered us or we it … When the winds mounted to 60 miles an hour, no matter what the direction, the hut trembled as though in an earthquake and the constant blast of sand against the arched roof sounded like torrential rains. Sand was everywhere—in our shoes, heaped on our beds, [and] hidden under the maps on which we strove to draw neat isobars. The hut itself was deluxe. Large wooden lockers to hang clothes, wide sink with running water (when the pipes weren't frozen) … storm hall at one end, [and a] 20-gallon tank with spigot set on top of the stove for hot water.[7]

Pilot Thomas Erickson remembered one night when "The wind got so fierce that the six of us in our Quonset house thought that we—and the hut—were going to be blown away. When the hut started rocking a little we all pushed against the windward interior wall. What probably saved us was the snow that built up on the outside of the [hut]. The next morning we had to dig our way out." (From his partial memoir on file at the National Park Service, Alaska Regional Office, Archives, Unprocessed Collections, Alaska Veterans Files.)

There were variations of the Quonset hut. One was a wooden version used by the army called a Pacific hut, which was valuable because it used much less strategic steel, and its wood construction provided better insulation from the cold.

There were other prefab buildings in Alaska which used more traditional square- and rectangular-box shapes such as the Yakutat hut and the Stout House. Robert Brown described the latter: "[They] were made of sort of a pressed cardboard or some sort of composition type of thing, and easily erected by those construction crews out there [near Attu]. And you could poke a hole in the wall. They were that flimsy. But we lived with it [until steel Quonset huts became available]."

It can get really cold in the Aleutians when the wind is involved. Generating enough heat in living quarters, especially in tents during the coldest months, was a challenge. Oftentimes, off-duty men had little choice but to crawl into their insulated sleeping bags to stay warm even during daylight hours.

Army pilot John Pletcher said, "I have slept in one of those sleeping bags in full winter uniform, in my flying suit … and was just barely comfortable. And the wind would be blowing, and, of course, the tent would be flapping and [letting] the hot air out as fast as we could heat it up … We had a little old stove for heat, that's all we had."

From what I gather, coal- and wood-burning Sibley stoves were used to heat the tents. Coal was available from mines in the interior of Alaska, delivered in bags. Sometimes it had to be warmed up before it would burn.

Frank Davis described:

The little pot-bellied stoves [that] were rigged with stove-pipes which ran up through [the roofs of the tents] … Several schools of thought [developed] as to the care and feeding of these little soft-coal stoves. It was early determined that [hunks] of tundra would not burn like peat, and frequent trips to the coal pile remained a necessity. The most [vexing] problem was the frequent choking of the [chimney] pipes with soot. This challenge was met in several ways, none entirely satisfactory.

The pipe-bangers would clang on the stovepipe, usually bringing the whole rig down in a cloud of soot and sections of pipe. The boiler-men preferred to toss half a canteen-cup of water onto the coals, slam the lid, and let her blow. This was generally the most effective technique, unless an excess of water also put out the fire. An antiaircraft artillery liaison man later assigned to us tried a variant of this technique with a little gunpowder, which not only brought down all sections of pipe and all the soot, but blew out the fire, cracked the stove, and gave the inventor a rather nasty bruise … when the door flew off. My personal preference was the acrobatic technique, which required the would-be chimney sweep to climb up one corner of the tent and drop a hunk of coal down the pipe … In addition, a good laugh could always be had by sending a greenhorn up the leeward side and watching him grope his way down with a face full of soot.[8]

Pilot John Pletcher on Adak disagreed with the comment about tundra:

We set our stove up, first time. We set it up, got a fire going [and] pretty soon we noticed steam coming out of the ground about three feet back from the stove. And we discovered that we were on tundra and the … bottom of the stove had gotten hot enough that the tundra under the stove was smoldering … We learned … yeah, that tundra will burn![9]

Neil Fugate's tent at Dutch Harbor used "a stove which burned Presto logs. The logs in the stove would send … sparks up the chimney which fell back down and burned holes in the canvas tent roof. During the night, as the soldiers slept, the falling snow would sift through the burn holes and build up on the inhabitants of the beds below … Sometimes it might be several inches deep on [the] beds by morning."

Despite his tent's stove, pilot Royal Sorensen recalled that "In the [winter] mornings the pail of water on the top of the stove turned to solid ice."

Ray Galloway, on Unmak Island in 1942, wrote, "Our tent heaters were fired with coal as a rule but a few men devised an ingenious but very dangerous method of burning 100-octane gasoline. Not surprisingly, we had a few tents burn down and also had some singed eyebrows."

Quonset huts could hold heat better than tents. Roald Forseth remembered that "we had logs of compressed wood chips for the Sibley stove … The wind pulled air through the hut like a vacuum pump. A load of logs would burn furiously and turn the stove cherry red. Then the stove pipe would turn red, and the intense heat would drive everyone to the far corners of the hut. In a little while the fire would die down, and the cold would creep in, and we'd crowd closer to the stove. That's the way it went every night until we crawled into our bunks."

Because oil used in some hut stoves was often too cold and viscous, army Lt. Col. James Havron related how GIs in one hut widened a stove's burner hole to get the oil to flow, using an ice pick or other tool:

That was fine as long as it was cold. But when the oil stove had been operating for about an hour, everything warmed up. The oil began to flow [faster]. All the soldiers had left the hut … to go on duty. [The oil] flowed over the floor and caught on fire … In almost [an] hour's time—the whole thing was gone.[10]

At many locations along the islands, pit toilets or latrines were all the army or navy offered, and they weren't exactly hotel quality. Also, they were often located a long distance from living quarters.

Pilot Thomas Erickson on Amchitka Island wrote, "More than once I would trudge through a foot or two of snow on a wild winter's night to get to one, then have the discomfort of icy blasts of sub-zero Arctic air attack a part of my body that was unaccustomed to such treatment" (from his partial memoir on file at the National Park Service, Alaska Regional Office, Archives, Unprocessed Collections, Alaska Veterans Files).

Not everyone had Erickson's gumption. Robert Brown noted that "in the wintertime people didn't go more than two feet away from their stout house for that evening pit stop."

The tent for a three-hole latrine used by Charles Pinney at Cold Bay, which he had to walk a half block to get to, blew away so frequently that his bunch gave up reerecting it.

Sgt. George McBride said, "The usual procedure [when sitting in our latrine was] to remove gloves, wipe, and get the gloves on as fast as possible … to avoid frostbite."

Bill Fry recalled that on Adak, "One day we had a pretty strong wind but no matter the weather if 'you gotta go,' you go. I was one that had to go and while [I was] sitting to get the job done, one guy had just finished [his] 'paper work' [and] dropped the paper in the hole and soon the wind blew it up through an empty hole, [where it] circled around and stuck [on his] face."

As for cleanliness, on the outermost island of Attu, navy airman Garvin Germany Jr. described sometimes going a month without bathing. They did have a shower, but it was inside a muddy Quonset hut.

Mac McGalliard, the army air force mechanic, remembered that "When we took our baths we would go outside and scoop up some snow in our helmets and set the helmet in the hole on the stove, and wait until [the] water was warm enough to wash our armpits and crotch and then shave in the same water. A wonderful way to live. This we did for about two years regardless of [the] temperature outside."

Van Vechten told about "[filling] our metal helmets with water and [heating] them by strapping them to the stove pipe that rose from the … stove in the center of our tents." The water was then poured into an old tin washtub. "We drew lots as to who would be first into the tepid six inches of water, and by the time the last man on the totem pole roster got in, he literally could walk on water, with apologies to [Jesus]."

Describing impromptu washing and shaving in a letter home was Edward Thomas: "First I need a pan of hot water which I fetch from the stove. Then I make sure no one else takes it before I'm ready to use it. Then I place the pan on a chair or table if no one is using it and proceed with ablution."

Walter Kellog on Attu might've broken a record: "I saw that they had found an old steel washtub at an old fisherman's campsite. Not having had a bath in five months, I cleaned up the tub, heated water on the oil heater stove, and took a bath. The next time we saw the tub, it had been converted to a bass fiddle by … a Chicago musician."

A GI recalled an elaborate shower an inventive soldier planned and built at one location on Kiska where there were no bathing facilities. Using a complicated setup of pails and warm water, squeaky-clean GIs emerging from the contraption hardly recognized each other.

"In one Quonset hut," according to an *Air Force Magazine* article, "the boys had fixed up a drum of cold water on a platform, which fed into a tank on the stove, thence to a sink—all made from hydraulic lines out of junked airplanes."

Conditions could only get better as time went on, and improved toilets and laundry facilities became available. Navy radioman James Doyle on Adak said his showers in a Quonset hut were nice and warm.

Billy Wheeler's 36th Squadron war diary mentioned that in 1942, "the new bath house at Umnak was installed and opened for use. Convenient hours were scheduled for officers and men. This new order ends days of taking showers in a tent with water that is neither hot nor cold, and never the way you expect it to be."

As hinted by the name given to a group of the outer islands—the Rat Islands—rats came to be a problem in the Aleutians, both to humans and especially to native sea birds.

Roald Forseth had some bouts with the rodents:

The rats were everywhere. Every ship brought in more rats ... and there was garbage all over the island. Those rats dug through the floors to get into our huts. They must have smelled the food, and a rat will kill itself to try to get food. We wished we had a dog, but only the officers had dogs.

I woke up one night because something was crawling on me. I looked up and saw a hairy Norway rat sitting on my chest. I flinched, and the rat sprung at me and bit my nose. I roared, and the rat ran.

I wanted revenge, so I rigged up a deadfall in our hut. I baited it with garbage, and used a pitchfork powered by a stretched inner tube to try to spear the rat. He was too fast, and always snatched the food without getting hit. I figured I'd try something different. I'd use electricity. Nothing can outrun electricity.

I tapped into a 220-volt line ... Then I set up the trap so that the rat would complete the circuit when he grabbed the garbage. That worked. There was a big flash, and the rat bounced a few times as he was electrocuted. Unfortunately, the hut stunk for days, and the guys all got mad. But I got the rat.[11]

Eventually, through the use of traps, special dogs, and the help of natural predators such as hawks and foxes, the rodent population was reduced.

Chapter 6
Flyboys, Bad Weather, and Flamboyance

It was not uncommon for planes to land after long missions—or after great difficulty in finding an airfield—with only a few gallons of fuel left in their tanks.

Flying was the most convenient way to travel the chain of Aleutian Islands—which stretches over 1,000 miles—but it had its perils, mostly due to the cold, windy, foggy, and cloudy weather. Beyond the transport of goods, mail, and personnel, planes were used for patrols and attack missions. During the early days of the war, electronic navigation aids were virtually nonexistent in the Aleutians (perhaps with the exception of early radar systems), so finding an airfield or making a landing was often dangerous and iffy.

On the other hand, wartime aviators often had a sense of adventure and derring-do. They were usually quite young, and dying in an accident seemed remote, but nonetheless happened often.

Navy flier Lewis "Pat" Patteson wrote about his first trip into the Aleutians:

There was one airstrip [on Adak] made from perforated steel matting laid on a tide flat. After landing we parked on packed sand alongside the runway, shut down our engines, and climbed out to survey our surroundings. And as on previous occasions when we first landed on a new island, we said, "Who in hell picked this place for an air base?"

Across the runway from us we could see a hillside littered with tents, and even from a distance it was easy to see that this tent city was located in a sea of mud. A mud-covered Jeep came speeding across the runway and skidded to a stop alongside our plane. A mud-covered guy jumped out and reached into the back of the Jeep, dragging out a mud-covered box containing GI mess kits. "See that tent across the way? That's the mess tent. They are feeding over there right now. Grab a mess kit and get over there if you want to eat." … We couldn't tell if the guy was a general or a buck private but he seemed to be the supreme authority and official greeter for Adak, and he didn't give us a chance to argue or question.[1]

Much was asked of ground personnel servicing the planes on the islands, again due to the oftentimes bitter weather and lack of facilities. Often, this maintenance or repair work was done out-of-doors, in bitter cold or under storm conditions, and even at night.

Damaged planes were cannibalized for parts to keep other planes going. An article titled "The Rambling Wreck" in a December 1943 *Air Force Magazine* described:

A bomber limped into Aggatu from a mission over Kiska with the leading edge of a main wing spar shot up and a de-icer boot badly damaged. There were no parts in stock so [the] line chief put his men to work on the carcass [of an earlier crashed

No heated maintenance hangars for these men on Attu servicing a Martin B-26 bomber (apparently shown with the pilots they served). *Photo by Bruno Kozlowski and courtesy of Andy Kozlowski*

plane] … They braved a 35-knot gale through an entire night removing hundreds of little screws to [remove parts of the wreck]. They then fitted the [cannibalized parts] onto the wounded bomber. They worked by the uncertain rays of flashlights and Jeep headlights without any shelter from the storm.

Two weeks later another B-24 returned from a Kiska mission with one prop feathered and an engine frozen stiff [so again] the ground crew pounced on the [wreck], wrestled an engine from its nacelle and substituted it in the crippled plane … Tarpaulins partially protected the men from the sleet that bit like steel. Crew chief stands and workmen were hurled to the ground by the frigid blasts [and] the plane was lashed to a tractor and a Jeep to hold it on the ground.[2]

Joe Baldeschi, based on Attu and part of a support crew, said: "When we had a mission … they had us up at 2:00 in the morning [to get planes ready] and man, I tell you some mornings it was so stinking cold and we didn't have any face masks. You walk down … maybe a fifteen-minute walk—I tell you, half way down, your tears come out of your eyes and they freeze on your cheek, it was so cold."

Army air force mechanic Mac McGalliard wrote, "The first one and one-half years in Alaska we had no hangers … [so we changed engines] in a tent. Many times we changed plugs, radiator, oil cooler, or generator in a snow storm. We had gloves, but you couldn't feel the nut with gloves on so we took them off and [worked] for five minutes and [then] went to warm up for ten."

Robert Buchanan, in an oral interview, explained that "it was our job—the mech's job—to get in the plane and start the plane up and run the engines, check the engines out, check the plane visually all over … When the pilots would come out, why, they'd get in and you'd tell them everything was all right; that would be it."

Fires were often kept burning in open-top fifty-gallon drums near waiting planes so plane crews could warm up before takeoff.

A crew refuels a navy PBY plane the hard way on Ogliuga Island. *Courtesy of Bill Maris via National Park Service*

From the Garfield archive:

[Airplane] hydraulic fluid wouldn't flow at minus 30 and 40. Even at less cold temps, the fluid became so stiff that airmen had to sit with their feet braced against the landing-gear operating valve [when flying] to lower and raise the gear. [Also,] the spark plugs wouldn't heat [and] the oil supply to the engines was cut off because moisture ran down into the oil-tank sump and promptly froze. Hundreds of feet of [airplane] control cable were useless because the grease in the system froze as solid as concrete.[3]

As for flight crews, Billy Wheeler noted in his squadron's diary that they were kept so constantly busy that when one crew landed, for example, "It was their first chance to change clothes in a week."

A note found in the Brian Garfield archive indicates: "These two days are to be remembered vividly by all members of this flight because … we have seen little or no food. [One crew member] felt like offering a half interest in hell to anyone who could have produced food."

Occasionally, pilots and crews had the chance to spend some time off on the mainland. Bomber command tried to rotate remote bomber crews though more developed locales, including Elmendorf Air Force Base near Anchorage, so crews could look forward to some rest and recreation. An airman quoted in the Garfield archive indicated: "Anchorage is the metropolis of our part of Alaska and the desired mecca of all men tired of rain, mud, sauerkraut and wieners."

If it was cool to cold at sea level, it was much colder at the high altitudes many planes flew in. Large World War II-era planes used in the Aleutians usually offered no cabin heat, so frostbite was often a possibility.

Also, getting a plane badly iced up during flight was among a pilot's worst fears. Ice buildup on wings could reduce lift and add weight, so pilots were advised to fly low if possible. Garvin Germany Jr. wrote that airplane carburetors could ice up from the cold temperatures and high humidity, causing engine failures.

According to pilot Royal Sorensen, "We could fly three hours at a time, and with 60-degrees-below zero temperatures and no heater in the C-47, our knees and hands became numb. All winter long I would wrap my feet in paper, put on two pairs of wool socks, and wear sheep-lined bedroom slippers inside my flying boots. Later we received down-filled jackets and pants, which were a godsend."

Bernard Mehren, a weather observer based on Shemya, wrote about dressing for flying in the cold:

General Electric has solved the hazard of low temperatures. Since the [planes] are too large to be heated adequately, electrical outlets are strung from nose to tail. Just plug your "zoot suit" in and adjust the [temperature].

Dressing for these [flights] is a major operation. First comes long woolies [and] over them your … shirt and trousers. Add … electrically-wired trousers and jacket.

Over this goes your A-9 flying trousers—alpaca-lined—and B-9 jacket with hood. As a finishing touch you put on heated gloves and—for those who have small feet—heated shoe inserts topped by flying boots.[4]

On the other hand, some pilots froze because they got too warm and perspired too much, reducing the effectiveness of their trousers' and jackets' insulation.

Some pilots couldn't resist providing impromptu aerial acrobatics to liven up the day for landlubber GIs. Harry Bailey, serving on an army cargo barge, wrote about "a group of P-40s [which] buzzed low, went aloft to loop and roll and then dropped over the ships at a slow speed … [and then] wiggled and dipped their wings. As all this unfolded before [our] eyes, one had to have a feeling of pride."

At other times, wrote Bailey, pilot theatrics were a bother:

Flying crews both army and navy with visions of aspiring to become the likes of General Doolittle … took to the air. Their mission: to scare the hell out of our barge people. One afternoon … I was taken outside so I might see the effects of a B-25 that buzzed us earlier in the day. It had taken three feet off the top of our mast.

Sometime later … we were about equal distance between Attu and Shemya … Off toward Shemya, maybe ten miles away, a [large seaplane] was just above water level and as the distance grew shorter there was no doubt of their intentions. They were about to give us the full treatment … Tex was shouting a few choice GI curses and I jumped off the chart rack and ran to the back of the ship [before dashing] back to the pilot house. About now you could see figures in the cockpit … I said to Shorty, "He will never be able to pull up in time … " It appeared he just sort of hung in front of us [as] a slow—oh, so slow—uplift carried [him] over. The Texan said he could see their grins as he shook his fist at them. Fortunately, this was our last exposure to summer fun and frivolity.[5]

At Dutch Harbor, seaplane crew member Bill Maris was watching a movie indoors "and someone hollered 'air raid'—the doors got torn off [their] hinges as we all evacuated the theater only to find it was a false alarm as we recognized our F4Fs putting on an airshow for us."

A bomber pilot in the Garfield archive mentioned buzzing his airfield after takeoff as a salute "to those lads who stay on the ground but who make it possible for us to fly."

Aleutian wisdom found in the Garfield archive: "Fighter pilots are said to be either old or bold; never both."

Airmen felt part of an elite group. There was one-upmanship to be sure: navy versus army pilots, and so on. For example, according to the Garfield archive, navy pilots were jealous that army pilots received swift promotions—if they survived. It was said that youthful fighter pilots looked down on staid bomber pilots. On the other hand, bomber pilots liked to call fighter planes "peashooters."

A B-25 pilot recalled years later with embarrassment that the first time he flew into Amchitka, his formation first buzzed the airfield to impress a squadron of P-38s already there.

Aleutian airmen in cold weather gear in a lighter moment. Bill Maris is at far right. *Courtesy of Bill Maris via National Park Service*

Garvin Germany Jr., a navy airman, told about the time he and fellow flyers were stranded at Cold Bay and made off with an army Jeep to go see a movie, then left it stuck in snow on the way back to barracks. Later, MPs ordered them up from bed and demanded to know who stole the Jeep. No one spoke. Another time, he and airman buddies were sleeping late in a barracks. A bosun's mate tried to exert some discipline by pulling an airman out of bed, but the fellow slammed the mate on the floor and told him never to bother him again. So the mate left, returning to install a clock with a clapper gong on the wall. They promptly disabled it, evading the mate's work details, making it plain that flying planes was all they did.

There could be some games in the cockpit as well. Consider the following from the Garfield archive:

Kaiser, the pilot, was flying at wavetop level and said to the co-pilot, "OK, Justanski, take over." But before he reached for the unattended wheel, Justanski … stopped to [religiously] cross himself. During this interval, the plane dipped toward the ocean and Kaiser had to grab the wheel to keep from crashing into the sea. This became a ritual until one day, flying a bit higher than usual, Kaiser said, "It's your airplane" and took his hands from the wheel. True to form, Justanski paused to make the sign of the cross. [But] this time Kaiser didn't touch the wheel; and when Justanski reached for it, Kaiser batted his hands away and said, "No, let's see how the Lord flies this airplane." After that, Justanski grabbed the wheel first, and then crossed himself.[6]

Trying to recreate the bravado of the Eddie Rickenbacker days of World War I, some pilots affected white scarves and old-style flying helmets. Airmen liked to emulate the trimmed-mustache look of the popular and irreverent Colonel Eareckson. The élan and belief in one's luck were probably necessary. In the Garfield archive, pilot Frederick Ramputi related that "our orders were to seek out and destroy Japanese war vessels, even if our fuel would not allow returning. Obviously, they were suicide missions."

Mel Plate, part of an antiaircraft artillery crew at Cold Bay, saw American bombers returning that were so shot up he was amazed they could still fly.

There were a few instances of patrol aircraft coming upon Japanese vessels. Here's a description written by TSgt. Lester O. Gardner:

[I] dropped my right hand to the toggle switch [which would release our bombs]. The pilot straightened out and I toggled about ten times … We passed over the bow of the destroyer. Horrified, I saw tracers and "pom-pom" [antiaircraft fire] coming at us. We had to climb quickly to avoid ramming the mast. I saw a gaping hole in the stern, smoke pouring out … There was a trail of tiny figures in the water, a few clinging to wreckage.

We started home, the plane undamaged. We came in over the field at dusk, circled and landed … I jumped out of the plane, bent over and patted the ground, my knees still weak from excitement. It was sure good to be alive. [Sometimes] I'll think back to the scene of that battle [and] remember the most perfect bombing run I ever saw, actual or practice.[7]

Another pilot remembered sinking a Japanese ship and feeling some remorse afterwards.

A PBY seaplane, sent out to look for and attack a reported Japanese cruiser, instead ended up checking out a radar blip. Navy navigator Bob Larson indicated:

We picked up the target again and [flew below the cloud ceiling of 200 to 300 feet] to investigate … Visibility was about one to two miles. Suddenly we sighted a surfaced submarine, apparently charging its batteries … [Our] 500-pound SAP bombs could not be dropped from less than 750 feet … without endangering our own airplane. The [clouds were] so low that we could not get up to that altitude. We headed for the sub anyhow, intending to strafe. Suddenly a sharp explosion changed the situation. Holes appeared all over the plane and the starboard engine caught fire. Our first thought was that we had been hit by [antiaircraft] fire. We figured that if the sub could do that much damage with one shot it was not very prudent to let him have a second try.[8]

Later, the PBY crew realized they'd accidentally dropped a bomb, causing their own damage. Able to extinguish the engine fire, they repaired as much of the plane as possible on the trip home. "The large holes were plugged with boards and rags, while the small ones were stuffed with pencils and bits of wood," wrote Larson. "One piece of shrapnel had come through between the two pilots." The fate of the Japanese submarine wasn't noted.

Sometimes bombs wouldn't release from bomber racks over targets, so someone had to go back to the bomb bay and manually kick them out. Also, inexperienced air crews were known to bomb whales swimming close to the ocean surface, thinking they were submarines.

A beached PBY seaplane on Adak that was probably scavenged for spare parts. What led to its predicament in June 1945 isn't known. *Alaska State Library, US Navy Bureau of Aeronautics, Adak 1944-45. ASL-P545-64*

Overall, a lot of air crew members and planes were lost. According to the Brian Garfield archive, by October 1942, the 11th Air Force in Alaska had shot down thirty-two Japanese planes and destroyed thirteen on the water, and had lost only nine planes of its own due to combat. However, sixty-three American aircraft were lost to other causes—including crashes upon landing or taking off, crashes into other planes while airborne, running out of fuel and ditching in the ocean (often due to not finding an accessible airfield in time), flying into mountains, and mechanical difficulties.

One pilot was quoted as saying, "I'd rather face a Zero in the air, than zero-zero [visibility] on the ground."

Navy seaplane radioman Kenneth Skinner said during an oral interview, "We lost quite a few men, which was pretty hard to take … VP-46, the squadron that relieved us in the fall of 1943, lost about half their men. That was pretty rough because I had quite a few friends in that group."

It was said that some pilots, hypnotized by flying over featureless gray seas for hours, simply flew into the ocean.

A Garfield archive note dated January 1943 indicated: "Four B-24s were lost in bad weather on an [aborted] mission. Two disappeared completely. One crash-landed on Great Sitkin [Island], and the fourth overshot the flare-lit Umnak runway and smashed up two P-38s that were parked there."

Due to the frequent foggy or cloudy weather, days suitable for flying from Attu ranged from eighteen in February to only nine in August, according to the Garfield archive.

When his own plane was searching through fog for a place to land, Ray Galloway was wondering:

> How men faced death in such a manner. What did they think of? Did they pray; did they curse their luck? … I remember praying and asking God to spare us. There was an old adage that there were no atheists in foxholes. Neither are there any atheists in airplanes lost in the Aleutian fog.
>
> [Fortunately, we found an emergency airstrip to land on.] Before we rolled to a stop, fog enshrouded our plane again … Later, the fog miraculously raised for what seemed like minutes and eleven C-47s landed like a flock of ducks. The fog then closed and did not open for three days and nights.[9]

Even more subtle, invisible dangers could crop up. Bill Maris described becoming sick from carbon monoxide poisoning while running an auxiliary generator with an exhaust leak in an airborne PBY seaplane.

Pilot Bill Thies in an oral interview told the story of flying one night along the chain at about 2,000 feet altitude and asking his radar operator to call him when they passed a certain point. After a while, growing impatient, he complained he hadn't heard back. The radar man replied, "We're standing still … " It turned out the oncoming wind was so strong, it matched their airspeed, so they were essentially not moving in relationship to the earth below. Said Thies, "That was some God-awful weather."

Weathermen were highly depended upon to predict flying conditions, and performed pretty well without the advantages of today's satellite imagery, computer programs, and Doppler radar. One of the most respected seems to have been Cmdr. John Tatom, who sometimes worked with Paul Carrigan, a much-quoted person in this book. Tatom was able to predict the approximate time various airfields along the chain would be closed due to clouds and fog. Pilot Murray Hanson, writing in *Military Journal Online* (Issue 1) about himself as a third person, described taking Tatom on a meteorological trip:

> When they took off the weather wasn't bad, but as they flew westward over the north Pacific the ceiling lowered and rain and snow began to batter the plane. This was what John [Tatom] was looking for: he moved up to the machine gun turret in the bow where he could look out portholes directly into the teeth of the storm. Soon they were in it all together—the clouds closed down and the wind became violent … After about fifteen minutes of this, [pilot] Murray was ready to return to base. Not so [Tatom]; he loved it … "Onward," he chortled whenever Murray asked if he hadn't had enough.
>
> [Tatom] kept the flight bearing farther and farther into the storm, until after one horrendous lurch of the fuselage the plane captain in his tower reported that a spare generator had wrenched itself loose from its hold-down brackets and punched a hole in the fuselage on its way to freedom. Murray asked no further; he made a 180-degree turn and headed for home.[10]

There were fanciful bird stories mentioned in the Garfield archive. Said a ground-crew GI, "I watched a seagull swing in to a landing on the runway. It cocked an eye at the weather, turned and walked into a hangar." Also, a pilot flying 400 miles out to sea was said to have buzzed a seagull and shouted, "Now I know there's somebody else as crazy as me."

Seaplane crewman Kenneth Skinner said, "The weather was something else. You could be ten minutes away from Attu [and have] sunshine; you could see the island and be just great. By the time we got there and ready to land it would be all fogged in. We'd either try to go to Shemya [and if that was fogged in] we'd have to fly clear to Adak in order to land."

Landings could be hair-raising. One pilot was known for diving blindly for fog-shrouded runways and not pulling up until the last moment, nearly giving crew members heart attacks.

Said Joe Baldeschi during an oral interview, "When you couldn't see the island—because Attu looked like a cotton ball down there, always covered with snow or clouds ... half of the time we would come in blind ... You know you hit [the airstrip] when the pilot drops the yoke and you hear the wheels hit the steel mat. Now you know you're back."

If a plane ditched in the ocean, airmen in the water had to be rescued quickly to avoid hypothermia. Water temperatures in the Aleutians vary from an average of 38 degrees Fahrenheit during the coldest months to 50 degrees in the warmer months.

Hypothermia progressed through stages: The shock of being immersed in cold water would initially cause uncontrollably fast and deep breathing. When that response passed, the aviator would be fine for a short while, but then blood would move from the outer areas of his body to the interior, leaving muscles weak and uncoordinated, which could eventually lead to cardiac arrest. It's estimated the average person can survive in 41-degree water for only ten to twenty minutes. If the water's 50 degrees, it's just a somewhat longer process. If an air crew were to get into an inflatable lifeboat without getting immersed in the water, they'd have a far better chance of survival.

Navy navigator Charles Fitzpatrick described an ocean ditching while flying in a Ventura medium bomber. His pilot had taken a major chance by trying to fly from Umnak to Kodiak late in the day with a malfunctioning radio and no LORAN navigational aid. Day turned to night as strong headwinds ate up their fuel supply. The pilot, wrote Fitzpatrick in his book *From Then 'til Now, My Journal*, announced that if they didn't find the Naval Air Station at Kodiak within forty-five minutes, he'd have to locate a suitable place to set their plane down.

Eventually, the pilot

announced he was going to ditch [the plane] at the first place that appeared to have habitation ... "If there is such a place along this coast." There was never a thought we wouldn't make it [and I] never had the slightest thought I would fail to make dry land that night. [Two crew members] had said again they'd prefer to bail out [but the pilot] reiterated the fact that we were going to ditch [and] the subject was closed. After nearly two hours of searching in almost instrument-flying conditions, we spotted lights ahead. The arrangement of the houses and their reflecting lights sent us almost through the top of the plane. Certainly, that was a lighted runway below. It was a sickening feeling, very sickening indeed, when we realized those lights came from small houses running down the side of a hill at the base of a mountain.[11]

Reality set in as the pilot set their plane "down in a textbook landing in six-, maybe seven-foot seas in one of the darkest, stormiest nights ever. It was [9:45 p.m.]."

They were about a mile offshore, and were able to inflate, and then swim to a four-man raft. Six men made it there, but their combined weight kept it partly underwater. The water was cold, and Fitzpatrick was the last one pulled aboard. Wet, and in very dim light, they watched as their plane went vertical and disappeared underwater. Realizing winds were going to carry them away from land, they fired a few flares. They were missing their copilot. Fortunately, people from the nearby town of Karluk who heard them flying overhead assumed the aircraft was in trouble, and a missionary organized a rescue crew that rowed out in a 25-foot skiff.

Fitzpatrick wrote that on the raft,

[in] an effort to make a noticeable gain for shore, a paddle was broken. Now down to one paddle … we heard the greatest thing ever—unfamiliar voices calling to us out of the dark. On their way to us, our flashlight quit. They called for us to yell more so they could be guided by our voices.

[After the rescue, several of the villagers on the rescue boat] kept repeating for us to beat our legs and arms [to increase blood circulation] … I thought I was doing a job of it when a young fellow told me to hit my legs harder … Like a few of the others I didn't have it in me to move enough … Other than speak a little, I absolutely could do nothing for myself.

[As we arrived at the shore,] many of the town's people had come down to the beach to see the activity. For them this was a most exciting evening.

Our teeth were chattering so hard it was difficult to speak. We shivered violently.[12]

After receiving some donated clothing and being given places to sleep by the villagers, they were picked up by a navy vessel five days later.

From *Pacificwrecks.com* comes the story of a Lt. Kidder, who took off from Attu on a P-38 test flight in 1945, but, while trying to return to base by descending through clouds, was unable to find Attu. Losing all radio contact, partly because his main antenna snapped due to icing, he flew overlapping search patterns for four hours. Running low on fuel and not wanting to ditch in the water, he finally found Buldir Island, without an air strip. He safely belly landed on some flat terrain and was met by five American GIs serving at a remote weather station. They radioed for help, but didn't receive an answer. Fortunately, a ham radio operator in St. Louis, Missouri, picked up their distress call and notified the War Department. The pilot was rescued two days later. His P-38 was later recovered, rebuilt, and resides in the Hill Aerospace Museum in Roy, Utah.

A pilot watched an Aleutian bomber ponderously taking off whose pilot retracted the wheels too soon. Unfortunately, with not enough airspeed, the plane began to settle down and was soon careening down the metal runway on its belly, screeching and bending back the propellors. After overshooting the runway and grinding to a stop, the crew escaped and ran for cover. After a few seconds, the plane's 500-pound bombs exploded.

Murray Hanson, writing in *Military Journal Online*, said he "learned that Dutch Harbor's new [air]strip was probably the only place in the world where the wind blows simultaneously in opposite directions at the two ends of the runway … An incoming pilot had a choice of landing in either direction, but whichever he chose he would find himself landing downwind."

It was not uncommon for planes to land after long missions—or after great difficulty in finding an airfield—with only a few gallons of fuel left in their tanks.

At an unnamed Aleutian airfield in 1942, according to the Garfield archive, brass "ordered the three available PBYs [seaplanes] to take off and go [attack a Japanese task force nearby]. As luck would have it, one PBY suffered a flat nose tire, the second was rammed by a fuel truck, and the third was crippled by a torpedo accident—all before any of them could take off."

Perforated steel mats, called Marston mats, enabled the fast construction of Aleutian airfields by Seabees. After troops and machinery landed on Adak, for example, engineers drained and filled a tidal lagoon, laid the mats, and had planes taking off—all in the space of only twelve days. Both bombers and fighters could use them, but they were less than ideal. In a Garfield archive note, Capt. Russell Cone reported that "the mat laid on ... porous volcanic soil gave the effect of landing [his B-17] on an innerspring mattress." Some williwaw winds were strong enough to curl the matting up so it resembled potato chips.

Airman John Mullican remembered that "on our first raid with the 77th, we received some battle damage, and landed on Fox runway at Amchitka to check it out. Since the damage was minor, we prepared to take off and noticed people gathered on both sides of the runway. When asked what was going on, one of the people told us we were the first bomber to take off from Fox runway and they were curious if we could make it."

Beyond the weather, other phenomena caused problems as well. In the vicinity of the Islands of the Four Mountains in the chain, with volcanic peaks reaching between 5,000 and 6,000 feet high, the earth's magnetic lines of force were distorted, throwing compasses off. According to Murray Hanson, this could cause "passing vessels and aircraft to veer toward those islands ... It was said at the end of the war that bodies had been removed from a dozen or more [plane] wrecks found plastered against [those peaks]."

Weather observer Bernard Mehren remembered:

Magneto trouble delayed our departure so that we didn't get to [Port] Heiden until long after dark. We [had been cleared for stopping at] Cold Bay but the weather would not permit a landing. Heiden wasn't much better and was further complicated by a new tower operator who forgot to turn the runway lights on ... I can remember how glad I was that we had a chaplain for a passenger; how nice the cold, wet, muddy ground looked when we were finally on it; how the pilot's hands and the co-pilot's hands and my hands shook as we accepted the two ounces of straight rye whiskey prescribed by the medical department.[13]

Pilot Royal Sorensen recalled approaching Cold Bay to land:

I couldn't get the wheels down. The crew chief said the hydraulic fluid had leaked out and we had no [spare fluid]. I told him jokingly that the only fluid I had was in my body, and I was going back to relieve myself. The crew chief then ordered everyone on board, six or seven people, to urinate into a pail, after which we poured the contents into the reservoir, enough to get the wheels down and locked into place for a safe landing.[14]

Cecil Fuller of the army medical corps, talking about an airfield on Kodiak Island, related: "They had winds up there like you wouldn't believe. I saw medium bombers that would just sit at the end of the runway headed into the wind. They revved up these engines [and] didn't go more than a 100 feet until [they were] in the air because of the 50-, 60-mile-an-hour winds."

Army GI Floyd Erickson remembered seeing a plane go down: "I remember sitting there on the ship before we [arrived at] Adak ... There was an airplane up there—it was a fighter and I could see he was coming down awful straight. He must have been in trouble, and all of a sudden, he just hit a cove ... less than a mile away ... I don't see how he could ever have got out of that alive, but he went down right in the ocean ... Gosh, that was the first one of the things that we saw."

In an oral interview, army pilot William Hutchison remembered one day hearing "a plane grinding away in the fog, and pretty soon, I was outside, and I heard the motor stop and I knew that they had hit the mountain. They must have had a wonderful pilot because ... everybody on the plane survived; they all stepped out of the plane, and fell down the mountainside in one huge snowdrift. They were having a great time. I thought that was one of the happiest moments on Attu."

Navy air navigator Charles Fitzpatrick, in his book *From Then 'Til Now, My Journal*, had a poignant memory from Attu:

Selecting a cold, gray and brisk afternoon, I thought it would be nice for a walk and for listening to the crunching snow underfoot. While out at the point, I had the misfortune to witness a P-38 fighter plane crash. As the pilot approached Murder's Point, losing altitude fast, his engines sputtering and intermixed with some soft backfiring, he looked at me as though he were asking me to do something. His distraught face ... told everything. We both knew there wasn't a place to ditch or land ... As he approached he looked a little forward off his port wing at me, seconds long. Then when opposite me ... I was sure his lips were moving. Finally, turning his head quickly, kind of a fast glance looking over his shoulder in my direction and back equally as fast looking forward, facing reality ... his plane barely skimmed the crown of Murder's Point settling steeply into the rocky coastline amid the swirling waters. It all was so very fast ... Obliterating those seconds; that scene, from my mind took some time.[15]

Bill Maris, a navy flight mechanic, wrote about having to land their large PBY seaplane in Korvan Bay at Atka Island, due to bad weather elsewhere:

We landed in heavy seas and high wind [and] couldn't anchor due to the sea state, so we [taxied] out away from the beach and rocks ... We taxied the rest of day and night with sea anchors rigged, and the next morning ... at daylight, Mr. Decker decided it was safest for survival to beach [the] plane ... Trying to drive the [aircraft] nose-first up on the beach didn't work [so] we got a line ashore ... and tied the [aircraft] off to beached logs ... The beach was very steep and this caused the [aircraft] to heave and pitch every time a wave hit it. We salvaged all life-saving gear possible [and] set up camp on a flat spot behind the crest of the beach ... We improvised a tent out of one of the parachutes, gathered firewood, and prepared to spend the night. Ensign Arnold, radioman French and second mechanic Huppert started hiking for Nazan Bay for help.

Later that afternoon we heard a ship's horn sounding and spotted the USS *Hulbert* coming into the bay [which eventually managed to bring us aboard] ... We were treated royally, given dry clothes, a quick [medical] check ... hot food, two fingers of [liquor] in water, and a warm bunk.

The missing Ensign Arnold [along with] French and Huppert ... were finally found four days later, wet, cold, tired, and hungry.[16]

Chapter 7
The Welcoming Committee Visits Kiska and Attu

It was dark as they approached, and he could see the muzzle flashes and tracers from Japanese guns as his plane passed low through the Kiska harbor for only five or six seconds.

When the Japanese attacked Dutch Harbor in 1942 and then occupied the American Aleutian islands of Attu and Kiska (at the far western end of the chain), the generals, admirals, and their superiors left the invaders alone for a while. This gave the Japanese time to dig in, bring in supplies, build defenses, and try to create airfields. The Americans didn't know if the Japanese had further designs on the Aleutians and mainland Alaska, but were concerned about air threats to the northwestern United States.

Resenting the audacity of the Japanese to occupy a slice of the United States, the Americans didn't leave the Japanese alone on the two islands for long. Air attacks from the Dutch Harbor area against Kiska began soon, often depending upon slow and lumbering PBY seaplanes at first, a duty they weren't designed for, along with old bombers such as B-17s. Due to the long flight distances, these planes didn't have fighter escort.

A navy PBY taxying. Early on, they were pressed into service to bomb the Japanese on Kiska. Later in the war, PBYs were usually used for patrols and pilot rescue missions. "PBY" abbreviates "patrol bomber," with the Y designating its manufacturer, Consolidated Aircraft. *US Navy photograph*

In 1943, the army and navy picked the island of Adak as their forward air center and command post and set up a major base there. Flying from Adak, the flying distance to attack Kiska was greatly shortened. Later, American forces were unopposed when they built another large airbase on the island of Amchitka, closer yet to Kiska. Now the Japanese on both Kiska and Attu were the recipient of frequent air attacks from bombers and fighters and were on the defensive.

Newer bombers and better fighters were brought in. Multiple airfields on additional islands were built, offering other landing alternatives if needed. It was time for a conspicuous display of bravery and a considerable loss of life on both sides. And, as always in the Aleutians, the worst enemy was the weather.

Following are some air warfare stories centering on air attacks against Kiska and Attu. Keep in mind that most of the American pilots and crew were in their early twenties, perhaps for whom the term "baptism by fire" was coined. The antiaircraft fire from Kiska was intense.

Pilot Bill Thies in an oral interview recalled an early attack on Kiska:

Well, the commanding officer … said, "Bill, we think there's Japanese on Kiska but we're not sure, so go out there and take a look." So we get out there. I duck in and out of the fog bank and look down there and there was a whole Japanese fleet … So I go back up in the clouds and radio Kodiak … I thought, I've done my job. I'm gonna get the hell outta here and get back. [But the commodore radioed me to bomb the enemy ships.] So, I got with … the navigator, and I said, "We've gotta figure out some way to save our necks before we carry this order out." Bob thought for a while and he says, "I have a good idea." He says we'll duck down out of the clouds, and there was a big spit [of land] which was very predominant on Kiska. He says, "I'll find out exactly how far it is from that spit to where the fleet is. When we [pass over that spit], knowing where we were … I'll time it, and when we get over the main body of the fleet I'll tell ya—I'll call you up and we'll drop the bombs manually." That's what we did.

I got a picture of the ship we sunk. It was a Japanese transport. That's when [I was awarded] the Navy Cross.[1]

Thies added, "We lost nine … out of twelve airplanes in the first thirty days, mostly due to weather. I was one of the lucky ones to come through."

SSgt. Roger Vance, who was later missing in action, wrote in a letter home about participating in some of the first Kiska raids:

I was just a kid with a new toy playing at a new game. But now I've seen some of those toys broken. It's still thrilling but it also is a terrible, bloody business. I've seen our planes [head] out and come back shot full of holes, and one came back dripping good red American blood … I know not what guardian angels fly with us, but there are other wings than ours … in the air over Kiska … A higher power than our 100 octane gas … pulls us through.[2]

Vance described approaching Kiska: "I could feel the tightness growing, especially in my throat and tummy, and I knew the others were feeling the same thing." It was dark as they approached, and he could see the muzzle flashes and tracers from Japanese guns as his plane passed low through the Kiska harbor for only five or six seconds.

Two bombers on their way to Kiska came upon a Japanese ship and made a very low approach to bomb it, to avoid antiaircraft fire. One pilot warned the other that he'd gone so low he was skimming the ocean waves and kicking up spray.

An *Air Force Magazine* article in 1943 described a B-25 mission against Kiska. On this attack, bombers approached the island from the west instead of the usual eastern approach. One group of planes flew up and over a ridge and down the other side, into the crosshairs of Japanese gunners. The lead plane, piloted by Lt. Ray Stolzmann (an accountant in private life) released its bombs. They were supposed to have delayed fuses, but instead exploded instantly, seriously damaging the following plane, wounding its pilot, piercing its wings with holes, and forcing it out of position. Bombs in its open bomb bay were now jammed and one 500-pounder was caught vertically. The bombardier was tenaciously able to work that bomb free and reposition the other bombs.

"Five of the six planes met at the rendezvous, and four of them were damaged," stated the article. Upon returning to home base, one of the planes had to make a belly landing due to landing gear damage. The attack left a Japanese oil dump heavily damaged.

Capt. James Beardsley, an army air force navigator, wrote an introspective poem titled *Kiska Mission*, reminiscent of the helicopter attack scene in the Vietnam war movie *Apocalypse Now*. Following is an excerpt (the full poem was published in the October 1943 issue of *Air Force Magazine*):

> *The flash of cannon was our welcoming sign;*
> *The sound of their shells, and the bullets' whine;*
> *Presenting a glimpse of man-made hell,*
> *Of death amid the battle yell—*
> *A holocaust of fire and flames.*
>
> *Our vengeful fingers stoked smoking guns.*
> *Down dropped our bombs in whistling tons,*
> *Missiles of death, of fire and hate,*
> *Destruction most articulate.*
> *We burned and maimed and slew.*[3]

In contrast, navy flier George Sinclair wrote in his diary: "April 4, 1943 … Beautiful day … Bombed Kiska" and on April 24, "Nice day … Bombed Kiska with forty tons of bombs."

Capt. Irving Waddlington wrote in *Air Force Magazine* about another low-level bomber attack, this one led by Col. Eareckson and escorted by fighters:

> We were about four miles from Kiska's North Head when I saw firing off that point. There were two large guns and they were following us up nicely. One shell hit directly below our ship, throwing a huge geyser of water that nearly touched our belly. [The island of] Little Kiska opened up.
>
> The leading P-39 dived on one large gun emplacement, silencing it with a single burst … The cross fire from Little Kiska, North Head, and South Head seemed impenetrable, and ships anchored in the harbor were throwing a large amount of fire … Just before we reached the Head, a Jap machine gun sprayed the water in front of us.[4]

An Aleutian fighter pilot (probably in a P-38). *Courtesy of Walter Dalegowski via National Park Service. Image 741*

Waddlington's plane was hit in the wing and rudder, with one shot barely missing his side gunner. He saw a float-plane Zero take off nearly vertically, only to be blown apart by fighters. On the other hand, two P-38s pursuing a Zero collided and went down in flames. Waddlington's group left an enemy camp on fire, and all their bombers returned home.

Another bomber pilot said that attacking Kiska was like running a gauntlet, with tracer bullets whizzing by, and as all his plane's guns fired, the noise level was incredible.

In a February 1984, *Air Force Magazine* article titled "The Forgotten Front," mention was made of "seven heavy bombers, five [medium bombers] and six fighters [which] attacked Attu from their base at Adak. Weather closed in and six of the eighteen disappeared without [a trace]."

The army air force and naval aviators pressed the attack about as often as weather permitted. When it didn't, airmen languished. Some hated the waiting more than being shot at during bombing runs.

As Billy Wheeler's squadron diary put it, "No single factor has as bad an effect on morale as being grounded and at the same time kept on continual alert status. Patience is a virtue rarely present in the makeup of a flier … Contract bridge [has] become the reigning passion. Three tables are running at any hour of the day and most of the night. Terrific winds have fanned the ten-inch snowfall into a continual blizzard."

Consider this passage from the Brian Garfield archive, quoting Herbert Ringold:

It's harder to get used to the waiting. You spend half your time waiting for the weather to open so you can do some flying. Fighting the Japs wasn't bad at all—it was the sitting around, waiting for the chance to fight. Sometimes [our airbase was] only twenty minutes from our target and [yet we'd] wait for weeks to [get airborne to] get to it. We used to stay in bed so long we had a tournament to select the sack champion. A fellow named Hanson copped the honor with twenty-six hours in bed.[5]

Tommy Olsson of the army air force wrote that they typically got up at 4:30 a.m., arrived at the alert shack at 5:30, and then were on standby until 6:00 p.m. "The usual manner of spending the morning [on standby]," said Olsson, "is to carry your sleeping bag over and find a cot to get some more sleep. The afternoon is spent reading, writing letters and taking part in bull sessions."

Navy flight mechanic Bill Maris wrote: "[I] would watch the B-24s take off with a full load of bombs for Kiska and almost run off the end of the new 10,000-foot Marston matting runway, dropping a little down into a gully as they climbed for altitude and headed west. [I've] seen a PV-2 run off the runway on takeoff, catch fire and burn; all were saved and air evacuated [to] Anchorage for treatment."

The Japanese were never given the opportunity to build functioning airfields on Kiska and Attu. To defend themselves from the air, they had only float planes able to take off from water, including a potent version of the Zero fighter.

One of the first skirmishes with a Zero float plane took place when PBY pilot Lt. J. E. Litsey tried to photograph a new Japanese heavy cruiser anchored at Kiska. He was approached by an enemy plane, which he assumed was an observation plane. Instead, it turned out to be the new, fast Zero, attacking with guns blazing. Litsey was able to escape into cloud cover. When he returned to Dutch Harbor, sixty bullet holes were found in his plane. After that scare, PBYs were no longer used to closely approach Kiska.

During a naval bombardment of Kiska, Lt. Raphael Semmes Jr. and another pilot were flying ship-launched, old-fashioned scout planes to help direct fire. John Rodgaard wrote: "While Semmes could hear the ships' guns over the roar of his Seagull's radial engine, cloud cover obscured his view of the targets. [The two pilots] flew their planes over Little Kiska Island, just east of the harbor, hoping for a better view of the falling shot[s]. Instead, the pair of Seagulls were spotted by two Japanese Zero float planes, which promptly dove toward them."

Semmes himself wrote, "I … commenced a flight maneuver which the instrument instructors at Pensacola had told me to be sure never to do. I made a steep … power spiral through the overcast and leveled off at 200 feet to find that the fighters had not followed."

Other old scout planes that participated were not so fortunate: one was lost and three others had a total of one hundred bullet holes.

Billy Wheeler wrote about a photo-reconnaissance mission with a B-17 over Little Kiska Island in the 36th Squadron war diary:

> We ran into a little excitement today … Coming away from Kiska, one Zero paralleled our course just out of .50 [caliber machine gun] range. A few bursts of our waist gun dissuaded his one or two attempts to cut in on us. Shortly after … we saw two more Zeroes flying under the cloud base at three o'clock. Captain Wernick turned to the right on a head-on course to the Zeroes. One Zero, evidently completely surprised, pulled up and disappeared into the overcast. The other attacked from about 11:30 o'clock—pressed it fairly close, but he could have come closer with greater effect. He put one explosive 20 millimeter shell through our left bomb-bay door, cutting a fuel line and just missing the nose fuses of our 500-pound bombs.[6]

John Mullican of the 406th Bomb Squadron recalled arriving at the Umnak air base before moving on to Adak, and then Amchitka, with B-25s. They made several very low-level attacks on Kiska; during one, Mullican counted more than three hundred antiaircraft bursts. The plane next to his lost an engine due to a hit, but the plane was able to limp back to base. In the Garfield archive, Mullican remembered that "there was not one day in which we were not scheduled for a mission."

Tommy Olsson of the army air force reported that among the planes returning from one Kiska raid "every medium [bomber] was battle damaged. One was shot down, but the crew was saved ... One plane landed without brakes and went off the end of the runway."

A Garfield archive note indicates that one attack on Kiska in April 1943 involved 112 planes dropping 92 tons of bombs.

The Americans even bombed at night using the illumination from burning incendiary bombs.

For those craving excitement and danger, attacking Kiska by air provided plenty of both. It's a testament to the construction of the bombers and the grit of the air crews that so many survived the gauntlet of antiaircraft fire and occasional attacks by Japanese fighters.

As mentioned before, American aviators' worst enemy was the weather. Capt. Ira Wintermute, flying a B-24, wrote about one incident:

Halfway to Kiska we ran into a solid front of fog. We couldn't see anything and felt hemmed in by some evil genie ... [I] said to the crew, "We're lost." There was a dead silence.

We dropped our bombs to lighten our load and make our fuel last longer. There was no way of knowing whether we were north or south of the island chain. Hour after hour, we flew in wide circles, trying to catch a radio signal or sight of land. Nothing!

We had been flying fourteen hours and were exhausted. It was time to ditch ... The eight of us gathered on the flight deck near the emergency-exit hatch and started to nose down. The plane plowed into the sea and upended on its nose ... The next thing I knew, I was on top of the water. I swam to a wing and thought I saw all of the crew swimming. [However, we soon learned that] two were gone.

We were on ... two rafts, tied together, for eighteen hours without food or water. Soaking wet, we huddled together to escape the bite of the freezing wind ... No one slept—just sat there like dead men.

The next morning, we brought out paddles and started to push toward what we thought was land. Suddenly, someone yelled, "I hear a plane." A big navy [PBY seaplane was] headed our way.[7]

Another ditching at sea was described by John Stavinoha:

We made several passes on Kiska and pretty soon I heard chuck, chuck, chuck. Engine died [in my P-40 fighter] ... We was headed back to ... Amchitka where we were stationed. But I didn't make it. About halfway in between, I decided I'd have to ditch and so I ditched. And I was in the water, 30-degree water. Lifespan, twenty minutes ... My [airborne companion plane] threw me one of his life rafts. And I crawled in, but that wind and everything was colder than the water.

[A PBY seaplane] came in and landed ... So they pulled me in and said, make ready for takeoff. That was the scariest one ... So [the PBY attempted a takeoff in heavy seas] and he bounced a couple of times and then he hit a big one ... [The seaplane] had sprung 400 rivets in the hull and was sipping water by the time we tried again and he got up there and ... away we go. He made it.[8]

A PBY pilot went to the rescue of another P-40 pilot who lost power and ditched after a Kiska attack. Water-taxiing over to the floating pilot, the crew found the pilot already too weak from the cold water to climb aboard of his own accord. The 12-foot waves made their takeoff difficult. Such flights were called Dumbo missions.

An article about the role of fighters in *Air Force Magazine* (1943) told the story of a P-38 pilot whose best chance for survival (when his home base was fogged in) was to land in a lake on an island near Kiska. He was able to swim to some rocks and wait for rescue. A PBY rescue seaplane had to land out in the ocean 3 miles away and get to him with a rubber life raft.

An excerpt from Col. Lawrence Reineke's poetry indicates:

From here out to Kiska and back …
Your propeller comes to a stop, your engine it has quit.
You cannot swim; the water's cold; the shore is far behind;
[You're] a tasty dish for the crabs and fish; but you will never mind.[9]

Paul Carrigan wrote about battle-damaged planes returning to base:

[A few planes] came in on one wheel and this drew everyone's attention … By manipulation of controls [pilots] kept rolling on an even keel until speed decreased to the point at which the plane simply fell over on the wheel-less side. This usually caused the plane to spin round and round as it slid until it either hit something or came to a jolting stop on the runway. Occasionally the one down wheel collapsed quickly upon landing and this usually resulted in a bad crash.

Many planes were almost out of fuel. A few, completely out, came in dead-stick with feathered props. These planes all had to land NOW and they did … On several memorable occasions we watched fighters landing simultaneously from both directions.[10]

The story is told of a bomber over Kiska that had already received battle damage when a shot came in through the cockpit, throwing bits of metal into the copilot's hands and piercing the pilot's foot. With both pilots mostly incapacitated, they still managed to fly the craft. The copilot, with his hands mangled, manipulated the plane's rudder and brakes with his feet, while the pilot managed the throttles and control column with his fingers. In this fashion, they managed a landing. When the copilot stepped out of the plane, his flying trousers were covered with blood.

In another incident, a .30-caliber shell hit a pilot's radio, bounced off the rear of his armored seat, hit a portion of the windshield and, now spent, fell into his lap. Picking it up with his gloved hand, he put it into his rear pocket as a souvenir.

Similarly, from the Garfield archive: The illustrious Col. Eareckson, while on an advance observation flight, had a .50-caliber bullet come through the bottom of the plane into the cockpit, where it bounced off the colonel's leg and fell to the floor at his feet. He picked it up as a souvenir. Unlike some "armchair officers," the colonel didn't mind putting himself at risk.

Airmen Brickett and Albanese had a battle incident described in Billy Wheeler's 36th Squardon war diary. While circling over Kiska amid small-caliber fire, bombardier Brickett was concentrating on his bombsight while Albanese was kneeling behind his gun. A large bullet entered the nose of the plane, drilled into Brickett's calf, and exited from his thigh. From there, it tore through Albanese's forearm and then through the upper portion of the same arm before zipping out through the top of the plane. After treatment, Brickett was able to return to air duty, but Albanese, who had more serious bone damage, was returned to the States.

Navy flight mechanic Bill Maris: "Watched a crippled B-24 make an emergency landing after being shot up over Kiska … He had no brakes, so he ran off the end of the 3,200-foot runway, crushing the [plane's] nose around the wounded bombardier. The bombardier was critically wounded from antiaircraft ground fire while over Kiska and died, but the other wounded [men] survived and were taken to the base hospital."

Nonetheless, for some GIs on the ground, air combat seemed flashy and exciting. There's the story of a cook for a B-25 outfit on Adak who longed to be a flyer. He had never flown before, but he finally got the commanding officer to make a gunner out of him … On his first combat mission, the B-25 suffered landing gear trouble … and all men aboard except the pilot parachuted … Back on the ground, the cook quit combat and returned to cooking.

In the army's *Adakian* newspaper was an article titled "As Others See Us":

Bundled to the ears in fur flight clothes, handsome young Lieutenant Frank Rasor stamps his feet as he awaits the order to get into his sleek Billy Mitchell medium bomber for the twenty-one-minute run to Kiska. "This goddamned war business sure isn't what it's cracked up to be," he complains. "In every damn movie or dime novel … a pilot takes off, has a whale of a flight, knocks down a Messerschmitt or something and then flies back to a bottle, a girl, or both.

"Now wouldn't that be the right way to fight a war? But look at us. We fly over Kiska and drop bombs. Maybe they hit us with ack-ack and maybe they don't, but there's never any planes for us to fight. And what do we fly back to? This muddy island, some warmed-over macaroni and some cold stewed tomatoes."[11]

Reportedly, every military pilot flying missions in the Aleutians during the war had an undated death certificate on file. Whether due to the enemy, the weather, or mechanical failure, the more flights under your belt, the greater the chance you'd become a statistic and there'd be one less body in the chow line.

Chapter 8
Come Payday, All-Night Poker Games

Our spare time was mostly occupied [by] playing poker. The normal game was ten-cent limit and I've seen games last all night. On foggy days games would go on all day.

In the wartime Aleutians, I gather that some men played cards—maybe bridge or cribbage—in a gentlemanly way without money on the table. On the other hand, throughout the war, other men of all grades and stripes made life a little more exciting by gambling with hard cash. Whether it was aboard ships, in tents, or Quonset huts all along the chain, the arrival of payday meant it wasn't hard to find the sounds of thrown dice or the slick sound of shuffling cards.

If a guy was single and didn't have dependents back home needing his paycheck, he was free to do whatever he wished with his money. Meals, bed, medical, and clothing were free for enlisted men, so why not dial up a little excitement?

Paul Carrigan, the meteorologist, wrote:

What time we had was spent sleeping, reading anything we could find, writing letters, attempting to study, [or] sitting in on the nightly card game … Some nights the preference was poker; other nights it was blackjack.

There was usually about a thousand dollars floating around the hut. The money continually changed hands, ending up in the pockets of various current winners. Not infrequently, two nightly winners … cut cards to determine that night's overall victor. After five or six hours of painstakingly smart poker we did not consider this a dumb way to end the session. This … provides insight into our overall "what the hell" attitude.

Card games would cease or be penny ante for a while when a big winner slipped off to the post office and sent a money order home. Although we had all done this and the losers acknowledged the wisdom of the move, they at the same time considered it an extremely horse**** act.[1]

One night, a Japanese officer's sword from Attu was bet and lost in a poker game.

GI James Liccione wrote that gambling technically wasn't allowed at military facilities, but in the Aleutians, commanding officers would look the other way and games could last into the early morning hours.

Ottis Littlejohn said during an oral interview, "I remember one night I played poker until midnight. I had to go on watch … from midnight to 4:00 a.m., and I went back down there [afterwards] and the same game was still going … so I sat down and played then until breakfast time and I won $100 … The next night I lost it in fifteen minutes playing blackjack. Easy come, easy go."

Ray Galloway remembered: "Our spare time was mostly occupied playing poker. The normal game was ten cent limit, and I've seen games last all night. On foggy days games would go on all day. There were, however, some old regular army men who played no-limit games, and I've seen pots with hundreds of dollars in them."

One enterprising gent went one step further and received permission to turn a Quonset hut into a gambling hall. He was one of the chief beneficiaries of the move, regularly increasing his monthly income.

There were some compulsive gamblers. Navy man James Doyle said, "A few of the guys were real gambling addicts, you might say. The minute they got those extra bucks in their hands [on payday], it was down on the floor with the dice … Some would lose their entire [paycheck] and have to wait a month. [Maybe they had enough money left over to] buy a milkshake at the army PX."

Harry Bailey, an army barge man, told about a cook from Louisiana named George "Rabbit" Daniels:

> He had had poor gambling success … but … went ashore at Attu after receiving his pay and proceeded to the monthly big game. Thousands of dollars would change hands that night. He returned in about four hours and the first question asked him was how much he had lost. We should have been a little more observant. He was not too steady on his feet and had a smirk on his face. It appeared he had celebrated with a few snorts of someone's tent-made, fruit-flavored alcohol.
>
> We assisted him aboard and sitting him down, we went through his pockets. After a total count of all denominations, it appeared he had won approximately $1,300. The following night, his confidence at the highest, he made ready to go ashore for some more rolling of the ivory cubes. Charlie, the skipper, insisted he only take a small amount of money, perhaps no more than two hundred dollars. Most agreeable, [Daniels] departed. Within a little more than two hours he shouted for the ladder to be laid to the dock. After crossing and coming inside he put his winnings on the table—a tidy sum of approximately seven hundred dollars.[2]

Like the cook, there were winners and losers. On the losing side, it was mentioned that a GI moaned and groaned so much over sixty cents he lost in a crap game that his tent mates raised and gave him sixty-five cents just to keep him quiet.

Army man Bailey said, "Money used to change hands … One guy would [win it all, then] somebody'd … find somebody he could borrow $10 from and they'd have another game and all the money would transfer to somebody else. I don't know how many times it'd pass through my hands and go to another fellow a week later when we were … rolling dice."

On shore, or on ships, it wasn't uncommon for a GI to win $600, which was a lot of money in those days.

Air force mechanic Mac McGalliard remembered moving from base to base so frequently that his monthly pay couldn't keep up with him. Finally, said McGalliard, "I got seven months' pay all at once. It lasted three days. I guess you might say I was a poor poker player. OK, say it. The only good thing to come out of my time in the Aleutians was that I had $70 [withheld from my pay] and sent home. That was the only money I saved or sent home in the twenty-eight months I was up there. Boy, the crap games they had [were] wide open—no restrictions."

He also remembered "one of our guys [who] traveled around from outfit to outfit, gambling. Supposedly he carried around $20,000 in a money belt. He was found one morning in a Jeep, upside down, down an embankment, dead." McGalliard wasn't sure if his money belt was still there.

Gambling cliques, and especially compulsive gamblers, created the need for GI "bankers" who made loans, mirroring the outside society at large.

Then there were those who only flirted a little with Lady Luck. Pvt. Edward Thomas wrote, "A few days ago under the influence of beer, I gave my gambling luck a very small test ... in a crap game ... I lost the great sum of $4.00. This was disturbing enough to make me mumble over and over to myself that gambling doesn't pay. Most of the fellows around here, though, aren't affected that way. Some lost as much as $250 with a few rolls of the dice without seeming to care very much."

George Sinclair wrote in his diary, "I've quit all gambling."

Chapter 9
Whaddaya Have to Do to Get a Drink?

[There was a] slight, bespectacled corporal who ... had majored in chemistry ... before becoming an army weatherman. This "professor" was resident brewmaster when not standing office weather watches.

In the Brian Garfield archive, I found the story of Sgt. Edward Newman, who "was offered a fortune for a bottle of Coca-Cola—it was the only one on the island." Instead, Newman ended up giving it to a GI who'd received a Dear John letter.

If some Aleutian Islands GIs were that desperate for a Coke, many more were desperate for alcohol.

Men enjoying Cokes while working on an amphibious plane. *Courtesy of Craig Stolze (probably the person on the left) via National Park Service*

Fortunately, in built-up and established bases like Adak, enlisted men could buy beer at a PX. Navy radioman James Doyle said, "Radio City men could drink beer at a bar at the army PX. You showed an empty beer can and then you got a new full one, so you wouldn't carry it off."

Navy seabee Earl Long described the opening of a beer hall on one of the islands:

The catch was that the bottles were all sold pre-opened and had to be consumed on the premises. As you might expect, however, it wasn't long before one of the wise guys in the group tried to break the rules. He stuck three bottles of beer in his belt and concealed under his jacket as he walked out of the beer hall, but the shore patrol was onto him, and as soon as he stepped out of the door, they struck him across the midsection with their billy clubs, busting the bottles of beer. As you can imagine, the results were messy and embarrassing. After that day, I never heard of anyone else trying that ploy.[1]

On Shemya, army air force man Jim Schroeder mentioned having a ration of six cans of beer a month. Officers, however, had a monthly liquor ration, and on the more developed islands, they had an officers' club with liquor. Charles Fitzpatrick, a navy air

WEEKLY BEER ISSUE
Good for two (2) bottles
from Jan 20 thru Jan 26.
C. C. Lander
Welfare Officer.

A beer ration ticket issued to enlisted men by the navy on Adak. *Harry Paul Jr.*

navigator on Attu, admitted that "The liquor rations per officer was phenomenal."

Pvt. Edward Thomas wrote, "A couple days ago I tasted my first beer in about eight months. All the boys in my hut had to be transported by truck about four miles through dripping wet darkness to a mess hall outside of our area to get this beer, [where we] consumed our quota of three bottles per man."

The very ingenuity that led men to solve everyday problems like keeping aircraft flying was also employed toward finding drinks more potent than beer. Often, they tapped into whatever other alcohol might be available. Seaplane pilot William Thies talked about "torpedo juice":

All torpedoes for the navy and [army] planes were stored and loaded at Umnak. There was a navy chief torpedo man in charge. The "fish" in those days ran on ethyl alcohol. The alcohol was spiked with "pink lady" so that if anyone drank it, they would get diarrhea. This enterprising chief drained all the torpedoes, built a still to remove the pink lady [and then] recovered and sold the pure alcohol! His court martial punishment was a reduction in rank to seaman second class and "banishment" to stateside!!![2]

That the chief drained *all* the torpedoes may be an exaggeration.

One GI, drunk on torpedo juice, ran nearly naked out of his hut with a rifle, yelling that he was at war.

Joe Baldeschi tells about using a different chemical:

Somebody had warned me that there'd be a great party—and there was ... We [had] anti-icing fluid for deicing the wings [of our plane], and they found out that this was grade A [alcohol] ... They didn't have any booze up in Attu, not even beer. So they drained it and replaced it with grade C. They took the grade A and had a good time [drinking it] for a few days.

That was deadly too because at one time the commander of the base held an inspection because two [GIs] died from drinking that stuff. Because what they did [was], they took the grade A and took a glass and put about four slices of bread over and filtered the grade A through the ... bread. Then they'd mix [in] some orange juice or whatever and drink it. So those were the people that really missed alcohol.[3]

Roald Forseth was quoted in the *Baltimore Post-Examiner* as saying a man nicknamed Whips "convinced us to buy cases of canned-heat Sterno and big cans of grapefruit. Back in the hut, he showed us how to squeeze the Sterno through a sock—preferably clean—and then swallow the extract with a grapefruit chaser. I survived ... and we all woke up the next day with splitting headaches."

Reportedly, two wartime GIs were buried in the Amchitka Island cemetery after dying from alcohol poisoning.

Navy men on Adak celebrating the promotion of one of them to chief on his twenty-first birthday. *Courtesy of Bill Maris via National Park Service*

Air Force mechanic Mac McGalliard remembered, "We had a young man by the name of Terry. He must have had [a] connection with the hospital because about once a month he came home with a five gallon can of grain alcohol ... Terry sold a fifth for $100. Everyone was glad to get it. There was no other place to spend our money; no PX, no girls, no anything. One guy would buy a beer bottle full [of the grain alcohol] for $25 then nurse it for a week. [If] he drank it straight, boy I'll bet he has no belly left today. It was 180 proof."

Army pilot Royal Sorensen remembered that "one day, Col. Chennault [the son of Gen. Claire Chennault of Flying Tigers fame] had everyone bring anything 'worth drinking' to a central washing machine and we poured everything together into it, then after a little mixing, we all helped ourselves."

Some drinkers were shameless. Men would line up at sick call, claiming bad coughs and asking for cough medicine. The medicine contained codeine and alcohol.

Then there were skillful men with more patience and caution. Guys with a little chemistry, biological, or brewing experience carefully set up makeshift stills where everything from potatoes to fruit to raisins—with some yeast added—fermented away, yielding alcoholic beverages of varying quality. Brewmasters with a consistently drinkable product, often called Sneaky Pete, were considered valuable resources.

Harry Bailey wrote, "Ashore and on some ships, enterprising people were [creating] some decent high-potency, flavored alcohol. It was being distilled from most any type of fruit or vegetable. The use of potatoes was quite common, but the most talked about, with perhaps having the bouquet of wine, was a fine-flavored alcohol that was started with grape jelly. The army, for whatever reason, never had any other kind."

In his memoir, Harry Sperling related a great story. He said none of the crew on his ship had any experience moonshining, but through a trial-and-error process were able to concoct a "tundra juice." During the fermentation, they stored their ten-gallon jug in their ship's heated furnace compartment.

After moving to a dock at Adak, they figured their batch of "juice" was about ready for taste-testing. However, they weren't too pleased when notified that Gen. Davenport Johnson was soon due to inspect their and others' vessels. Unfortunately, their almost-ready jug exploded the night before the inspection, and the ventilation system pumped the odor throughout the entire ship. The smell, said Harry, was like being in a bar that hadn't been cleaned or aired out for a month.

Since the general was due within a few hours, they frantically turned the ship's vent fans up to full blast, with little effect. Someone suggested they get some Aqua Velva shaving lotion to cover the odor, so Harry and his executive officer went to the PX to buy a whole case. They soon learned they were limited to one bottle each because men had been drinking it for the alcohol. They informed the PX manager of their critical situation, so he authorized a full case but insisted on coming along to verify the story. The crew emptied most of the lotion into the ventilation system and sprinkled the remainder all around the compartments. Then, instead of smelling like an old bar, it now smelled like a very "dingy bordello."

Their ship was in the middle of a group of three and after inspecting the first vessel, the general stepped onto their boat, wrinkled his nose and said, "Keerist, what's that smell?" then went on to the last boat. Returning afterward to their vessel, he said to no one in particular, "I know something's been going on here, but I'm not about to check it out."

Robert Boon, who served in the army band at Dutch Harbor and was the group's supply sergeant and company clerk, also served as their brewmaster. They strengthened their Sneaky Pete concoction by removing some of the water through distillation. Also, said Boon, "There was a rumor going around that some [other] people had taken a .30-caliber machine gun and used the [water-cooled] barrel to cool the steam, but I never actually saw that operation happen."

Paul Carrigan had another story:

[There was a] slight, bespectacled corporal who ... had majored in chemistry ... before becoming an army weatherman. This "professor" was resident brewmaster when not standing office weather watches. His distillery was a large oaken barrel placed close to the oil stove in the army hut. A sheet of plywood covered with elegant cloth camouflaged this moonshine still and made it look like an innocent writing table.

[Master Sergeant] Cox provided sugar, raisins, apples, pears, yeast, or whatever was available and his corporal-chemist brewed with loving, meticulous care. Spare weather thermometers hung suspended at different levels in the working mash … Periodic fermentation tests were made as the working mixture bubbled and was babied to perfection.

Cox, in his position, knew well in advance when his superior officers intended to hold barracks inspection [so] two electric fans … were started several hours before inspection to flush out the odor of fermenting fruit …

The brewmaster [had] told Cox that it was time to siphon off the first batch of joy-juice. Cox graciously invited all off-duty [meteorologists] to a party … When a group of us knocked and entered the army hut that night … [a poker game] was already in progress … It was a scene straight out of a gambling casino.

Cox rose and gave a warm greeting to his navy guests. The … game was suspended as siphoning preparations to tap the barrel began. The brew was carefully drawn off into sparkling clean gallon jugs. It was a surprisingly clear liquid of the palest green color. Canteen cups were filled all around and a toast was made. Approving sippers expressed delight at the magic wrought by the corporal-chemist-weatherman. Someone exclaimed that the concoction tasted like California champagne.

A festive air reigned. Small groups engaged in conversation while others sampled delicious hors d'oeuvres Cox had set out on a snack bar.

[Later,] most of the army and navy enlisted weathermen, some weather officers, and many other army and navy personnel acquired jugs of the brewmaster's product. Although the brew earned the nickname "Green Death" because of its color, each batch was consistently excellent with an alcohol content of about twenty percent.

After the inaugural blow-out there were no other large parties at the army hut, [but] individually or in groups of two or three we sometimes stopped by at night for a quiet drink, conversation, or gambling. The brewery was in constant operation and Cox always had a supply on hand. If one visited or came to play cards or dice, he generously served a drink or two. If one wanted a jug to go, the price came high.[4]

Similar to what happened at Dutch Harbor, where some men made off with officers' liquor stores, GIs elsewhere rarely skipped a chance to score some hooch.

Paul Carrigan wrote about the time when officer Leslie Gehres (probably a navy commander by then—and not generally liked by enlisted men) was moving his unit or office to Adak:

There were four cases of Canadian VO [liquor] from Gehres's private stock sitting on [the deck of the seaplane tender/destroyer *Gillis*]. [One man] shielded the view of the busy [officer of the deck] while a crewman was successful in putting eight [bottles] inside his foul weather jacket and getting into the fireroom air lock undetected. This booze remained untouched that day and well hidden. [The] remainder of the four cases disappeared somewhere betwixt and between deck and stowage. That night the 8–12 watch on the after gun got put on report … for being drunk. They couldn't officially be charged with theft of the liquor but they paid the price nonetheless.[5]

Here and there, other libations were liberated. In one instance, Seabees filched twenty-five cases of beer from a freighter at Dutch Harbor.

A court-martial record at the National Archives at Seattle revealed two men were charged and convicted of breaking into a medical dispensary on Attu and taking whiskey and medicinal alcohol. They received bad-conduct discharges. Tracking the culprits down wasn't difficult because a bunch of drunken men had been discovered drinking the stolen loot.

Harry Bailey wrote about beer being stolen from power barges bringing cargo to Attu and Shemya: "The record haul was 100 cases, taken [from] one barge. This was a monumental feat at the time." The men hid the beer in the engine room. But eventually all the largesse came to an end—pilfering ceased when a military policeman was posted on deck.

There was a bush pilot who flew whiskey and beer to grateful GIs on one of the islands. The beer went for five dollars a bottle and booze for a sky-high one hundred dollars.

An army shrink speculated that some enterprising merchant marine sailors brought in and sold liquor and marijuana. Similarly, said Harry Bailey, "If you had fifty dollars one could purchase bona fide low-price whiskey—Schenley, Fleishmann's, and Seagram's 7—from freighters up from the States and other smaller boats that occasionally came from Seward or Kodiak."

In several courts martial cases, navy men found drinking from a gallon of red wine—and another sailor found with brandy—all said they bought the alcohol from army guys.

Air force bombers returning from repairs in Anchorage sometimes carried cases of whiskey in their bomb bays, enabling GIs to get, yes, thoroughly bombed.

A Canadian chaplain had to return home after he was caught selling communion wine to troops.

Army pilot Royal Sorensen told about a major beer run:

I had the brilliant idea of flying to Dutch Harbor to see if I could talk the army out of several cases [of beer]. As soon as I'd landed … I went to the officers' club where I met the supply officer and asked him for some beer. He told me that he could spare only three cases … so he pointed me to the navy supply officer, who asked how much I could carry in the C-47 [transport plane], and I told him 10,000 pounds. We loaded the plane full, and when I took off I had to use the entire runway to get in the air. Back at Umnak [Island], I called operations to inform them that I had a planeload of beer. The commanding officer couldn't believe it, and said a party would be held that night and that I would be the guest of honor.[6]

Ray Galloway mentioned that after a liquor-drinking bout involving three gallons of liberated whiskey, guys were taking target practice in a tent, taking turns shooting through a playing card handheld 10 feet away.

Paul Carrigan wrote about some moonshine being passed around in a weather unit:

Giles couldn't hold his liquor as well as some, and he became extremely argumentative at these times … [On the other hand,] Strong was argumentative even when sober. Shortly before the jug was emptied, Strong and Giles got into a heated argument.

Giles grabbed a shovel, raised it and advanced on Strong. Strong backed warily away, reached above the workbench and took down a crosscut hand saw. The fight that ensued was not only the most bizarre I've ever witnessed but also one of the bloodiest and most frightening.

Giles swung and jabbed while Strong used the saw like a swordsman. Most of Giles' swings missed but some of his quick thrusts struck Strong's upper body, including face and head. One long jab lifted a patch of flesh and hair that partially scalped Strong. Whenever Gile's thrusts were parried, Strong's sharp saw slid down the shovel handle and lacerated Gile's hands. Other saw swipes, thrusts and slashes opened jagged, ugly wounds.

The fight ended when the two men were so bloody they could no longer see and [were] so exhausted we were able to disarm them and get them to sick bay.[7]

Carrigan himself fell victim to the devil in the drink after visiting their unit's Green Death distillery. He and several friends were on their way back to their hut in the driving sleet when

we were about to pass the weather office. My none-too-bright idea was to visit our army buddies and navy shipmates on watch. Emmett thought this was a splendid idea. Roberts did not … His mention of Hassell stuck a pin in my happy bubble and sent me off on a tangent of drunken fury. Rather than avoid the office, I announced that it was an ideal time to tell that little runt off.

Hassell was seated at his desk at the back of the office when I burst in and made, more or less, straight for him. Dispensing with formalities, I shouted that I was going to break his scrawny neck. All work in the office ceased. Everyone was immobilized except Hassell. Cat quick, he jumped up and ducked under my outstretched arms. Coatless and hatless, he sprinted out into the icy gale with me hot on his heels.

I chased [him] all over our cliff-ringed mountaintop that stormy winter night, all the while shouting in a scream to match the wind. Upon tripping he almost fell into my clutches but finally found a hiding place.

Roberts and Smith caught up with me. Panting, out of breath, and in my exhausted stupor, they had no trouble leading me to our hut and my sleeping bag.[8]

The next day, Hassell approached Carrigan, saying, "I know you've had several close calls lately flying in this atrocious weather … I'm glad you let off some steam last night. We all must do that occasionally or we'd explode … No need to apologize."

Another time, Carrigan was pulling a weather watch with others on a stormy night, when a drunk but otherwise well-respected senior officer barged in, interrupting Carrigan's careful preparation of a weather map:

Hassell leaped to his feet and ordered, "Attention!" … Hassell advanced to greet our unexpected guest but he was silently waved aside. We were surprised by the unusual night visit but mostly by the condition of the visitor [and] we remained rooted at attention.

After steering himself to the map desk, the officer attempted to climb atop the high stool I'd just vacated. My proffered arm lent to steady him was pushed aside. He made it astride the stool and attained balance … He then carefully selected one of the special fountain pens used for entering [map information] and began to draw a meandering isobar … This line was not only strange but it was being drawn with a permanent ink pen. This was highly unusual because maps are analyzed lightly in pencil accompanied by much erasing as one goes along … But not this man. Most impressive was even in his state no study … was required before he drew the heavy ink line in a matter of seconds. Lord, I thought, the man is truly a genius, especially because the ink line encompassed the Bering Sea and most of the North Pacific Ocean where weather reports were nonexistent.

"Do you know what this is, youngster?" he asked. "That's a goddamned bunny rabbit!"

With a startled look I saw it sure as hell was exactly that—in black ink—all over my precious map.

My mind was trying to untangle what had happened when it was further short-circuited. As the officer slid off the high stool and stood up he swept the map up in his hands, ripped it not quite in half, wadded it into a ball and threw it on deck. Without another word, he lurched out the door and was gone.

[Outside, the officer's Jeep] sputtered to life, over-revved, and with a clash of gears the Jeep took off down our steep mountain road. In the weather hut we did not hear the crash far below. MPs estimated the Jeep must have been doing at least 50 mph when it came off our hill spur onto the main arterial. At that junction it hit a ten-wheeled army truck head on.

It took over an hour to extricate the more-dead-than-alive officer from the wreckage.

Except for one permanently gimpy leg, he recovered fully from severe multiple injuries and returned to active duty.

It was not only the lowly but often the lofty who fought off [craziness] by succumbing occasionally to alcohol.[9]

One Christmas Eve, some GIs had a beer party, then headed up a hill for some stronger stuff. "It was quite [a] Christmas," said navy flight mechanic Bill Maris. "A couple of the guys didn't show up so we went looking for them and found them asleep in a snow bank … And so ends another year."

Air force mechanic Mac McGalliard recalled:

Did we have a party, man o man. I can only tell you about our Quonset hut … Someone said something somebody didn't like and it went [on] from there.

We had two coal stoves in the hut … and of course they were full of black soot. They came down with a crash and rolled north and south. As for the wrestling that went on, no one really got hurt. Soot, blood and beds all over the place. When the fun was over we looked around and someone said, "Get a mop." [That was of no use because] the floor was black, black, black!!!!! Then someone … suggested turning the floor over … So over it went, stoves reset, bunks in order, beds made, and guess what, the whitest, cleanest-looking floor you ever saw.

In comes the [commanding officer] for inspection ... He looked around, grinned, and said, "Did you have a good time?"[10]

In Billy Wheeler's squadron diary, he describes a scene proving that real life can be funnier than fiction:

Colonel De Ford, our new bomber command CO, gave a party, [believing] in friendly get-togethers among the officers of his command—and we were enthusiastically in accord with his theory ... With Colonel Cork's experienced assistance in obtaining whisky, Colonel De Ford located two cases of bourbon [to which was added grapefruit juice] ... Everyone had a rip-roaring time, singing songs, listening to jokes, falling over the portable organ, etc. ... At an early hour the colonel called an official halt to the festivities and remarked that for the rest of the night we were on our own.

About ten men, in company with Colonel Cork, went to the squadron operations hut and started all over again with a fresh supply of whisky ... [An officer named] Pete was eager to have a confidential discussion with Colonel Cork and began ... to stalk him. Pete had been spending a quiet half hour drinking everything he could see and cleaning his fingernails with a Bowie knife. Of course, the colonel couldn't be expected to know that Pete merely wanted to talk to him, [so seeing] the knife was too much. The chase went merrily on until someone opened the door as Colonel Cork passed it on his thirty-sixth trip around the stove, Pete still at his heels but not gaining an inch. On the lucky thirty-seventh [pass], Colonel Cork made the other side of the room while Pete went through the door and made [his] mark on the great "outdoors."[11]

Paul Carrigan had a scare that made him a teetotaler—for a month:

Some off-duty squadron radiomen came into our living quarters tent one night to hold a party. They had acquired a gallon jug of 190-proof pure grain medicinal alcohol. While one clutched this precious commodity another lugged a full case of ... grapefruit juice.

After an hour or so and Lord knows how many full canteen cups of the potent mix, it became necessary for me to go to the head. My speech wasn't impaired and other than a slight facial numbness when I'd lit the last cigarette, I thought I was completely sober.

I sat up and slipped into my flight boots to go outside. When I attempted to stand up, I fell heavily to my hands and knees. Try as I might I could not get up. I was paralyzed from the waist down. At first everyone thought I was joking. Finally, I had to be helped outside then back to my sleeping bag. No one else was affected this way ... Extremely frightened by the thought I might be permanently paralyzed because I didn't feel the effects of the alcohol in any normal way, I just lay there ... I was afraid to test my legs and eventually fell asleep. When I awoke in the morning my legs were back to normal and I wasn't even troubled with a hangover.

I was sobered in more ways than one. Although it wasn't so in this instance, some unscrupulous person could easily substitute wood alcohol for grain alcohol.[12]

Of course, if a man found himself on the Alaskan mainland in Anchorage or Fairbanks on some temporary mission, he would have found authentic bars with cheaper pricing.

In ending this chapter, two little stories remain. In the first, Lt. Eliot Asinof told the story of visiting his officers' club, whereupon the barrel-chested bartender, a native Aleut, asked, "What'll it be, lieutenant?"

"Scotch," replied Asinof, "a double, please."

The bartender poured from a bottle of Chivas Regal. Behind him were bottles labelled Stolichnaya, Canadian Club, Wild Turkey, and so on. The ongoing joke was that, in reality, the only liquor on the island was tequila.

Navy air navigator Charles Fitzpatrick in his book *From Then 'Til Now, My Journal* wrote about another way to sneak liquor into the islands:

Dad had sent me a canned fruit cake [for the holidays] which when opened was more like a sponge than a fruit cake. It was soaked. I can assure you there wasn't a gram of water in [it]. That delicious … cake had been drowned in fine bourbon. When I opened it in the privacy of my Quonset hut … the pure aroma of dad's fine bourbon at once permeated the Quonset's warm air. [I] had guests to arrive almost immediately. The small canned cake lasted but minutes.

As I sit and write about it, I wonder: Did mother know of it? I'll bet she didn't.[13]

Chapter 10
The Navy Often Had It Better

God, the navy had nice food compared to the army. I always remember [they] had honeydew melons and cantaloupes. I didn't see one of those things for three years up there.

To this day, the advantages of serving in the navy versus the army are argued. In the Aleutians during the war, the subject came up frequently.

Earl Long, a Seabee, wrote:

> Our [navy] accommodations had changed from canvas tents … to Quonset huts, which was much to our relief and comfort. My reason of bringing this up at all is to illustrate the difference in treatment of personnel from one branch of service to the other. The army units were right next to us, and although they had been in the area for many months, some even eight or nine months before our arrival, they were still forced [to] live in tents. They took their meals in mess tents and ate out of mess kits. We had a wooden mess hall, had our meals served on metal trays, were allowed to eat all we wanted, and had galley crews to do all the cleaning up. When we left the island several months later, the army units' living conditions had not changed one iota.
>
> I remember that later on that year when the movie house was built, the unfairness continued. The army and navy personnel formed separate lines, navy going in first, and then if there were any seats left, the army guys were allowed in … I always did and still do feel that the inequality was wrong. Perhaps the most disturbing incident of this sort occurred when we were about to return to the States. A lot of our unneeded clothing and blankets, some of it even unused, was loaded on navy trucks to be destroyed. Army men came to our area and asked for some of it, but our brass had given orders to refuse their requests. Things like this saddened me.[1]

Army man Harry Bailey in an oral interview recalled, "The army did not give you clothes that were adequate for being on a ship. We were always trading with the navy. We'd give them something in [return] for one of their jackets."

Walter Anderson, a navy guy, recalled, "My mom wrote and told me that one of the neighbor's boys was up there in Attu in the army and she gave me his outfit's name and I went to look for him. He was in the battle of Attu. We used to call the army guys 'dog faces.' I found Joe up there and he looked like a dog face … These guys lived in a cave. They were with the mountain group."

In the Garfield archive, an army flier commented, "[A navy Seabee] took me to his quarters on Adak and to the officers' club. After I had completed the visit and [after] a wonderful meal … I returned to our tent and told the boys about how high on the hog the navy lived and they did not believe me."

Army band members found a way to enjoy navy food, as related by Mack Collings:

The navy was … all well fed and we were in tents living on mess kits. We'd go get our food in our mess kits and go back to the tent and eat it. So, on Monday—or on Wednesdays and Fridays—the navy would always have chicken and steak and all we had was canned Spam … So … I would go down and pick up a Jeep and then about four of us [would] take our instruments and we'd go down and entertain the navy in their nice barracks and buildings … and then they'd feed us. Oh man, what a deal![2]

Army man Harry Bailey, again, said:

God, the navy had nice food compared to the army. I always remember [they] had honeydew melons and cantaloupes. I didn't see one of those things for three years up there. The naval officer who [I sometimes worked for] … gave us a couple of melons which was … his way of saying that we did a good job supporting them.

White tablecloths, stewards, and fancy table settings in a navy officers' mess on Adak. *Harry Paul Jr.*

[Also,] I know a story of a couple [army] air force people that heard about the good food the navy served. They were flying people and pilots [that is, officers] and they went over to the navy officers' mess hall to eat one night and they [were] treated … alright but [their uniforms were dingy] … All the naval officers from the lowest one to the highest one were dressed in their dress uniforms and white shirts and ties. [The army men] felt out of place … But I guess they made their one trip.[3]

Bailey said he preferred to shop at the navy ship store which had more goods than the army's PX.

Somewhere out on the islands, army GI Ward Olsson washed his clothes in a navy shower. He wrote, "We're living in a Pacific hut very much crowded [with twelve men], with no place to wash except in the hut. After seeing the way the navy fix[es] their huts and latrines up, our things look sick."

Navy Lt. Rudy Leach said, "The army got the work, the navy got the food, [and] the marines got the credit." It seemed that marines had a knack for getting newspapermen to write that marines did most of the heroic wartime fighting.

Navy man Bill Hutchison and a friend "had our navy-issue fleece-lined green parkas stolen as we ate at the army mess. In retaliation we borrowed an army Dodge command car and kept it hidden for two months. I later saw our wonderful coats hanging on the army mess coat rack. We took them back, but kept the command car."

My dad wrote home, "Most of the men here believe the army and navy should merge. We could sure save a lot of money if they would merge. The navy has things much nicer than the army, and that may be one reason why the navy big boys don't want to merge, but I can see lots of advantages."

Sometimes the equation was reversed. At Cold Bay, navy men had to steal tools and equipment during a "midnight requisition" from the army to build a communications system. Their largest acquisition was a generator.

Navy Seabee Howard Rummel, on Attu, noted that the "exchange of services and supplies between the army and navy were made by the primitive barter system ... From the atmosphere of barter relations ... the army and navy developed a spirit of mutual cooperation."

According to navy man Joe Baldeschi, there were arguments about who made the best pilots—army or navy. They sometimes shared the same airfields.

Before the war began, there had been infighting between the naval and army air forces: the navy didn't want the army doing long-distance patrolling over water, and in fact seemed to resent the army air force being in the Aleutians at all. However, *Air Force Magazine* in 1943 pointed out that "on many missions both army and navy planes participate. The navy sends out a PBY rescue plane which has saved many [army air force] lives."

On a more formal level, according to the Brian Garfield archives, the services exchanged intelligence and motion picture films, both services' stores sold to all servicemen, and clothing was worn interchangeably by all services—at least in the Aleutians.

Chapter 11
Blood in the Snow

"You know," he said, "I think those guys are trying to kill us."

After the Japanese attacked Dutch Harbor and then occupied the Aleutian Islands of Kiska and Attu in 1942, American forces began to bomb those islands from the air base at Adak Island. Later, bombing missions were flown from a new and closer American air base on Amchitka Island.

Naval bombardments also harassed the Japanese bases.

When it came time, after eleven months of Japanese occupation, for an American ground force to try to wrest one of the islands away, the invasion flotilla from Adak bypassed Kiska and went on to Attu. If Attu could be retaken first, that would isolate Kiska and make it harder for the Japanese to resupply it, starving it out, and possibly forcing the Japanese to evacuate.

Col. William Eareckson, the flamboyant leader from the 11th Air Force, which had been attacking Attu and Kiska, wrote a ditty expressing mixed feelings about the enterprise:

When viewing Attu's rocky shores
While planning how to take it,
This thought emerges more and more:
The Japs should first forsake it.
Since Attu's not worth a hoot
For raising crops or cattle,
Let's load with booze and take a cruise
And just call off the battle.[1]

Nonetheless, in May 1943, thousands of troops, mostly from the army's 7th Infantry Division, headed for Massacre Bay on the southeastern side of Attu Island in an armada of ships. It would be the first amphibious island landing ever by the army's infantry. Smaller groups were to land on the northeastern side of the island. The idea was for all groups to meet in the middle of the island and then push the Japanese defenders into smaller and smaller perimeters until their backs were against the sea.

The best that can be said of the operation was that it was a learning experience about amphibious landings and how to properly prepare for weather, terrain, and a resilient enemy. The worst to be said is that in their haste to push the Japanese out of the Aleutians, the army messed up royally, with insufficient intelligence, planning, and preparation.

The 7th Infantry Division had been training in California for desert warfare. When their war assignment was changed to Alaska, the division received poor training for cold-weather fighting, and soldiers were generally given clothing that was unsuited for the cold, windy, and wet Aleutians.

American generals expected to overwhelm the enemy and win the island in several days, so troops involved in the initial fighting had very limited food rations and shelter. Instead, the battle dragged on for twenty days, brutal in every way. As a result, the battle for Attu was the second bloodiest battle in the Pacific, only exceeded by Iwo Jima—in terms of percentage of deaths.

The flotilla arrived off Attu on May 11. The invasion had already been postponed for one day because of poor weather, and this day had its problems too—fog problems. In May, full daylight arrived at about 6:30, but there was considerable light before then.

Dean Galles of the 7th Infantry, in an oral interview, said:

> We climbed over the cargo nets [of the troop transport ship] to get in the landing craft … at about 3:00 in the morning, and then we rendezvoused out in the heavy fog. We couldn't see. I don't think we could see 25 yards … And we circled and circled, and they were hoping that the weather would break … Finally, at 4:00 [in the] afternoon, they sent [us] a seaplane that had a compass. None of our landing crafts had [a] compass. We didn't know which was north or south or anything, so they sent this seaplane in, and it [taxied on the water, leading us all to the beach].[2]

Landing craft with troops circle in the fog off Attu before finding their way to the beach. *San Francisco Call-Bulletin Collection, Alaska and Polar Region Collections, Elmer Rasmuson Library, Univ. of Alaska Fairbanks. UAF-1970-11-56*

Maj. William Jones, writing on the American Veterans' Center website, recalled:

> We were to hit the beach at 8:40 a.m., but were delayed by a dense fog … Radar was then in its infancy, and few ships had it … After circling the area in our Higgins boats for hours, the navy control officer finally located a small frigate that had basic radar, which was able to identify the direction of the beach. The directions were duly pointed out … and off we went.

Approximately at the center of Massacre Bay … is a large rock formation … about the size of two conventional automobiles, protruding above the water about five or six feet … About eight feet to the left of our craft was another landing craft, which smashed into the rock as we sped on past … Several of the standing soldiers [fell] forward out of the craft [and into the water]—our first casualties of the Battle of Attu.[3]

The most emotional description of the landing was written by Lt. H. D. Long of the Australian army, who related:

Our beach came into view. As it did, the mist lifted a bit and we … saw Attu Island.

It was something prehistoric. Cold, cruelly broken, mountainous … Attu seemed devoid of life. Not a tree, an animal, or anything else … moved. And yet we knew that death lurked in the fog … As we approached the beach for the landing, breaths tightened, stomach muscles curled, and men prayed. They prayed … for noise, any kind of noise. Dear God, please make a noise of some kind.

Then it came. Not the Japs, but a sparrow. He sat on a bump above the beach and sang his lungs out, and an explosive gasp [came from] hundreds of throats. The spell was broken; the world hadn't died around us.[4]

Men had to wade into cold water to get to shore. When some landing craft struck protruding rocks, some troops carrying full packs jumped off into watery depressions and drowned before they could reach land.

Both troops and cargo went ashore at Massacre Bay. Reportedly, of the ninety-three landing craft and boats used, after a week only three were still operational. The others were the victims of rocky hazards, high winds, and surf.

Smaller numbers of troops landing on the north side of Attu were dropped off from submarines and had to paddle 4 or 5 miles to shore using inflatable boats. In a windy sea with waves and tidal currents, that's a lot of paddling.

As happened with some later Pacific amphibious landings, there was no immediate Japanese resistance on the beaches and nearby lowlands. The Japanese merely used the classical tactic of holding the high ground—nearby ridges and mountainsides—and waited for the Americans to come to them. They were well dug in with plenty of ammunition and warm clothing. Oftentimes the fog obscured their positions. Things soon got hairy.

As Allied soldiers proceeded up a valley away from Massacre Bay, Japanese snipers from above began to take their toll, and the advance stalled. Meanwhile, the wet, muddy muskeg and the cold wind began to take a toll, too—especially since most of the GIs were poorly provisioned and clothed.

Army veteran Dean Galles remembered:

We were so ill-equipped, clothing-wise. We had leather Blucher boots, and by being continually wet all the time, they just fell apart. After [many days] of fighting, they called us back to the beach, and they said, "Take your shoes and socks off . . . " I was so amazed. My feet were black with, I guess, fungus or mold … We wiped that off, and they brought in twenty-five-pound buckets of lard from the navy, and said

"Coat your feet with lard, put on dry socks, [and] new boots … and get going again."
Well, this resulted in what they called immersion foot up there, which is a combination
of frostbite and fungus. And some of the guys, when they would rub the mold off,
[their feet] became infected and gangrene set in, and there was some amputations.

The light jackets we had were just nothing for what we needed. We needed
parkas, … we needed something we could put up over our heads in the wind and
the storms and stuff. And we never did have [full] gloves. [Also,] we didn't have
any … sleeping bags until … a good two weeks after we were on the island.

By sleeping on the cold wet ground all the time … our groin became inflamed … I
don't know what it is. Anyway, it was so painful when you'd try to stand up in the
morning … the majority of our guys had to crawl the first little bit. And once you
get up and get going, then you could work it out pretty good.[5]

The deficient boots worn by most of the troops had been issued to many of them aboard
ship, and they weren't broken in. Once wet, they were difficult to dry out. The preferred
shoes for those conditions were rubber-bottomed, leather-topped shoepacs, but the initial
troops didn't have them.

Rubbing one's feet was recommended to keep blood circulating. Joseph Sasser remembered
that "we would get in our foxholes [at night] and take off our socks and we would put our
socks close to our body and then our body heat would dry those socks out overnight."

The average high temperature for that time of the year on Attu is 39 degrees Fahrenheit,
and nighttime lows average 30 degrees. Of course, the constant Aleutian winds would've
created lower wind-chill temperatures. As the troops inched their way up ridges and mountains to higher altitudes, temperatures would've dropped. Officers urged their men to occasionally move around at night to keep their blood circulating, but some men slept solidly
and woke up with frostbite.

Army infantryman Frank Bosak wrote that in desperation, some GIs wore the clothing
of dead Japanese soldiers to keep warm. William Anderson said, "I picked up an old coat
that some Japanese had that looked like a fur coat, and I wound it around me … I went to
sleep in a foxhole … I woke up and there was a man with … a rifle standing there looking
at me. It just happened to be one of the warrant officers [who thought I might be Japanese]."

Some GIs also found and ate Japanese rations such as dried carrots and canned salmon,
according to Sgt. Barney Laman.

Lt. George Reeder Jr. wrote about living off C- or K-rations, which might include
hamburger with rice, a couple biscuits, a piece of chocolate, and Vienna sausages.

Joseph Sasser, a combat engineer, said he heard that scout companies landing on the
north side of Attu went three days without anything to eat or drink, saying, "They were
eating snow to get some liquid into their system." Some men vomited green bile.

Sgt. Emmett Mull said he had no shelter and no change of clothes for seventeen days. Most
GIs, however, carried so-called canvas shelter halves—which, when two were connected together,
and supported by two poles, could form a pup tent barely large enough for two soldiers.

Gaylord Tapp remembered, "We tried to put up a tent one night, a great big tent so … six
of us [could] sleep in it. We couldn't get the thing to stay up, it was so windy. Raining. Wind
blowing. We just left it lying down and got underneath of it … It was horrible."

In the book *The Capture of Attu*, mention was made of men wrapping shelter halves around themselves to keep the wind at bay and sleeping all in a pile.

Barney Laman said that during their first night under fire, they tried to rest—probably in a foxhole—but water would seep in and they were always wet.

A GI remembered, in *The Capture of Attu* book, about having to overnight in a battle zone: "It was late, and the cold was intense. It made you ache dully all over; it was a wet cold. We tried to sleep but it was fitful. We would wake up with spasmodic shivers every little while." The fog was so thick, "it eddied around a man like water."

Gaylord Tapp, in an oral interview, said, "[A] lot of infantry lost their hands and feet. They froze to death up there, a lot of infantry boys ... Yeah, I felt sorry for them."

According to an army report, the troops' backpacks were often left back on the transport ships because they were too bulky to be carried ashore during the landing. They contained sleeping bags, which the troops could've put to good use. Stated the report, "Few troops ... received [sleeping bags] before the fourth or fifth day, and until that time the men had no protection during sleep, when sleep was possible, except from the shelter halves which they had carried ashore."

The report concluded that "there is evidence that many of the troops found the cold, damp, wet weather harder to endure than the enemy fire." It mentioned that at the end of five days of fighting, one battalion still had 320 men who weren't killed or wounded—but of those, only 40 were still able to walk, due to cold-weather ailments.

A GI sheltering from Japanese fire during an uphill push during the battle for Attu. *San Francisco Call-Bulletin Collection, Alaska and Polar Region Collections, Elmer Rasmuson Library, Univ. of Alaska Fairbanks. UAF-1970-11-45*

As troops moved inland, they came under increasing fire. Fog played a role: rifle and machine-gun fire was only accurate when one could see the enemy, and the fog came and went, sometimes offering cover for an American attack, but also making it more difficult to spot the Japanese. GIs were sometimes asked to do what was nearly suicidal: attack uphill into the maw of Japanese fire. Men would seek shelter in shallow depressions as bullets passed within inches overhead. Sometimes GIs got within 25 yards of camouflaged Japanese dugouts but still didn't see them. Fighting would continue on during the night.

Allied mortar and rifle fire during the final days of the battle for Attu. *Library of Congress*

Cpl. Jerome Job said, "I was up against a rock, and one bullet went over my head [by] maybe an inch, another went under my leg, and another splattered against the rock under my armpit. We decided to withdraw and cool off."

Lt. George Reeder Jr. said he fought with bayonets. He had a friend with a wife and baby back home who was killed by a sniper.

A GI named Gonzales quoted in *The Capture of Attu* book, said, "One Jap gunner was slumped over his gun and his blood was running down and dripping off the end of the barrel. It made me feel good to see him. I thought that might have been the gun that shot two canteens off my belt during the day."

Sgt. Paul Plesha was part of a platoon going into position to set up their mortars when friendly fire killed two of their men. Elsewhere, there were instances of GIs being mistakenly strafed by their own planes and bombarded by their own artillery.

GIs were seen taking potshots at Japanese casualties or dead rolling down a snowy mountainside, just for the hell of it. When the fog cleared enough for ships offshore to heavily bombard the high ground, Japanese body parts literally rained down the slopes.

When some aging vets returned to Attu for a visit in 1993, Morton Solot, a wartime twenty-three-year-old platoon leader, remembered the way blood had looked in the snow fifty years before.

Lt. H. D. Long of the Australian army wrote about the fighting:

One of my biggest worries was trying to make my wild gang of gorillas fight with their weapons. They wanted to kill Japs with their bare hands, "just to show the sons of bitches we can do it." And they did kill them with their hands, literally beating them to death. I liked the spirit, but it was dangerous.[6]

There were stories of spontaneous heroism. Occasionally someone would boldly step out from stalemated troops and get the job done, seemingly impervious to bullets. A private reportedly got tired of being pinned down by machine-gun fire and singlehandedly forged ahead through snow with a rifle and grenades to eliminate nine Japanese firing positions. He returned to his lines to wave his companions forward.

Partway during the unexpectedly difficult battle to root out the Japanese, when rosy predictions of a two- or three-day engagement went out the window, the army's invasion leader, Gen. Brown, was replaced in disgrace after asking for more troops and seemingly lacking confidence. The new leader, Gen. Landrum, basically retained Brown's strategy and continued on.

Army sergeant Dix Fetzer said his group had to dig new foxholes every night. The Japanese threw a grenade into one of their holes, which the GIs threw back, and which the enemy quickly returned. It exploded in the American hole, killing three of Fetzer's buddies. Fetzer himself had shrapnel hit his knee, and his hearing was damaged.

Paul Carrigan wrote about an army sergeant who later "told his [Attu] stories matter-of-factly with neither braggadocio nor apology." The following is the sergeant's story:

US troops had gone ashore with orders not to take prisoners … After being trapped in [a] valley for five days while being slowly cut to pieces, the sergeant and his men were in a bloodthirsty mood and looking for revenge. They felt no qualm killing several badly wounded enemy.

A Jap hiding in a crevice must have known his unit's positions had been overrun. He was alone and about to die … Waving a white rag, he came out of hiding.

This was such a surprise, the sergeant and his men didn't shoot. With pantomime the sergeant indicated to the prisoner he should raise both arms and clasp hands atop [his] head. The white rag concealed a palmed grenade. This was activated when the Jap tapped it against his helmet. Before he could finish his throwing motion the semicircle of bunched GIs cut him down "with so much lead the bastard would have sunk with two life jackets." The grenade was a dud.

[Said the sergeant:] "I felt bad, … because my poor judgement could have cost lives … I should have shot that sonavabitch the moment he cleared the rocks."

[The sergeant told of] a grisly incident a day later at Point Able [indicating] the vow was kept … Six Japs in a bunker were cut off, out of grenades, almost out of ammo and surrounded. They surrendered, were rooted out, patted down for weapons, lined up and shot.[7]

[The Attu fighting, wrote Carrigan,] "was like stuffing an angry badger and a wildcat in a burlap sack and tying the neck. Options were reduced to one: annihilate or be annihilated. Can there be a more fertile ground for barbarism?"

Dean Galles admitted in an oral interview, "We were so conscientious in our job up there—anything that looked like a Japanese did not survive. And so [army intelligence people] pleaded with us, or gave us orders actually, to take prisoners. Well, we finally got one … and sent him back, and they interrogated him, and whether they found out anything … I don't know."

In the book *The Capture of Attu* the story of Pvt. Ira Clawson was related:

While under fire, he made a dive [for a Japanese hole]. [It was] a nice deep hole with a partial roof over it, and as he flopped down just outside he noticed a figure in it. "Hey, how about sharing your hole, buddy," said Clawson, and … he started crawling in. The little figure hunched down in the corner looked back over his shoulder at the two hundred pounds of Clawson about to crawl in with him. To Clawson's great surprise the little fellow, who incidentally had slightly slanting eyes and buck teeth, did not wish to share his hole … So he made a grab for Clawson's rifle. [After a scuffle, the Japanese then] made a grab for [a] knife. Clawson … kicked the Jap in the mouth. [Clawson's buddies] had watched the fun from the adjacent hole, and … they came over and shot the Jap.[8]

An American night patrol saw someone following them in the murk, assuming it was their officer, only to make out a Japanese, who they summarily killed. Similarly, a Sergeant Mason in *The Capture of Attu* book saw a Japanese soldier come toward his unit in near darkness, apparently slightly drunk, with a sack of dried fish and rice balls. When ten feet away, he saw the GIs and said in English, "Don't shoot; don't shoot," but was taking his rifle with a bayonet off his shoulder when they cut him down. Another GI said that sometimes the only way they could tell a Japanese from an American was that their entrenching shovels were different.

One GI referred to a Japanese sniper as "our friend, the Jap on the left."

First Sergeant Fenton Hamlin, in *The Capture of Attu* book, told the story of his unit being pinned down by Japanese fire. The nervous GIs weren't talking to each other. One broke the silence with, "You know, I think those guys are trying to kill us." Hamlin recalled, "He stated so calmly what was so terrifyingly obvious to everyone that they laughed. It broke the tension."

In the same book, Theodore Miller related holding a position in the dark

when we heard voices coming and three Japs carrying boxes of ammunition walked by within ten feet … They were laughing and talking in low voices … [Then] another Jap came along, [coming] close to where we were laying and then he looked out and spoke something in Japanese … He came a couple of steps closer, staring at us … I had my bayonet fixed so I stood up slowly and motioned to the Jap to come over. He moved a few more steps toward me, staring at me … Suddenly the Jap made a grab for his pocket. I lunged at him and caught him in the right shoulder with my bayonet. He fell down and screamed, rolled over a couple of times, then he got up and, still hollering, ran up the hill.[9]

War makes for some weird cultural exchanges.

Crawling in the dark, a GI tried to warn the man crawling just ahead of him about danger ahead by pulling on his pants leg. The leg turned out to belong to a big Japanese, which the GI duly killed.

In the book *The Great War and Modern Memory*, British poet Max Plowman wrote about being in the trenches in World War I in France: "In this sunshine it seems impossible to believe that at any minute we in this trench, and [the Germans in theirs], may be blown to bits by shells fired from guns at invisible distances by hearty fellows who would be quite ready to stand you a drink if you met them face to face."

As related in *The Capture of Attu*, a GI was about to enjoy his last K-ration cigarette when a Japanese mortar shell burst in front of him, cutting his finger and slicing his cigarette off flush with his hand. "And that's the last goddamn one, too," he complained.

In the same book, some American officers during an interlude in the Attu fighting were discussing which was better, scotch or bourbon, when they spied five live Japanese at a distance. They called in four artillery shells that completely obliterated the men. "It was just too damned good to miss the opportunity," said one. "We were all cheering like a bunch of high-school kids at a track meet."

A sergeant claimed to have killed thirty-five Japanese, and was very proud of it.

About 1,150 GIs were wounded at Attu and approximately the same number had weather-related injuries.

Bill Jones of the army artillery was one of those wounded. He was hit in the cheek with shrapnel and had a broken tooth, but was quickly treated and returned to the battle with some aspirin. Then on the seventeenth day he was wounded in the leg. It took him seven hours to crawl back to a hospital because the Japanese were shooting at litter bearers. Upon arrival, medics had to cut his boots off because his leg was swollen.

A GI in *The Capture of Attu* told about sharing a foxhole with "a wounded boy lying on top of us and asking where he was hit and what hit him … He died in just a few minutes."

Also in this book, 1Sgt. Fenton Hamlin related, "At [a command post] a cave had been dug into the snow and the wounded were lying in it side by side on shelter halves. Even when they were unconscious, their bodies trembled violently from the cold. Empty shell cases [and] ration boxes … had been torn up and consumed in tiny fires to heat the last packages of coffee and warm stiff fingers."

Sgt. Robert Rundle recalled: "When [Japanese] shelling stopped, I started looking around me. I saw another soldier sitting up in a trench with his eyes wide open. I thought he was looking at me with his mouth open. Then I discovered that the 'mouth' was his slit throat. I marked him for recovery by standing his rifle in the ground with his helmet on it."

Two wounded men were seen walking downhill toward an aid station, holding each other up.

The caption for an army signal corps photograph reads: "Medics massage the legs and feet of seventeen-year-old Pvt. Donald Lynch who was forced to remain in a water-filled trench at the front for over twenty-four hours due to enemy fire. At the time the picture was taken, he was credited with killing five Japanese soldiers. Pvt. Lynch was finally rescued by the medics and taken to the hospital."

An army report stated, "The first principle of treatment of cold injuries is that the casualties should not be permitted to walk, even if they feel able to do so. Many of the injuries sustained on Attu were so severe that the men were scarcely able to walk, but, because of the difficulties of evacuation, many of them had to walk; some of them crawled. The wheeled litters which had been brought ashore were useless and evacuation had to be by hand carry."

Not all the casualties were the physically wounded: The book *The Capture of Attu* described a corporal who had been near a Japanese artillery shell explosion. He was shocked badly and began to shake and weep.

Also, in that book, toward the end of the battle for Attu, a young GI was shot in the chest and

Captain Pence crawled over and half dragged, half carried the boy back toward the main body of the company. He was groaning. He was hit hard. Pence stopped and gave him a shot of morphine. [The boy] began to talk about his wife and child back in the States. He was nearly dead when they got to the company. He could recognize only Pence [and] begged him not to leave … Pence held the boy's hand for a short moment while he talked about his wife. He was silent then and shortly after, he died.[10]

It's a fact of life that most of the troops in a battle zone are support troops, providing everything from medical attention and food to ammunition. On Attu, one estimate had only one-fourth of the men doing the actual fighting.

Supplies piled up on the Massacre Bay shoreline, and men often had to carry them inland on their backs.

Lt. Darwin Krystall in *The Capture of Attu* book:

One little man in Service Battery, a fine worker and an excellent, cheerful soldier normally, was sodden with sweat and rain and fatigue when I saw him struggling through the mud uphill with a single [artillery shell] on his shoulder. Its fifty-four pounds pushed his feet almost to the knees in the sticky mud and bent his back.[11]

Other times, according to Gaylord Tapp, some ammunition was passed to the front lines by means of an old-fashioned bucket brigade.

Pvt. Morris Madison brought munitions to the front with a Jeep. As he returned to the beach for another load, a Japanese artillery dud furrowed the ground between him and another Jeep. The next shell exploded nearby. He also helped transport the wounded. Without improved roadways, vehicles had trouble negotiating the muskeg and mud.

War can bring out the best and worst in people. Cyrus Falconer Jr. wrote author Brian Garfield saying that after the Attu battle, he saw photographs showing Japanese troops that had been savagely mutilated.

Sgt. Dix Fetzer said he saw a GI trying to extract gold tooth fillings from dead Japanese soldiers.

Souvenir hunting was common during the fighting. Ceremonial swords, personal effects, Japanese flags, and Japanese weapons were all duly collected by the victors for personal collections or for sale. Rummaging through the clothing of dead bodies seems barbarous, but it happens in every war. There's interest in collectables, sure, but there's also the aspect of learning more about guys who were trying to kill you. Did they have wives and families? Were they willing combatants or scared conscripts?

A diary recovered from an unnamed Japanese noncommissioned officer on Attu revealed that his life was hellish too. He wrote that frequent bombardments from American ships and strafing by fighter planes often kept them in shelters for hours on end. They were running low on rations and sleep. Even with superior clothing, their hands and feet got cold, too. There were rumors and hopes of reinforcements coming from Japan which never materialized. "This is the time to endure hardship, and struggle through," wrote the NCO. The last entry before his death was, "Naval gun is constantly firing on us."

A well-known Japanese diary recovered from Attu was from a doctor named Paul Nobuo Tatsuguchi who'd been educated in the United States. In Japan with his family when the war broke out, he was conscripted into the army and ended up on Attu. He became the equivalent of a sergeant major and had medical duties.

The following are some poignant excerpts from his diary that tell a story from the other side of the battle. The diary was apparently first translated by the American "Northern 5216 Detachment." This is my edited and condensed version:

May 15. Continuous flow of patients into the field hospital caused by the ... bombardment [from] enemy land and air forces, also naval. The enemy has great numbers of Negroes and Indians ... I just lay down from fatigue. In the barracks facial expressions of men is tense.

May 17 ... At night ... under cover of darkness, I left the cave. The stretcher [bearer] went over muddy roads and steep hills of no man's land ... Sat down after every 20 or 30 steps. Would sleep, dream, wake up and go on.

May 18 ... About sixty wounded came to the field hospital. I had to take care of them myself all through the night. Everybody made combat preparations and waited. Had two grenades ready.

May 21. Was strafed when amputating a patient's arm. It was the first time since moving over to Chichagof Harbor that I went into an air raid shelter ... Nervousness of our commander is severe and he said his last words to his officers and men. He will die tomorrow. Gave all of his articles away. Hasty chap, this fellow ... Everyone who heard this became desperate and things became disorderly.

May 22 ... Air raid began; strafing killed one medical man. Medical man Rayki wounded in thigh (right) and fractured arm. During the night a mortar shell came awful close.

May 24. It sleeted and was extremely cold. Stayed at Misumi Barracks alone. A great amount of gunfire. Shells dropped by naval gunfire. Rocks and mud flew all around. The roof falls down. In a fox hole five yards away Hagaska, medical man, [was killed] by penetration of shell through heart.

May 27. [My] diarrhea continues; pain is severe; took everything: pills, morphine, opium and all, then slept well … There is less than 1,000 [men] left when there were 2,000 troops here [originally].

May 29. Today at [8:00 p.m.] we assembled at headquarters. The field hospital took part too. The last assault is to be carried out. All the patients were made to commit suicide … [I am] only thirty-three … and I am to die. I have no regrets … Goodbye Tocke my beloved wife, who loved me till the last … Until we meet again, grant you God speed.

[Daughter] Hisaka, who just became four years old, will grow up; I feel sorry for you. [Daughter] Takiko, born February this year … without seeing your father.[12]

It is assumed that Mr. Tatsuguchi was shot and killed, though where and under what circumstances isn't entirely clear. He was a Seventh-Day Adventist but clearly also adhered to the Shinto idea of the Japanese emperor being a near-divine entity.

A reference at the end of the diary is made to a desperate, last-ditch night attack by the remaining Japanese troops on Attu. GIs were caught by surprise, and the Japanese nearly attained their goal of capturing American artillery and using it to their advantage.

According to Bill Jones of the army artillery, the banzai, or suicidal attack, began around 4:00 a.m.

Flares had been sporadically lighting up a valley and GIs had gone to sleep in small tents, certain a Japanese defeat was imminent. American wounded were being cared for in larger tents. As *The Capture of Attu* book put it, all

hell broke loose. Grenades began to burst in the valley … and machine guns opened up. Japs, lots of them, began appearing through the fog in the glare of the red flares. They charged through the disorganized [American] company … The scattered pockets of [GIs] began falling back. The firing was becoming terrible, transforming the valley into a nightmare of flashes and noise and scampering shadows and death.[13]

Gaylord Tapp in an oral interview said, "We [had earlier gotten into] our sleeping bags. And just about sunrise that morning, the Japs … come up the ravine and they come in there shooting and bayoneting, just jabbing … us in the tents. They killed the kid beside of me and missed me. I saw a bayonet come in the tent four or five times while I was dressing. I don't know how he ever missed me, but he did. Cut the other kid's face about half off."

Some of the Japanese, nearly out of ammunition, grabbed discarded rifles and continued their charge with knives tied to the guns.

Dean Galles described the chaos, saying:

I was on Buffalo Ridge, which was the most advanced position, and [a group] came up to our place—they were all dressed in parkas. And I really thought … we were getting replacements … And so I walked right into them, and that's when I got engaged in hand-to-hand fighting, and I was bayoneted four times, once on the forehead, once on the wrist, and once in the ribs, and once through the thigh … I got a headlock on the next guy, and I found out one thing there. The Japanese had a peculiar odor … But anyway, that group was annihilated up on our … ridge.[14]

Sgt. Robert Rundle related, "They invaded our mess tent and killed our cooks. One of the cooks was in a foxhole and he managed to kill some Japanese but then the enemy lobbed a hand grenade into his foxhole and the cook was killed ... Then I was assigned to a machine gun nest in a gully to guard our camp so no more enemy troops could reach it. My closest buddy, Quinto Spinelli, was shot dead-center through his helmet. He was lucky. The bullet grazed his scalp and went out the back of his helmet. It knocked him out so the Japanese though he was dead and moved on."

Consider the following from *The Capture of Attu*:

[Captain] Pence had just stooped over to go out of the [command post] tent and had pushed the flaps back as a man barefooted and without his jacket dashed into the [command post] shouting, "The Japs are here. They've broken through." Then they heard it. A horde of Japs burst into the CP screaming and shouting. The wind had deadened the sound and then its full volume suddenly burst on them with blood-chilling, savage intensity. Pence shouted a warning and jumped out of the tent into the Japs. They were yelling and shooting, bayoneting, grenading—utterly destroying everything in their way.[15]

Cpl. Lawrence Kelly, in the same book, remembered:

We were in a bad spot. We were sure that there were Japs around us and we had no idea where friendly forces had held and where they had broken ... We spotted an American walking toward us across the open ground. It was Alvin A. Mahaffey and he wore a tight grin as he walked straight toward us ... We heard a bullet crack over our heads and Mahaffey fell about twenty feet from us. He began to swear, and ... rolled into the creek with blood running out of a gash in his arm. He had been playing dead in a hole ... all night, with Japs running over him every few minutes. He had been kicked and rolled over by three different groups of Japs, but miraculously none of them had jammed a bayonet into him.[16]

A story was related (as the third person) by Capt. George S. Buehler in *The Capture of Attu* book, taking place as the sounds of gunfire and shouting were coming uncomfortably close to his medical tent containing wounded GIs:

The first bullet ripped through the tent ... The stovepipe was hit with a crash ... The shouting was all around now, and a stream of running feet pounding the tundra passed the door. [Captain] Bryce was shaking [Captain] Buehler, "Wake up, the Japs are here!"
Buehler mumbled and turned over, [saying], "Too early to pull that stuff, Bryce."
[But] Buehler woke up [as] ... the stove clanged as a bullet crashed through it. ... Escape flashed through his mind first, but with the Japs milling around outside ... and the tent full of patients, the thought vanished ... The patients were asking again, "What are you going to do with us?" and Buehler told them all to be quiet, to lie down low, and not shoot under any circumstances. "Play dead."

Captain Bryce crawled to [a dead patient with a badly mutilated head on a] litter. Cautiously he moved him toward the door. The [tactic was] simple … Bryce pulled the man halfway off the stretcher and left him sprawled face up in the doorway so that curious Japs who peered inside could see this first and [lose interest in the rest of the tent] … [The dead soldier] will never be cited for valor, but [he] held his position against the door of the tent more valiantly and more effectively than he could have in life.[17]

Army cook Ray Gonzales in *The Capture of Attu* said, "We discovered seven Japs in Company D's kitchen. They were eating anything they could find. We threw some grenades, which broke up the meal, and a [Browning Automatic Rifle] man finished the Japs off."

During repeated advances, the Japanese almost reached their goal of the American artillery on Engineer Hill, but hastily thrown-together groups of GIs fought back and repulsed them in close-in fighting with whatever weapons were available. Finally realizing their defeat, almost all of the Japanese still alive chose to commit suicide with grenades. Their commanding officer was shot and killed. Of about 2,380 Japanese on Attu, only about twenty-eight survived as prisoners. In the area of the banzai attack, the ground was littered with bodies, some American, but mostly Japanese, resembling the worst American civil war battlefields. Bulldozers later excavated volcanic soil to provide pits for Japanese mass graves.

A lot of young men had their youthfulness, life's potential, and spirit sucked out of them because of calculations and decisions made by powerful older men thousands of miles away.

The lessons learned during the Attu debacle were applied when the army later made an even larger amphibious landing to dislodge the Japanese on Kiska Island. For a few weeks previously, pilots strafing and bombing the island had reported no visible Japanese activity or antiaircraft fire, raising the question: Was the enemy still there?

However, the navy insisted that no Japanese evacuation ships could've gotten through their blockade of the island. However, that's exactly what happened: under cover of fog, enough Japanese ships to carry the approximately five thousand Japanese troops home had arrived several weeks earlier, were quickly boarded, and then departed without being detected.

Unfortunately, the nervous American and Canadian troops who'd come ashore shot at each other. Other GIs were the victims of booby traps. Thirty-two died on the island. A navy ship hit a Japanese mine with seventy-one killed.

With Attu and Kiska taken back, there were no more land combat operations in the Aleutians during the war. One infamous battle was enough.

The military began to turn Attu into an air base which could attack the northern Japanese islands. Life eventually settled down into more of a routine.

Howard Rummel wrote that "in their leisure the Seabees acted as guides, arranging personally-conducted tours of the battlefield for the benefit of news reporters, merchant marines, and other late arrivals. A land-office business was done in Jap souvenirs, and as the original supply became exhausted, the Seabees learned to manufacture Jap flags, dog tags, and diaries [for sale]."

Navy man Vic Krtygowski said, "Once we got to Attu and the captain permitted the crew to go [ashore], I happened to be officer on the deck when the guys [returned]. And here they were coming back with rifles, mortars, grenades, all live ammunition stuff, and so I had to stop them."

Weatherman Paul Carrigan wrote about taking a long hike across the island with a friend to look for souvenirs. It was the middle of summer, and daylight hours were long. However, the going was more tedious than they expected. "Near the head of Massacre Valley," wrote Carrigan, "a soldier told us we'd be hard-pressed to reach any souvenir grounds on the high ridges before dark. He added that most of the 'good stuff' had been gleaned weeks ago."

Darkness closed in before they reached their destination, and they were half sitting, half reclining. Carrigan related what happened next:

An almost imperceptible sound I could not identify caused me to turn my head … toward Massacre Bay. I heard no further sound and was about to turn away when I saw him … a hurrying, bobbing, weaving figure choosing a path that kept him well below the ridge top … For a second or two I watched and wondered idly why the man would be running toward the interior western mountains when it was almost dark … As he drew closer he became silhouetted against the dim skylight and a cold, prickly chill shot up my spine. It was clearly a Japanese soldier … Unaware of our presence, the Jap kept coming. With [a] long overcoat slapping around below his knees and in a half crouch he was moving at a good clip with a curious … lope. Over his left shoulder … hung a bulging sack. His right hand held what at first appeared to be a long pole but frighteningly materialized into one of those overly long Japanese rifles … As fleetingly as some bad dreams come and go, the enemy soldier vanished into the dark.

After several headlong spills during the next five minutes, we burst into the first US tent camp and pantingly blurted out what we thought was our startling story. The soldiers, jaded members of an engineer outfit, seemed almost indifferent … "Nothin' ta get excited about," said [a] sergeant wearily. "There's still a few running loose … They steal food but don't do any killin.'"[18]

Chapter 12
Enlisted Men Must Salute First

The routine when taking over a new [Aleutian] island was [first, to build] the officers' club. Second was the runway.

The militaries of the world tend to be tradition-bound. Even though World War II was fought in new ways, with air power, amphibious landings, and radar—ending with the A-bomb—the inner workings of America's military system had changed little over the years.

As men were drummed into the army and navy, trained and shipped north to the Aleutians, the traditional officer and enlisted-men divide remained. Looking at the army, "enlisted" in the World War II era referred to GIs in grades private through sergeant while "officer" referred to commissioned officers—from lieutenant to general.

This feudal-like division caused problems. It's similar to lords and knights with their vassals, knaves, and serfs.

Navy officers conduct their weekly inspection of enlisted navy Seabees on Adak. Note the old-fashioned leggings, which were probably only worn for inspections. *National Archives at Seattle*

Enlisted men are trained to call officers "sir" and salute them when passing, with the officer returning the salute. In an October 1943 ad in *Air Force Magazine* aimed at enlisted men and headlined "Salute Proudly," a caption read, "The snap and precision of your salute, the bearing of your head, and the forthrightness of your glance reflect the pride you have in your army, your unit and in yourself." This doesn't quite jibe with the usual enlisted men's attitudes found in this book!

The assumption is that officers' orders will be carried out by enlisted men without question.

Navy aviation officer Charles Fitzpatrick wrote, "I recalled classes where it was taught the naval officer was not to fail his crew. Set the example, be forthright, firm in command, never show anxiety or fear but step forward and be the leader. I did attempt to exude all of the above and more."

Some have suggested that all officers should pass through the enlisted ranks first, similar to starting in the proverbial corporate mailroom, but in reality, most World War II officers were minted fresh, coming from service academies, college programs, and officer training programs. My father, a former teacher and former national guard enlistee, was given a direct commission as an officer during World War II after taking navy training at two universities.

A wartime Aleutian military newspaper offered this humor: "A captain and a colonel were walking across [a] field. They met many privates and each time the captain would [return a] salute, he would mutter, 'The same to you.' The colonel's curiosity soon got the better of him and he asked, 'Why do you always say that?' The captain replied: 'I was once a private, and I know what they are thinking.'"

At established bases, officers typically slept and ate at different locations than enlisted men. The officers' facilities in other than tent areas were almost always better. Officers, especially nurses, were given quite a bit more living space per person than enlisted men.

On Kiska, Quonset huts housed twenty enlisted men each, while officers' huts only had ten—and the officers' huts provided a partitioned room for each officer, plus a hut shower. The enlisted men's showers were in separate buildings.

On Shemya, officer Bernard Mehren wrote about his hut's rooms having closets and tables, with the beds having chests of drawers underneath.

A single exception to this officer-enlisted disparity was remembered by Paul Carrigan. An enlisted wheeler-dealer named Cox, who could procure nearly anything, turned one enlisted men's hut into plush living quarters, with thick carpeting, overstuffed chairs, sofas, and indirect lighting. The place resembled a club. "Even the officers' quarters looked like squatters' shacks by comparison," wrote Carrigan.

Naturally, officers were paid more than enlisted men, but the officers paid for their meals at officers' mess halls and for their lodging. Enlisted men received their food and lodging without charge. Under normal circumstances, officers bought their own various uniforms (including dress uniforms), while enlisted men's clothing was free.

"Lorraine Davis was granted a divorce ... from 2nd Lieutenant Bert Davis, 23, when she said her husband refused to carry groceries for her because it was unbecoming to his military rank." The story was carried on the Army News Service. *Artist: Oliver Pedigo*

Officers, including nurses, were cautioned against fraternizing with enlisted men socially, ostensibly to prevent the feeling that officers played favorites.

In his well-known book about the English military in France in World War I, *The Great War and Modern Memory*, Paul Fussell wrote that "there was the wide, indeed gaping distinction between officers and men, emphasized not merely by separate quarters and messes and different uniforms and weapons but by different accents … In London an officer was forbidden to carry a parcel or ride a bus … When a ten-minute break was signaled on [a] march, officers invariably fell out to the left side of the road [and] other ranks to the right."

There were many, many instances of enlisted resentment at the privileges given to officers. Typical complaints were that officers were given special shower hours, could attend USO shows without tickets, could have cameras, and that female USO performers fraternized with officers only.

According to GI Roald Forseth, only officers were officially allowed to have pets, although that wasn't always adhered to. In a letter home, SSgt. Roger Vance (later missing in action) described a colonel's dog: "I wish you could see that dog, he is a big husky, really a noble-looking animal, but the strange thing about him is his ability to distinguish between officers and enlisted men. He will allow the former to pet him and acts as frisky as a puppy. But when an enlisted man tries the same thing he stands stiff as a board, with his head high and proud, staring off in the distance with no show of affection whatever."

In combing through the National Archives in Seattle, I developed the impression that for the same offenses (such as drunkenness) Aleutian officers received lighter courts martial sentences than enlisted men. For example, a navy lieutenant junior grade in 1944 was charged with "conduct to the prejudice of good order and discipline." Convicted, he was to receive no reduction in grade or other punishment as long as he behaved himself.

In addition to living quarters, there were two major perks given to officers in Alaska: officers' clubs and a liquor ration. There were a few clubs for sergeants but the lower-ranked enlisted men only had their PXs, where the only alcoholic beverage was beer—if it was available.

Officers' clubs were satirized by cartoonist Bill Mauldin during the war. In one cartoon, two war-weary and haggard enlisted GIs stand in front of a "Red Cross Officers' Club," where a sign proclaims, "This establishment strictly OFF LIMITS." A spiffy lieutenant wearing a tie and holding a clipboard points a pencil at the chest of one of the men, with an expression that says, "You really expected to get in here?"

Nate White, a columnist in *The Mifflinburg Telegraph*, a Pennsylvania newspaper, had this to say in 1946:

> Why do enlisted men of the army and the navy so wholeheartedly and with near unanimity condemn their officers as a body? The answer is this: The complete adherence to the totally undemocratic theory of R.H.I.P. [Rank Has Its Privileges].
>
> At Adak, the main naval operating base in the Aleutians, I found that the officers of the navy had established a beautiful club … sporting many types of expensive hard liquors, beautiful interior decorations, a brick fireplace and chimney, and modern plumbing. There each night many base and fleet officers sought relief from boredom by getting totally drunk.

The point is, the transportation of those bricks, the plumbing, the liquor, and the comfortable furnishings for the club was accomplished at a time when the Aleutian campaign was in a critical stage, the Japs were still a menace, and enlisted men ... were living knee-deep in mud-surrounded tents.

At Dutch Harbor and Kodiak, the navy built the most fantastic officers' clubs imaginable ... [During the war] the officers at Kodiak were ordered to dress in their blues for dinner. They were served at spotlessly white, linen-covered tables with a beautiful silver service by Filipino stewards in white uniforms ... Seabees' orchestras furnished the music for "balls" and [civilian] civil-service girls in evening dresses enlivened the affairs.

This was all fine, many thought—for the officers. The effect on this extravagant display on enlisted men can be imagined.[1]

Dutch Harbor band member Robert Johnson said that the band's best gigs were at the officers' club, where female nurses were in attendance, and at the sergeants' club.

Enlisted navy radioman Ray Daves was allowed to visit an officers' club as the guest of an ensign, and he remembered that "the first time he took me to the O Club, I realized officers weren't that much different from the rest of us. They sat around, played cards, shot pool, and told jokes. I think they also drank a lot because I remember what happened when I asked the bartender for a 7-Up. He looked at me kind of funny and said, 'How do you mix that?'"

Navy seaplane crewmember Bill Maris, who later became an officer, wrote in 1942 that Ensign "Decker would invite us up to the [Officer's] Club for a round of cheer as we sat outside on the steps, as we enlisted men were not allowed [inside]."

Navy man Walter Stohler similarly recalled, "Of course us swabbies, we weren't allowed [in the officer's club]. The officers had it pretty nice. They had a real fancy Quonset hut."

Army air force officer Milt Zack wrote: "The routine when taking over a new [Aleutian] island was [first, to build] the officers' club. Second was the runway."

The other privilege accorded officers in the Aleutians was their liquor ration. Zack, again, wrote that "one of the perks of being an officer is that we could buy beer, liquor, and Coke at next to nothing. Depending on how much was in any one shipment, we could wind up with two or three bottles of liquor ... a couple cases of beer, and a couple cases of Coke in bottles. For those of us who didn't drink ... the liquor was bartered for supplies [or] ... could be sold on the 'black market' for $20 to $30 a bottle, by the guys who knew the ropes."

A psychiatrist wrote that the liquor ration "was deeply resented [by enlisted men]."

I found much more material about unliked officers than about popular officers. It's easier to complain than praise, but many of the complaints were legitimate.

To provide evenhandedness, the following are some stories about officers who were well-liked by their subordinates.

A leading contender for that honor was William Eareckson, an army flying officer who earned the appreciation of both enlisted men and fellow officers for leading bombing and strafing missions against the Japanese-held islands of Attu and Kiska, and for developing new attack tactics. It's said that he even joined infantrymen on the ground during the Attu invasion, where he was wounded. He was fiercely independent and not always liked by his superiors.

One of the upper brass who was generally liked was Gen. Simon Buckner. Beginning at West Point, he'd steadily moved up in rank and responsibilities until he was given command of the army in the Alaskan theater as a brigadier general. He was seen as tough but fair.

In the Brian Garfield archive, a letter by Maj. Gen. Archibald Arnold indicated: "[General] Buckner slept in a tent because he wouldn't take advantages his men couldn't have … He is reported to have slept on a cot with a very thin mattress and only a sheet for cover."

Air Force mechanic Mac McGalliard wrote that

General Buckner … always walked around with no aides, [wearing] a long GI overcoat, with no insignia or rank [showing]. (He said that way he could mingle with his troops and find out how they really felt.)

Buck [Burnett] was changing [spark plugs on a plane] and had gone to [the supply room] for plugs … When he got back, here is this long tall soldier in a GI overcoat standing at the foot of Buck's ladder. Buck strolls up the soldier and kicks him on the heel and says, "Move it, soldier, carry your ass." The tall guy smiles and moves on. Before long, the engineering officer comes running out to Buck and asks what went on. Buck told him and the engineering officer said, "You know who that was?" Buck made some unprintable statement and says, "Who cares."[2]

Seaplane pilot and navy officer Oliver Glenn gave Buckner a lift during the battle for Attu:

After takeoff, I invited him up to the co-pilot's seat and he asked me to fly him around the island a bit to see from the air where his troops were fighting. We cruised around the island for about an hour until he wanted to land. He was as nice a guy as you'd ever want to meet; he felt like a kindly grandfather. After we landed, he thanked me and said he'd invite me ashore to have dinner, but he didn't have mess set up and only had K-rations. I felt sorry; here he was with three stars on his [army] collar eating K-rations and I, a measly two-stripe [navy] lieutenant, was eating on a white tablecloth, [with] cloth napkins and two or three pieces of silverware on each side of my plate.[3]

Buckner, eventually promoted to lieutenant general, was later killed by enemy fire while commanding troops during the Okinawa invasion.

There were other officers liked by their men. Frederick Rust wrote in the 18th Engineers regimental diary in 1943 that their officer "regarded the accomplishment of our mission first [and] military formality second. [Our unit] has responded to this informal treatment by maintaining high standards of obedience."

Walter Kellog related an experience on Attu after the Americans took the island: "We had a general come and ask, 'Sergeant, where is your officer?' I replied: 'At supply, getting some supplies. Can I help?' He said he was there to see what was holding up the job. I told him we had only part of our crew there, we needed to dig 1,200 feet of ditch to bury the power cable, and we were understaffed. He did an about face and left without saying a word. At 6:00 a.m. the next morning, we had 200 infantrymen and officers march in, each with a shovel over the shoulder."

A navy officer with an enlisted man on Attu. *Library of Congress, Lot 803-17*

Mac McGalliard had this story

about [Captain Laven] … We … had a broken rear view mirror on our P-38 and Captain Laven had asked me to replace it … So off to salvage I went. Tools in hand, I located one on a [plane] that had belly landed. I got busy removing the mirror and some [master sergeant] came roaring out of the salvage hut and pronounced in no uncertain terms to get my hands off that mirror and get the hell out of there.

I left and proceeded to find … Captain Laven. The captain wore a sheepskin flying jacket with his bars on the underside of the collar. Well, here we came—me with tools in hand and Laven … [I] started to work again and sure enough the [sergeant] came roaring out of the shack once more and started telling us how he was going to hang our butts.

Now the fun part: Captain Laven just rolled up his collar and showed [his captain's bars]. Boy did that [sergeant] cool off—not a word—just walked back into the shack like a little lamb.[4]

McGalliard also wrote that his commanding officer "thought our morale was too low and wanted to do something to pick it up. He took a C-47 and flew back to Anchorage, [returning with] enough liquor to give each enlisted man a [fifth]. I don't know where all the money came from; I can only guess that the officers kicked in some … If you wanted a bottle, you came and picked up what you wanted—it was free."

Jim Schroeder of the army air force on Shemya said, "The officers were very nice, you know. You done no saluting or nothing like that ... they were just one of the bunch of guys with us."

Enlisted man Joe Baldeschi was on an island where only the officers had alcohol and remembered his pilot "knocking on the door one night ... and he [opened it up and pulled] out a bottle of liquor. I said, 'What are you doing that for? You know, if Commander David finds out, your lieutenant stripes are gone.' He said, 'I don't give a damn ... I'm going to have a drink with my boys. I fly with them, we risk our lives, you know; together we risk our lives, so I can have a drink with them.'"

Then, on the other side of the coin, there were plenty of stories about less-popular officers. Not all officers had the human touch and had the welfare of their men foremost in mind.

William Chesney wrote about "a captain that was a pain. He was always raising hell. And I said, since you're always raising hell with all of us, why don't you go back to the States. He said I'd love to. So I was on good terms with the chaplain, so I said, hey, can you give us a helping hand? He said, what do you mean, a helping hand? I said send the captain back to the States; he wants to go back anyway and he's a pain in the ass, sir. About two weeks later, he went back to the States."

Sgt. Hale Burge told this story: "We were sitting in [a bar] one night [and a] lieutenant come in. And he saw these two nurses with these two enlisted men and he started complaining to them that they're not supposed to do that. Well, they let him know right away that it was their business and told him to leave them alone. So we never did hear any more about that."

One GI complained that generals would fly in ostensibly to attend a conference, but would instead go salmon fishing.

Lt. Eliot Asinof coordinated the visits of movie actors and arranged USO shows, but the visit of classical violinist Yehudi Menuhin stumped him. How would he present Menuhin to young men who didn't appreciate classical music?

The first attempt was a performance at the post movie theater between two Betty Grable movies. Menuhin was summarily booed off the stage.

"I shuddered," wrote Asinof, who remembered muttering to himself, "Welcome to Adak." Asinof's next inspiration was to have Menuhin fiddle while the enlisted men ate in their mess hall. There, Menuhin took his Stradivarius out of its case, positioned the instrument, and told the men that if they didn't like the music, they needn't stick around.

Wrote Asinof:

He began to play. In the low ceiling, the sound was powerful, the tone so serene it appeared to stun them. Not only did they stop talking, they stopped eating. When he finished, they didn't move. No one left. No applause. They just waited for more.

Menuhin introduced the next number, but before he began, the kitchen door opened [and] the staff came out in chefs' white hats [and] aprons. KPs followed. They stood by the kitchen door, fascinated. He played for a half hour. It was beautiful and no one moved.

Then from behind [Menuhin and his accompanist] ... came the colonel, literally exploding into the enlisted men's mess.

"What's this? What? These men have jobs to do. There's a war on!"

Menuhin stopped [and] stood there like a man who had seen a ghost. He looked at me. I was helpless.

The colonel kept hollering at the men. "You're through eating, go back to work! It's after one. Go back to work. Goddammit."[5]

Asinof had yet another story about a killjoy:

[On] a typical dark, wet Adak day, we'd moved about the air base huddled under parkas, faces unseen, bodies beaten down by relentless winds. Suddenly, as if by magic, the wind shifted, clouds parted, the sky opened up, and there was the sun, a brilliant ball of fire. It was extraordinary ... Men poured out of huts, out of offices, the kitchen—all work stopped. We stood there, heads facing the rare, beautiful light. It was so magnificent we broke out laughing as we shed our clothes, danced in long johns like kids at a drunken party. We began singing, "*Wait 'till the sun shines, Nellie.*" The chaplain came out of the chapel, waving his arms to the sky, thanking God for this glorious moment.

Ten minutes, fifteen; it was too good to be true.

Then [the officer] came, driving his Jeep, yelling at us like an angry bull. "Stop this! Get back to work!"

The men glared at him. What was the matter with him? Didn't he see the sun? It was the sun! The sun! He turned his Jeep into the mass of them, threatening ... They retreated, scattered like frightened dogs. He wasn't satisfied. He got out of his Jeep, stared up at the sky, yelling at the sun, fist in the air. In seconds, clouds began to cover the blue, and slowly the sun faded behind them. It was frightening. He had to prove that he was more powerful than the sun.[6]

War training exercises were held on Adak as late as April 1945, when Japan was reeling from constant attacks, because a general had declared, "The defenses of Adak are unsatisfactory and not up to the standards required." Trying to convince officers and men that a Japanese attack was possible and that more training was necessary must've caused a lot of grumbling.

A psychiatrist noted in his report about conditions on Adak that "the men resented the fact that the officers who ordered them to string ... barbed wire, or dig dummy gun emplacements in a wet and freezing wind, rarely came to the Aleutians, or came only for a short time."

Paul Carrigan wrote about how his officer-in-charge, Cmdr. Tatom, told him and other weather personnel to build an officers' latrine. "Dig it here. Dig it deep, and make it a four-holer," Tatom ordered.

"Before this had been completed," wrote Carrigan, "Tatom had second thoughts and decided the location was too exposed to prevailing winds. [So Tatom then said] that the four-holer would be the enlisted men's head ... Tatom [then marched us] to the more sheltered northeast side of the hill where he selected a spot and ordered us to start digging. The entrance to the officers' four-holer was to be constructed so that a sitter could enjoy the panoramic view."

In another Tatom story, Carrigan told how a blizzard had been raging for almost thir-ty-six hours with winds over 80 knots … It was a time when [we] could take a few hours off and relax. Tatom had done just that and in the process he'd "tied one on."

[He] unexpectedly lurched into the [meteorological] tent. From a voluminous pocket of his snow-plastered parka he proudly produced a bottle of bourbon. He smiled broadly, made his way over to me, and proceeded to thump my back repeatedly.

"You're OK, Paul, no matter what anyone says. You not only do good work but by God I can count on you when the going gets tough … Let's drink a toast," said Tatom as he waved the bottle and called for glasses.

"Maybe you'd better sit down, commander," I offered.

"No, no, no, just get the glasses. One drinks a toast standing."

We raised our cups … As the fiery liquid slid down my throat I shivered and shook like a dog passing peach pits.

I finally convinced Tatom that he should turn in and get some sleep. He agreed [and] then quietly and politely bid me goodnight and unsteadily went out into a snow squall. After about five minutes I began to think that I should have assisted him [because] the temperature outside was well below freezing. . . I grabbed a flash-light to go check. I hadn't progressed 40 feet when I almost tripped over him … Half covered by snow, he was asleep and snoring [and] … might have frozen to death … Grasping him under his armpits from behind, I lifted, tugged, and pulled him into my tent [where I] got him into my sleeping bag and zipped up.

Upon returning to the weather tent, I wrapped myself in two old army blankets and tried to sleep on the plywood deck.[7]

Despite that tender treatment, Carrigan described how Tatom got soiled walking through mud near the enlisted men's huts after his Jeep stalled in a water hole, so the com-mander ordered the immediate construction of a walkway, adding:

"I … want that hole filled before nightfall."

[An enlisted man replied,] "The men are on what they consider a few hours set aside for their free time right now, commander. Can [we] wait until the storm eases?"

"G-------t," replied Tatom, "the men have no free time. They owe me twenty-four hours a day. I don't care how hard they work, it is going to be done and if I hear much more from you, you'll be first class again."[8]

An army air force mechanic on Shemya, Hale Burge, worked wonders rebuilding damaged aircraft. "So," wrote Burge, "when it came time to fly [a particular] airplane for a test hop, I walked around with the pilot and for about an hour he kept questioning me, [asking]: 'What'd you do? How'd you do this?' … And he took it and flew it. He come back an hour or so later [and even though he loved the way the plane flew] … he never congrat-ulated anybody or [gave] you credit for doing anything. It was always, 'hmmph.' Every time he said a couple of words it was, 'hmmph.'"

Army man Walter Howard on Kiska wrote about a new colonel who took command of his outfit who "planned an exercise … Before beginning the march, each man was issued two chocolate bars. At some point during the maneuver, there was to be an inspection to make sure that none of us had prematurely eaten the candy. I think I devoured the first bar before I was handed the second. [Later,] while serving on guard duty, I was reprimanded by the colonel for not standing and saluting him. He declared that if we were in combat, he could shoot me. I answered that if we were in combat, he would make a perfect target if an enemy sniper observed the salute.

"That night, two of my buddies strolled near his tent," related Howard. "One of them commented, loud enough for the colonel to hear, 'Have you still got your [bullet] for the colonel?' The other soldier replied, 'Yes!' It was not long after that the colonel was transferred off the island."

Elsewhere, a green lieutenant with little Aleutian experience ordered his men on a hike into the mountains in the winter, commanding them to carry only minimal packs and light clothing. The troops protested to no avail. A storm came in and stranded the men at high altitude. Many of the men and the officer had to be carried off on stretchers the following day with frostbite and other ailments. It was an unusual way for some to earn a Purple Heart.

Lt. Eliot Asinof wrote about a Col. Beckworth, who somehow outmaneuvered him at every turn. The story began when a boiler for the enlisted men's shower gave out, and Asinof was urged by the shower's enlisted caretaker to get the colonel to approve a new one, something the colonel was unlikely to do.

"[The colonel] wouldn't care. He was a what's-in-it-for-me man" who wanted a promotion to general, wrote Asinof.

But somehow a boiler was ordered and arrived. Meanwhile, however, the colonel had ordered a large antique Russian bathtub for himself, which went into a custom-built building—with a skylight—for which the existing boiler was inadequate. So the colonel blithely appropriated the new enlisted men's boiler for his own use.

Asinof felt so badly for the shower caretaker that he got the navy to donate an abandoned boiler, which was duly installed and connected. It exploded and killed the man. The colonel asked to see Asinof, and greeted him "with a vicious scowl, [saying] 'This is your fault, Asinof!'"

Wrote Asinof, "He was yelling at me like a madman; dozens heard him; he didn't care. I was brought there to satisfy his need to lay his guilt on me. [The caretaker] was dead because I made it so."

But the truth leaked out to the community of enlisted men. "That night the air base began to unravel," wrote Asinof. "A gang broke into the PX and looted it … It was done as a protest. Looting for the sake of looting. They were looting the colonel."

The next day:

[The colonel] came to breakfast like a mad bull, and I was his target.
"What do you know about this?"
"Nothing, sir."
"This is your problem, lieutenant. This has never happened before. Never!"
So, I was to blame again.
"Who did this? Find the stuff they stole. Find the men. I hold you responsible, lieutenant."[9]

At the dead man's funeral, wrote Asinof, the colonel took over the pulpit from the chaplain, saying the death was a sacrifice.

"[The colonel] paused as if he had to swallow his emotion," wrote Asinof. "I saw only the bullshit … 'Sacrifice,' he'd said. He did not know the meaning of the word."

But the colonel did promise to build a new and better shower, and he eventually delivered.

Later, when Asinof was discharged and returned to the States, he visited the dead man's parents to tell them the truth. They listened politely, then told him the colonel had visited them previously and given them a letter of appreciation. Said the father, "He had tried to get [our son] awarded a Distinguished Service Medal."

The colonel had told the father that he, Lt. Asinof, was "well liked by the men but … made trouble …"

"Now," said the father, "You have the nerve to defame your commanding officer. You've come here to start trouble. I think you'd better leave, lieutenant."

Wrote Asinof, "I was beaten … I could picture the colonel laughing at me … It was strange, the way he could beat me no matter what I did."

As with the PX raid, enlisted men did find ways to make their feelings known about certain officers. Henry Lesa wrote:

We had one incident. We had a couple of officers that felt they were better than everybody else, and they kept pushing people and so forth. We had a couple of Texans that got smart to this [one] guy … They were taking off pipe … about forty feet long [from a barge]. And they waited until his back was turned, and they butted him in the backside with the pipe, and they dumped him in the ocean … He came out of there spitting and sputtering. For the rest of the time, we didn't see him on ship again. He got the message.[10]

An Aleutian court-martial in 1944 found that navy enlisted man Clarence Windle struck an officer. Perhaps there was some justification for the act because there was to be no penalty if he behaved himself. If he didn't, he'd face one year of confinement.

Another court-martial found navy enlisted man Otho Ware guilty of assaulting and using disrespectful language toward an officer. He was confined for one year and then given a bad-conduct discharge.

Navy enlisted man Paul Carrigan was used to working around officers in the weather office. However, on one particular day, two officers from other outfits were conferring there with Tatom, his officer. Carrigan described what ensued.

"Carrigan," one asked, "turn that damned stove up and let's get some heat in this tent. Then step outside out of earshot for a spell."

Wrote Carrigan, "For six weeks, I'd been sharing a small office tent with an intelligence officer. There was little I had not been privy to. For [the officer] to imply that I was not trustworthy caused me to turn towards him and hesitate. [My boss] silently jerked his head sideways indicating I should comply quickly."

So Carrigan turned the stove up to full blast and went outside, while "burning with resentment and frustration."

"I'd been standing with my back to the tent for about five minutes," wrote Carrigan, "[then] I whirled around to see the tent on fire. Like a Roman candle, red-hot sparks were showering out of the chimney stove pipe. Numerous burning holes in the canvas roof were spreading."

There was a rush to save weather documents. "Goddammit," said one of the lieutenants, "I didn't tell you to burn the tent down."

"It was best to keep silent but I felt like telling him he'd demanded heat and gotten it," wrote Carrigan.

Sometimes things got more serious. Air force mechanic Mac McGalliard repeated a story he'd heard:

As the story went—this [commanding officer] was a mean and demanding so and so. No one liked him or respected him. By and by [men would] put as much [money] as you wanted … in the pot, for the guy who "got" the CO.

One day a [private first class or corporal] was digging a hole … with a bulldozer … Guess what, the CO came up in his Jeep and parked behind the [bull]dozer … The kid backed up, and too late—the CO was dead. Crushed in his Jeep. Accidental death was the finding. The kid collected six figures … Strange things happen in a war.[11]

Enlisted men of various specialties, even army band members, were pressed into service to unload ships. They got to see what was specifically being shipped to officer's messes and clubs. Wrote band member Robert Boon: "There would be a supply ship every so often and we would go help unload so we could steal some of the officers' mess meat."

Army enlisted man Paul Worley noted with some amusement that one day an air raid siren went off and a colonel with no shelter to go to had to jump into a garbage pit.

PBY crew member Bill Maris, in the Dutch Harbor area, remembered the

time I captured all the leftover canned chow from [a flight after] we were called back due to [weather] … [Officer] Bill Decker … gave me hell and said he had first dibs; I and the crew just chuckled. As far as I was concerned my crew came first. The officers were eating steak at Adak while we ate stew and ham and cabbage … Like the time I stole the fifth of scotch from Captain Gehres' box of liquor when I hitched a ride [on a plane] from Kodiak to Adak. Boy the s--t hit the fan on that one.[12]

Royal Sorensen, a pilot, remarked that "the wind had no respect for rank. At one of the islands, I got up in the morning to go to the latrine, and only wished I had a camera. There was no longer a tent, just a sign reading 'Officers' Latrine'—four holes with six inches of snow in them, and a forked stick holding a roll of toilet paper. The enlisted men's latrine was intact."

In the National Archives in Seattle, I found a court-martial record describing an event aboard the USS *Challenge* at Cold Bay:

[Enlisted man Gerald Minks] entered ship's galley for first sitting to dinner. The ship's cook (having been notified that there were two officer guests for dinner …) told Minks to wait for second mess. Minks stated to the cook in a very belligerent tone, "That kind of a deal stinks … " The cook stated, "If it stinks, you don't have to stay around the galley." Minks then stated to the cook, "You go to hell." The cook, who is a second class petty officer, asked Minks if he meant it and the reply was, "Yes, what about it?" Thereby the cook reported the breach of discipline.

[Later,] Minks was called at reveille by the security watch … but failed to get up … It is requested that the … man's case be investigated and disciplinary action be taken to the fullest extent of Captain's Mast.[13]

One place where the officer-enlisted divide lessened was in all-hands card-game gambling sessions, where coolness and skill counted for more than rank. It was one area where an enlisted man could enjoy a level playing field.

Despite officers' perks and privileges, their lives were not necessarily a bed of feathers.

My father, Harry Paul Jr., a navy lieutenant junior grade, wrote to his parents: "I don't exactly like what you said about officers being an awful lot … Some officers are unjust but I don't believe the percentage is as large as the percentage of enlisted men who you can't do anything with and you just can't please them no matter how hard you try … Some officers are terrible but so are some enlisted men."

In another letter he mentioned an officer "that I like so well—[he] was suspended from duty for five days and confined to his quarters for a little insignificant mistake. Things are tough here and morale is zero."

In a third letter, my father wrote:

This is the worst place I believe I have ever worked. You go to work expecting to get bawled out and we usually do, and of course you can't talk back. The other day the chief of staff said that one of the … chief warrant officers had to be assigned to extra duty for punishment for some little thing. But he had to back down on that because an officer can't be assigned extra duty. I think the whole trouble is that the skipper has been passed over twice for promotion and if he doesn't make good and get promoted this time he is all done in the navy.[14]

According to *Wikipedia*, "The navy … introduced an 'up or out' system in 1916," which was still in effect during World War II. That meant that remaining in one's rank for too long resulted in being unceremoniously dismissed from the military.

There was an incident where a B-25 pilot was ordered along with other pilots to take off in thick fog. The pilot taxied into the lead position but could not bring himself to take off, disobeying a direct order. After some long and tense moments, the flight was cancelled.

Harry Bailey, the army barge man, wrote about an army enlisted man who by default became the skipper of their vessel when they arrived at Attu. However, "when [this man went before a board to obtain a warrant officer rank], I guess he was supposed to present himself by name and say 'reporting as directed.' And he didn't. And he didn't get his warrant for that reason. And he ended up being demoted and then we took on a warrant officer who had no capabilities to be in charge."

One Christmas Eve on Amchitka, a navy steward's mate—most stewards were black—refused to turn the hut lights out because he couldn't find his watch. A fight ensued, and the man threatened the others with a razor. Another GI grabbed a gun, which ended up in the hands of a petty officer, who told the steward to stand back. The man advanced, saying the officer wouldn't dare shoot him, but that's exactly what happened, and the man died. The officer was not court-martialed.

A naval wing commander with his headquarters in Kodiak issued some unpopular orders for his flying officers, according to Murray Hanson in his *Military Journal Online* article titled "The Aleuts: Flying PBYs with VP-61 in the Aleutians":

> He required that only [a] complete regulation coat and tie could be worn in the wardroom and mess hall at Dutch Harbor—no flight gear [was allowed], not even for an early, early breakfast before takeoff for a dawn patrol. So flying officers and chiefs had to go to breakfast in complete uniform, carrying their heavy, fleece-lined flying suits, boots, helmets and gloves; eat breakfast and then make a quick change into the flight gear in the lobbies of the mess halls. Then they proceeded to their aircraft, leaving coats, ties, caps and sometimes pants hanging in the lobby. The procedure was reversed when they got back from their flight. Some war![15]

Even within the officer corps, there was a clearly defined pecking order. Navy air navigator Charles Fitzpatrick in his book *From Then 'Til Now, My Journal* wrote about an encounter with higher ups in an officers' club:

> There was a way [to obtain a staff car to go to a distant movie theater] but none of the group [of us junior officers] would pursue it. While we mulled over the subject, the bar at the officer's mess had been encircled by heavy brass ... Commander Wayne was among them; thus it was obvious he wouldn't be needing his command car that night.
>
> [The other junior officers were too timid to approach Wayne, so one said,] "Fitz, it was your idea—why don't you ask the 'old man'?" I gave it some thought. What could he do but say no ... "What the heck," I said, standing up.
>
> As I sidled up to the bar I ... waited for [Commander Wayne] to recognize me. A junior officer always waited to be recognized; he never interrupted his superior. I waited some more ... [The senior officers' eyes began to bear down on me as if to ask] "To whom does this ensign belong?" [Then,] Wayne looked ... and asked ... "What in the name of hell do you want? You don't belong here mister, you're not welcome."
>
> "I beg your pardon, sir. I apologize for the intrusion, Commander Wayne; we got back late from our mission and missed the transportation to the movies."
>
> "Is that what you wanted to tell me, mister?" He was madder than a wet hornet.
>
> "No sir. I wanted to ask permission, if I may, sir, to use your vehicle to take six of us to the John Wayne movie."
>
> Some of the brass [were] laughing; others offered a bit of mild needling. My demise had arrived, I was sure. In his very loud voice, he said, "The ensign wants to borrow my transportation." More laughter and jokes.
>
> [But Wayne added,] "This son of gun ... is the only one in my squadron who has the guts to ask me for my transportation. Hell, ensign" ... He stopped ... then tossed his keys on the bar. They slid right to me.

Arriving at the movies, we pulled into the commander's parking spot ... Rank has its privileges; even the door to the movies was held open for us.[16]

Army air force officer Milt Zack wrote: "It took me awhile to get accustomed, as an officer, to going to the front of the [movie theater] line to pay my 10 cents, even if there was a long line of enlisted men waiting. And we had our own section, which was center back of the theater; the best seats."

There are two cartoons revealing the divide by famed cartoonist Bill Mauldin. In the first, a Jeep has driven between three enlisted GIs shoveling a muddy road, spraying mud on them. In the rear of the Jeep, an earnest young officer in the passenger seat looks back at them, yelling, "Damn fine road, men!"

In the other, two officers in bulky winter clothing stand at a lookout, admiring brilliant shafts of sunlight falling on distant craggy peaks. One says, "Beautiful view! Is there one for the enlisted men?"

An officer peeling potatoes in a rare scene. *Photo by Bruno Kozlowski and courtesy of Andy Kozlowski*

A poem by Aleutian GI Fred Ellis titled "Reconversion," written in 1944, presented a fantasy probably harbored by many—that upon discharge from the military an enlisted man might run into his former commanding officer or CO, now selling peanuts and cigars.

"So be kind to working people," ended Ellis, " ... for the guy that's washing dishes may be your old [CO]."

Chapter 13
Aboard Ship in Often-Rough Seas

My first glimpse [of the ship] was utterly shocking. The bow had just plummeted downward, disappearing into the oncoming wave, [and] her twin [propellers were] churning only air. I was startled, believing I was about to witness the demise of the entire crew and ship as it dove into the depths of the sea.

Army GIs going to the Aleutian Islands via troop transport ships discovered what seasickness was all about. Floyd Erickson related that a trip on the USS *Harris* "was horrible … A guy came down and said, 'Eric, you're on gun guard.' And I as much as told him, 'You might just as well throw me overboard, because … I'm just sicker than a dog.' Oh, I was sick … I mean, I was so sick I didn't care what happened."

Later on, talking about being transported on the *Yukon* from Kiska to Dutch Harbor, Erickson said, "We all got sick, more guys than you can ever imagine. Oh boy, it was hard to go down to the kitchen and smell. I think what kept me alive was candy bars. I'd lie in the bunk there and just eat candy, and forget going to the mess hall … Somebody said there's waves out there fifty feet [high], and I believe it. I didn't go out to see; I just stayed in my bunk as long as I could."

The most revolting story about taking a troopship to the islands came from an interview with Roald Forseth by his son Mark Forseth, which was published in the *Baltimore Post-Examiner*. The article described Roald heading north in the slow SS *Cherokee* where he and his fellow GIs were "kept in the hold, and [slept] in bunks stacked five high. The bunks were in long rows, so your feet were always in somebody's face, or their feet were in your face."

Forseth had remembered that the stench caused by sweat and body odor in the hold was "horrendous." If a hatch was opened to allow outside air to clear out the smell, "there would be this blast of Arctic wind, which just seemed to make everything smell worse."

"[Seasick] guys would be vomiting in their beds or in their shoes … Guys were walking around with dried puke on their shirts."

Then there was the head, or bathroom, on Forseth's ship. Toilet seats resided above a long trough, and the slop of feces would slosh from one side of the trough to the other as the ship rolled with the waves, sometimes spraying into the air. "It's a wonder we didn't all get cholera," Forseth said. As a joke, when several men were sitting on the holes, a guy would wad up toilet paper, set it afire, and release it into the rushing swill, where it would singe the sitters' butts. "Everyone would have a big laugh," related Forseth.

The final indignity, said Forseth, was when "They made us take a shower. I guess they wanted us to look our best when we landed in the Aleutians. They marched us up on deck and made us strip. Then they gave us soap and hosed us down with saltwater straight out of the Bering Sea. That water is actually below freezing … I'll never forget that."

In an interview, former Seabee Earl Long described his voyage:

Only a few nights before we had made it to Dutch Harbor, we were passing from the north Pacific to the Bering Sea. The weather was bad, and Unimak Pass is not the best place to be … [Our] ship began to make a terrible noise and started to shudder and vibrate … I scrambled out of my bunk, grabbed my life jacket, and went topside. Others had the same reaction … I was to discover that the cause of this frightening sound was that the seas had become so rough that the ship was being pitched in and out of the water from bow to stern. When the ship's stern raised out of the water, so did the giant blades of the ship's propellers. Without the water around them … they spun wildly, causing a great vibration all along the hull. Even a ship as large as the *Yukon* can be little more than a cork bobbing on the sea.[1]

Long remembered that once they were docked at Dutch Harbor, "The winds … picked up and were slamming into the island … Our ship … was by no means a small vessel. Yet within minutes, the lines holding it to the dock simply snapped with a loud crack. The end result was that throughout the night, we had tugboats doing all they could just to hold us against the dock and prevent us from being beached."

During storms, the northern Pacific Ocean and Bering Sea can become dangerously rough. Destroyer escort duty in the wartime Aleutians was described in *Battle Stations!* magazine:

Huge waves drenched watch standers and the officer of the deck on the open bridge, forty-three feet above the waterline. Tons of water repeatedly blasted the weatherdeck and superstructure. In [this] type of sea conditions, life rafts were tossed about, gunshields flattened, and on … the *Engstrom*, several depth charges broke free and careened about the deck.[2]

Ottis Littlejohn recalled that sometimes the seas were "so rough, they couldn't even cook in the kitchen and we'd get cold cuts."

Gerald Doescher described eating chow aboard ship in rough weather: "You had to hold your tray in the air with one hand while you ate with the other. After a while it became second nature. Every once in awhile, someone would lose his tray and it would come sliding down the table. We just … let it pass by, and continued eating."

Doescher's ship was in place off the Japanese Kurile Islands in 1944, ready to rescue downed pilots, but when a typhoon swept in, they headed north to make a run for safety. Wrote Doescher:

The wind hit 170 mph and the waves were crashing over the deck. The sea was so rough I had to tie a rope around my chest and anchor it to a stanchion to keep from falling overboard. The ship tilted so much I saw footsteps on the side of the bulkhead … We lost four or five ships in that storm; they just capsized and sank.

There were several ways a ship could get in trouble. If too much ice collected on the superstructure, it would get top heavy and capsize. Another concern was hull construction. Our ship had welded seams as opposed to rivets. Welded seams were not as strong as rivets. At one point, we had five seams separate, but were able to get back to port before they endangered the ship.

Once in a while, the engine that turned the rudder would stop. We took turns serving on special teams that would turn the rudder manually when this happened. This was critical in high seas. If the ship couldn't head into the waves [at a 90-degree angle], it might be broadsided by a large wave and flip over. If you didn't drown upon entering the water, you were going to die of hypothermia within minutes. The water was so cold and death so certain, that we had a saying: "If you go over the side, just start swimming for the bottom."[3]

Marine William Ellis was a gunner's mate on a Liberty ship. On one trip they frolicked in some snow that fell aboard ship, but the snow was replaced with typhoon-force winds and waves. The ship's deck plates split in places, and they could see down into the holds. "It was getting to be a pretty serious situation," remembered Ellis. Some Jeeps and other vehicles being transported in the ship's holds lost their tie-downs—and some of the crew were given the dangerous job of going below to secure them again before they banged through the side of the ship. The ship's captain called it the worst storm he'd seen in twenty-two years.

In rough seas, Dominick Budnick said his ship met five-story-high waves that would completely swamp the deck. "How that ship didn't crack in half, I don't know," he wrote. "At times we were underwater seventy-five percent of the time."

In high-wind situations, said Harry Bailey, boats or ships dropping anchor to sit out a storm could find their anchors being dragged.

Adak's Sweeper Cove provided good anchorage and protection from the weather for a great variety of ships. The armada that sailed to attack Attu was organized here. *National Archives at Seattle*

Navy air navigator Charles Fitzpatrick wrote about being on a plane searching for a missing American destroyer during a lengthy and powerful storm in the Attu area. Radio contact had been lost with the ship. Thanks to his hunches and course plotting, they eventually spotted the beleaguered vessel. Fitzpatrick in his book *From Then 'Til Now, My Journal* wrote:

My first glimpse [of the ship] was utterly shocking. The bow had just plummeted downward, disappearing into the oncoming wave, [and] her twin [propellers were] churning only air. I was startled, believing I was about to witness the demise of the entire crew and ship as it dove into the depths of the sea.

That converted and weary old WWI [ship] was valiantly fighting a sea she should have forgotten about many years prior … With [the arrival of the peak] of each wave she precariously hesitated, perfectly centered, with both her stern and bow clearly out of water. Perched thus, hesitating but for seconds … [she then slid] into the trough below, plunging her into and through the next oncoming wave.

As her bow burst forth, decks awash, she strenuously dumped water from her soaked decks.

What men are created for such punishment? … We located [them] at the peak of their tribulation; we found them early in their fourth week [of riding out the storm].

[Our sending them] short messages [via a signaling light] was their only outside contact in weeks. We advised them of their position … They understood, replying only, "Thanks."

[Then, they signaled back,] "Returning port, severe hull damage."

"Roger. What port?" was our reply [as] we circled about for any additional word.

"Attu—Adak—the States."

"Roger." The next time around they asked for the weather [prediction between their position and] Attu. We knew they had to be all smiles at learning [that] starting late that night they would be seeing [clear, calmer weather] and stars … Subsequently, they thanked us for coming out to see them … Surely that crew was thankful [that] somewhere, someone cared.

Eventually, we learned that old refitted WW1 [ship] had to return to the States for repairs. Besides her twisted hull there was considerable above-deck damage.[4]

Ottis Littlejohn remembered coming "in to the harbor and [our] ship was just covered with ice and … the safety cables … were about four to five times the size they should be and everything was solid ice, and it was so heavy we were even sinking down into … the water. And we got into port and they passed the word: 'All hands chip ice' … So we were up there chipping ice off the entire ship … all the way down to the water line. There was so much ice."

There were some fatal accidents. In one, a man fell overboard from a small vessel, and some life buoys were thrown to him, but the ship never stopped because it was in Japanese waters with lurking submarines.

Mac McGalliard, an army air force mechanic, wrote about a similar incident during the initial mass landing on Adak:

In the flotilla of ships they had two or three tugboats pulling barges. The one in question had … drums of … gasoline all tied down nice and neat. On the barge were two .50-caliber machine guns. One on each end of the barge. Two men attended each gun … So what happened, the rough sea got to the barge and turned it over and the four guys with it. The cable pulling the barge was cut loose and the flotilla went on its merry way. I guess in the middle of the night, and the sea as rough as it was, how were you going to see the men in the dark anyway? Like all soldiers, they were expendable. That was one rough night.[5]

One of Gerald Doescher's shipmates got into some of their vessel's medicinal alcohol, mixed it with pineapple juice, and was "feeling no pain. He was talking with us when, out of the blue, he yelled, 'I'm a depth charge,' and jumped overboard. Luckily we were in port at the time … and [he] climbed back on board."

No one was killed on Doescher's ship, the *Pasco*, due to enemy action, but they lost four sailors at Dutch Harbor when the men missed an evening ferry to return to the ship and tried taking a small rowboat suitable for two. "[It] floundered and sank half way to the ship," wrote Doescher. "The young men, none older than twenty, tried to swim to shore. With the cold water, big waves and heavy clothing, they didn't stand a chance." One of the men got as far as a dock, but a desperate grab by a bystander missed and the man slipped under to his death.

The aging battleship USS *Idaho* was on duty near Attu at night when an unexpectedly large wave swept over the deck, carrying a man overboard. He was recovered by a nearby destroyer but died from hypothermia. It was left to his distressed best friend to gather his belongings and send them to his family.

High winds with accompanying high waves put many a ship in peril in the Aleutian area. Several broke in half. Shown is the tanker SS *Sackett's Harbor*, towed to Adak Island in 1946. The crew was saved but the front half of the ship was lost. In the same year, a Russian ship also broke apart, with sixteen lives lost. *Navy photo courtesy of Harry Paul Jr.*

Sailors had to have some confidence that their ships would survive the battering of Aleutian waves, but the ships were vulnerable. My navy father on Adak wrote in a March 1946 letter:

A Russian tanker, *Donbass*, broke in two out there south of us. A merchant ship, *Puente Hills*, found the after half and started to tow it … Then another Russian [ship] found the forward half and took it in tow and was going to Dutch Harbor, but a storm came up and the tow broke. The last I heard she was still looking for it. Fifteen people out of sixteen on the forward section were lost.

Then the *Sackett's Harbor*, a big … US merchant ship broke in two southwest of here … Then last night [yet] another ship out here radioed she was in distress and almost without any power.[6]

According to the Brian Garfield archive, in December 1942 "the minelayer USS *Wasmuth* sank after two of its depth charges broke loose in a storm and blew up, breaking the converted destroyer in two. All hands were saved."

Ottis Littlejohn in an oral interview recalled how thick the fog could be in Aleutian waters:

I had just come down from the bridge [of our ship] and I happened to look up and saw that thing coming at us. It looked like a battleship. So I yelled on the bridge, right quick, "Ship on the starboard side." So … we tried to go reverse and they tried to steer starboard, but they rammed us and knocked a big hole in the side and then … knocked another big hole in the rear, and the fog lifted right away and there they were sitting out there with [their] bow turned 90 degrees … The same thing happened to two other ships in the same fleet at the same time.[7]

Staying dry and warm while pulling deck duty was a challenge for Littlejohn. "[Our] gun watch," he related, "was four hours and you had to spend four hours in the weather regardless of what it was. Now, we used to take turns going down below … to the ammunition room and get warmed up a little bit and … you'd come back up and let somebody else go, but there was no real good way to keep warm. We'd cover up with these big canvas gun covers … but that was your duty and you had to do it."

Gerald Doescher described pulling guard duty on his ship in inclement weather, saying he and his fellow sailors wore "a thick coverall that you stepped into and zipped up in the front. Along with the suit, we wore galoshes, several socks, gloves and a wool hat. It was good protection and kept you warm, but after a while the wind-chill factor took its toll."

There were both American and Japanese submarines in the waters around the chain of islands. Many of the American subs were World War I-vintage S-models, and undersea duty could be unpleasant.

Submarine watch duty outside required wearing layers upon layers of wool clothing to keep warm, but once back inside the vessel, men's clothing grew moist due to the muggy air. Condensation formed on the inner walls of subs and permeated bedding (men shared bunks on a rotating basis).

On some trips, the submarines spent a good deal of time submerged, especially during the long-daylight days of the Aleutian summer when they might be vulnerable to air attack. They would mostly surface at night to run their diesel engines to charge batteries (which provided the power for underwater travel). While submerged, air quality deteriorated as carbon dioxide levels rose, which could cause headaches. One rather primitive method to deal with excess CO_2 was to spread out a chemical absorbent.

The quality and availability of potable water on subs was a problem as well.

In a US Navy publication, *Medical Study of the Experiences in 1,471 Submarine Patrol Reports in World War II*, one Aleutian-area submarine reported that after enduring a depth charge attack, "brandy [was] rationed one ounce per man … not to quiet the nerves but to try and stop people from shivering."

Submarine S-27 was on a reconnaissance and patrol mission near Amchitka before Americans built a base there. The sub was on the surface charging its batteries in thick fog when it ran aground on some rocks. Diligent efforts to back off were unsuccessful, and S-27 was abandoned, with the officers and crew making it to an abandoned settlement on shore. There, they awaited rescue. The crew thought it amusing that their officers still had them fall out for a roll call every morning, as though someone might want to go AWOL. Luckily, they weren't hurting for food. Six days later, an American seaplane spotted them and began the process of evacuation. Because the navy didn't want the nearby Japanese on Kiska Island to gather intelligence from the grounded and battered submarine, its loss wasn't announced until three years later.

S-27's captain, Lt. Jukes, was later charged with dereliction of duty at a court-martial. However, his career didn't end with this misadventure; he went on to command two new submarines. Smith, his executive officer, also commanded another submarine.

A positive account of S-submarine duty is found in weatherman Paul Carrigan's memoir. Carrigan volunteered (or was volunteered by his boss) to pull weather observation duty off the Japanese Kurile Islands during the summer of 1943 on submarine S-35. Perhaps the warmer summer weather and lack of storms made going easier. His tour lasted twenty-seven days and gave him a good view of sub life.

The old submarines were small and cramped. On his trip, the usual four officers and thirty-eight crew were supplemented with extra men aboard for training. One of the positives about the sub, wrote Carrigan, was the excellent food being served. Soon after departing Attu:

> I feasted on the best meal I'd eaten during my seventeen months in the Aleutians: pork chops, green beans, mashed potatoes, cream gravy, apple sauce, fresh baked bread, and ice-cold milk. I could go back for seconds if I still had room. Coffee and a chocolate sheet cake with white frosting for dessert.
>
> Day or night, submariners had access to a huge refrigerator crammed full of goodies. Snacking anytime one wished in [a] ship's mess hall was unheard of in the navy I was accustomed to, and I'd quickly taken advantage of this privilege.[8]

Carrigan met with S-35 skipper Lt. Cmdr. Henry Monroe soon after departure. Carrigan wasn't easily impressed by officers, but "the captain had a good firm grip and I liked him immediately … Six-foot-four, ruggedly handsome, lean and tough-looking, determination

[was] written all over his face … He was a born leader who could make correct decisions under great stress … I could not help thinking Monroe fit my concept of what a tough, seasoned submarine skipper should look like."

Carrigan soon established a rapport with the crew. "S-35's officers and crew seemed an unusually happy, friendly lot," he wrote, "not just where I was concerned but among themselves, too. This camaraderie was similar to that of our flight crews but to an even higher degree. There was an absence of peevish bickering so often present among crewmen aboard ships. I was told that fights occasionally broke out on submarines, but when they did it was usually toward the end of a long, uneventful patrol. Boredom and the cramped, sunless life exposed a few nerves now and then."

At first, Carrigan had to spread out his sleeping bag on the floor of the torpedo room, but with all the foot traffic on an adjacent catwalk, sleep was difficult and he sometimes catnapped in the mess hall. Later, perhaps because the chiefs recognized that his weather reports were the main reason for their trip, they allowed him to use their various bunks when they were on watch. Finally, Carrigan was able to catch up on sleep.

His job was to take four weather observations daily, encode the reports, and give them to the radio operator to send back to Alaska, probably to help plan American bombing flights from the Aleutians. Unfortunately, when the sub arrived on station alongside the Japanese island of Shimushiru, the nearby Japanese picked up their radio transmissions and soon determined what S-35 was up to. Soon, Japanese ships and planes were gunning for them. As Carrigan put it, "The Japanese were about to be handed a license to shoot fish in a barrel." Even Tokyo Rose mentioned their mission.

The submarine's orders were not to torpedo Japanese ships, but to maintain a purely defensive posture. For example, on their way to their assigned location, they encountered, then played cat and mouse with, a probable larger Japanese submarine. After a tense standoff, the two cautious subs finally separated and went their separate ways without ever seeing each other except as radar blips.

Once on station and trying to move about to confuse the Japanese, they nonetheless were attacked by air:

The Mavis came winging directly toward us. Although we had been expecting this there wasn't much warning because the [Japanese] flying boat was at extremely low altitude … [Our sub] crash-dived. There was momentary cavitation as the screws came out of the sea and the whole boat shook. … There was time for S-35 to claw her way downward while making a sharp turn before the depth charges exploded. I thought the first two went off right on top of us but the crew said they weren't even close. The final four, which exploded several minutes later, seemed a considerable distance away even to me … Submerged, we slunk along and missed [a weather observation and report].

[A] 36-hour respite ended when [another] Mavis found us. … Lookouts saw the low-flying bomber in time for Monroe to dive and take evasive action. The Mavis pressed home the attack and dropped six depth charges. None did any damage but all were close enough to jar the boat.[9]

Later, Carrigan wrote, some small sub-chasing vessels pursued them:

S-35 took a pounding. Depth charges exploded much closer than during any other attack. Monroe's evasive action would gain a temporary reprieve only to be impaled again by probing sonar. S-35 was kept [submerged] for almost 24 hours. Each time she poked her head up, radar picked up either a ship, a plane, or both. Air in the boat became foul. Breathing became difficult … [and] our batteries became drained … Monroe was forced to surface … It was night and there was blessed fog. Radar indicated an empty ocean and sky. Life-giving air gushed into the boat.

On her broadcast that night, Tokyo Rose announced, "We regret to inform the American naval command … that … Japanese forces sank the American submarine which had been sending weather reports."[10]

Another time, three Japanese fighters were seen in the distance, but they didn't see the sub.

During their trip, S-35's crew told Carrigan about a previous attack mission where they were the first to penetrate into the Sea of Okhotsk as they looked for large prey. In his memoir, Carrigan retold the story:

[S-35 skipper] Monroe's search … was rewarded when he found a large ship anchored in only 70 feet of water. This vessel … was a floating fish cannery … No other vessels were in sight. Monroe crept closer, taking periodic peeks through the periscope while he kept the target broadside to S-35's bow … Monroe fired [two torpedoes] at the close range of 800 yards. At the predicted run time there came two tremendous explosions that rocked S-35. As Monroe ordered "up scope," several additional explosions occurred. When the scope broke water, Monroe viewed a scene straight out of Dante's Inferno. The processor ship was a mass of towering flames and black smoke. She was already beginning to slowly settle.

When Monroe returned to the scope he was horrified to see a Japanese destroyer emerge from the dense smoke [but] instead of turning tail, Monroe took S-35 almost directly under the torpedoed ship … The destroyer's sonar soon located S-35 and the old boat was subjected to a fearful pounding. . . Depth charges continued to rain down. Some exploded so close the submarine was bounced off the bottom.

After a forty-eight-hour ordeal, Monroe escaped the trap. With considerable minor damage, S-35 arrived back at Dutch Harbor in mid-July 1943.[11]

On the next weather trip without him, wrote Carrigan, the submarine developed serious engine problems, especially when a large driveshaft broke. As the crew limped back toward the Aleutians, they apparently caught sight of the three large Japanese ships that had evaded the US blockade and evacuated troops from Kiska. Unfortunately, S-35's engine difficulties made an attack impossible.

In turn, there were American surface vessels devoted to hunting down Japanese submarines. Gerald Doescher described one:

Our sleeping compartment was below the water line. I was lying in my bunk half asleep when a sub came so close I heard our sonar ping off its hull. I jumped out of my bunk and ran for my battle station, but the sub stayed below the surface and left the area. [Another time,] we were on convoy escort when sonar picked up a submarine not far from us. We turned and chased it down. We were sitting on top of it, so our captain gave the orders to fire a salvo of hedgehogs … You can fire up to 24 at a time in a circle pattern. Unlike depth charges, which detonate after a certain time or depth, a hedgehog only explodes when it hits the submarine.

One exploded. After hearing the explosion, the sonar guys listened as the sub sank. A submarine can only go down so far before it implodes. The sonar guys heard the crushing sound of metal as it went past the point of no return. We couldn't stick around to confirm the kill because we had to return to the convoy, so never got credit for sinking the sub.[12]

Dominick Budnick wrote about the constant vigilance on his ship for Japanese submarines' periscopes slicing through the water. On watch duty one time, he spotted a periscope about a half mile away. "I was so excited I screamed into the phones and told the bridge what I saw," wrote Budnick. The ship turned directly toward the sub and dropped a dozen depth charges. Later, they saw oil and debris on the water indicating a possible kill. "The joke on board for the next few days was not to give me earphones, just let me yell and the whole ship could hear me," said Budnick.

According to Bill Maris, after the USS *Casco* seaplane tender was torpedoed by a Japanese sub, the sub was sunk by depth charges. Two of the sub's crew managed to escape, were captured, and interrogated at Dutch Harbor.

There were occasions of particularly dangerous duty. Dominick Budnick was recruited by his ship's captain to go on an admittedly suicidal mission. While the ship was unloading cargo in a bay, Budnick and others agreed to set out in an open whaleboat with depth charges attached by ropes. If a submarine was detected by the ship and the whaleboat was near it, the men were to release the depth charges, set to explode at a depth of 40 feet. This would obliterate their whaleboat. As they set out on their mission, "There were a lot of good-byes [from shipmates] and 'fellows it's been nice knowing you,'" wrote Budnick. "There was a lot of joking."

Surviving that test of his mettle, Budnick was promoted.

Budnick had another job which was equally dangerous: placing large shells in the breech of a large-caliber gun on the bow of their ship. If it had been fired often, the gun would become quite hot—and if one of the shells was a dud, the red-hot unexploded shell would fly out into his arms, protected with asbestos gloves. He would then run to the side of the ship and throw it overboard.

Living conditions aboard ship varied. Gerald Doescher wrote about Aleutian duty in the Coast Guard aboard the USS *Pasco*, a small patrol frigate. His communal sleeping compartment had no windows and was "crammed full of bunks stacked four high with eighteen inches between them. There was no privacy, but that didn't bother me."

"To avoid rolling out of the bunk when the seas were rough, you draped your arms underneath the bunk and hung on."

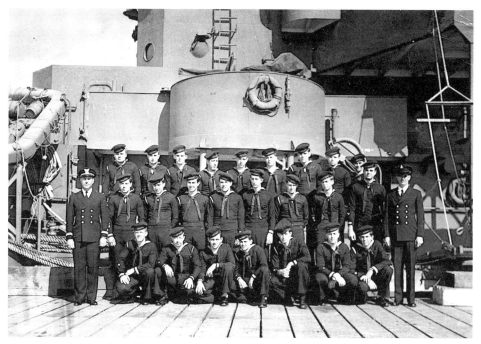

Crew of patrol frigate USS *Albuquerque* while docked at Attu in 1944. The ship performed escort and patrol duties in the Aleutian area. Toward the end of the war, she was given to Russia under the lend-lease program, and later returned. *Courtesy of David Hendrickson via National Park Service*

For entertainment, said Doescher:

> With almost 190 guys on board, something was always going on in the mess hall … Once in a while we would set up the projector and watch a movie … I had a friend in Oakland who serviced jukeboxes for a living. He would remove the old records and replace them with new ones. Before [we left on] our war cruise, he gave me an armful of records, and I put them in the ship's jukebox.[13]

Everyday life aboard the destroyer USS *Hatfield* was described by Dale Standley in an oral interview. The ship was so small it didn't have a mess hall, and meals were eaten in the sleeping quarters after the bunks were folded up against the walls.

Standley said one sailor made himself unpopular by not washing his clothes or himself. "He was always running around in his clothes that had old gravy spilt on 'em from days before and it was sour, it was just nasty" said Standley. "We … put him in [the shower], clothes and all, and then brushed him, washing his clothes right on his body. That straightened him out; he was a pretty good boy after that."

Naval radioman John Fahey related in an interview that on-and-off watch schedules could result in only six hours of sleep. Recalled Fahey, "I can't recall getting a full night's sleep in the navy … Hell, I actually would fall asleep copying [Morse] code; in the middle of the night, it's not hard to do." At least as a radioman, he didn't have to do outside work on the deck.

Famed author Gore Vidal was the first mate aboard a supply ship in Aleutian waters during the war, and his first novel, *Williwaw*, provided a vivid picture of shipboard life. In the novel, long-running personality conflicts result from power struggles and the privileges of rank. When other entertainments ran out, wrote Vidal, sometimes the only remaining activity was talking, and the longer a man was in the northern waters, the longer his stories became.

Sailor Raymond Brittain said that during one stretch in the Aleutians, he spent six months aboard ship without ever stepping on land. There must be a joke somewhere about such a man stepping ashore and his stomach turning queasy as he becomes "landsick."

Chapter 14
Working in (or for the) General

What GIs really hated was senseless work.

There were hundreds of different military jobs in the Aleutians lacking the glamor of piloting planes or the adrenalin rush of hand-to-hand combat. Somebody had to build barracks, dig ditches, pull guard, cook meals, string electrical lines, and ensure a healthy water supply.

Clint Goodwin, an army engineer on Umnak, talked about Aleutian construction work where "you had to be young, strong and bite the bullet. And if you were thirty-four or thirty-five, you couldn't make it. They'd send you back. They were too old."

On the other hand, some officers grew tired of young draftees with no work experience. Navy Seabee Clifton Davis in an oral interview said he was in a construction outfit where the average age was fifty-four because most of the men were former construction workers.

"SOMETIMES I THINK SCIENCE IS STANDING STILL."

Artist: Donald Miller

Seabee George Judy started out digging ditches and did other dirty work at Dutch Harbor and Amchitka, but a buddy said, "I'm going to teach you how to drive a truck ... or you are not going to make it." So Judy ended up driving for the remainder of his tour.

According to the Garfield archive, some Seabees arrived on an island to build huts and facilities. "Water had to be [brought to them in] cans from three miles away. For six weeks they dined from mess kits beneath leaky tents [before] the mess hall was erected. It was a month before a shower hut was finished and they had their first bath."

Army aviation engineers swarmed onto Amchitka to build airfields so fighters and bombers could attack the nearby Japanese-held islands of Kiska and Attu. An article in *Air Force Magazine* in 1943 described their toil:

Snow fell. The muck was up to [their] shoetops ... Getting heavy trucks, caterpillar tractors, trailers, scrapers and other machinery ashore through the surf was a real problem ... A mess truck made the rounds of workers in the field with hot food and drink. To keep the trucks and other machinery rolling, mechanics put "duck boards" down in the mud and lay on their backs [underneath the vehicles] to make repairs. The Japs attacked [by air] ... and several lives were lost in bombing raids.[1]

When construction began on a second bomber runway, the engineers were still working twenty-four hours a day. Meanwhile, other construction groups began to erect tents, a mess hall, and the infrastructure to supply aviation fuel and bombs.

In charge of this work on Amchitka using one hundred workers was a young communications lieutenant with no construction experience. He found that tracked vehicles were the best option for transporting supplies over the spongy and muddy muskeg, but even they got stuck in the muck from time to time. As *Air Force Magazine* put it, "Rain fell. The men were soaked. An army physician said he treated ... bruises, cuts and pulled tendons from slogging through mud. Weights up to 2,000 pounds were carried on the shoulders of as many men as were able to get round [a] box and lift it."

As soon as the runways were completed, B-24s flew in. After a hot meal, their crews took off the same day on a bombing mission against the Japanese.

Wilbur Green, in an interview, described being the skipper of an airplane crash rescue boat based at Attu. Sometimes when directed to a watery crash site, all they found were bodies or body parts, and blood would get all over their deck. It helped aviators' morale to know they had a chance of being picked up, but sometimes weather would prevent such boats from reaching a crash location, and if an airman couldn't get into an inflatable boat, he wouldn't last but minutes in the frigid water. On a happier note, Green and his crew sometimes took pilots out on fishing trips.

What GIs really hated was senseless work. There were complaints of combat troops being used to unload ships, and in one case, unloading a ship only to put the same supplies back aboard again.

According to Frederick Rust, writing in the 18th Engineers Regimental diary in January 1943, morale among the Seabees went down when there was only piddling work to do and improved when they had real, relevant jobs.

Some navy men, including James Doyle, were stationed at so-called Radio City on Adak, where they intercepted and copied down coded Japanese radio transmissions. Their's was a secret operation, partly because the navy didn't want the Japanese to know their codes had been broken, so Radio City was off-limits to others. Doyle and other young men, fueled by coffee, worked eight-hour shifts using special typewriters, listening intently through static, and trying different antennas to get the best reception. They never knew what the Japanese were saying, because the coded messages were handed over to navy higher-ups to decipher. From time to time, Doyle and his coworkers also coordinated with listening posts elsewhere in the Pacific to pinpoint the locations of Japanese stations. There was once an opportunity to go out on a naval task force to copy enemy Morse code, but, said Doyle, "I didn't want to go out there and hang myself over the side of a ship," getting seasick. Another section of Radio City was super-secret: they listened to Russian transmissions, according to Doyle.

Standing guard was one of the most thankless jobs for GIs. Men would have to stay awake at all hours, officers would come out to inspect them, and staying warm was a challenge. Another strain on guards was false alerts of Japanese attacks.

Navy weatherman Paul Carrigan was assigned the unusual duty of being one of the first to land on Adak before the main contingents of men and equipment arrived. He and a radioman were dropped off by seaplane and proceeded to set up a tent and radio transmitter near the beach to send weather and ocean reports to the navy and army. It was Carrigan's job to hand-crank a generator to power the radio. They were concerned that a few advance scout troops already on the island didn't know they were there and might shoot them.

Carrigan wrote about their experience:

My aneroid barometer started a nosedive that afternoon ... By midnight ... we were in the grip of a gale. With loud reports which sounded startlingly like rifle shots, violent gusts began to rattle and snap the tent fabric. Driving rain transformed our site into what some might consider a vacation paradise: a tent with a small stream running through the middle of it. With dismay we realized our site had been ill-chosen ... Slipping and sliding around on hands and knees, we set to work. With driftwood sticks we dug and scraped out a crude but deep trench around the ... sides of the tent. This diverted most of the water. In the process we became drenched by the cold rain.

From an opened case of field rations we ate our third cold meal of the day. Our craving for a hot cup of coffee was intense ... The wind continued to mount in fury and howl forlornly. On one observation I recorded a southeasterly wind speed of 52 knots [or 60 miles per hour]. It was a miserable night without sleep but fortunately our tent didn't blow down.

Dawn ... was more a greying of black. We stepped outside into horizontally slashing rain. [The bay's] waters were whipped into a white froth. At six-second intervals, swells that I estimated to be seven feet high were crashing with a roar onto the landing beach. I took an observation and we transmitted. Afterward, we relaxed, certain that the occupation of Adak would be postponed because of surf and weather conditions.[2]

Whether the admirals and generals got the gale warning or not, the occupation force soon arrived and began trying to land men and materiel. According to Carrigan, most of the initial landing craft sank and many troops drowned in the surf, often because of their heavy backpacks. In press coverage of the operation, the loss of life wasn't mentioned. A *Life* magazine article, for example, stated, "As the lighters and landing boats headed for shore, a gale blew up and piled men and barges into the surf ... The men stood in waist-deep icy water passing boxes and bales hand-to-hand to the strip of beach ... In an hour helmeted US soldiers were careening along the beach in army Jeeps."

Despite loss of life, the landing was completed. The lack of concern for weather conditions, however, was a preview of the ill-fated battle for Attu.

Later, as Carrigan later helped set up the full navy weather operation on Adak, the Japanese learned of the Adak occupation and for six consecutive nights sent a single plane nicknamed "Washing-Machine Charley" over the Americans to drop a single bomb. Wrote Carrigan, "When the air raid alert sounded the first night, I slipped into boots and jacket, grabbed my [Browning Automatic Rifle] and sprinted through the tent flap out into blackness. I promptly tripped over a tent guy line and fell sprawling face first into the mud. The bomb landed a half mile away ... " After that, he and his tent mates grew increasingly blasé, and "On the third nightly bombing, most of us didn't even bother to get out of our sleeping bags ... It was much safer to lie flat in our bags rather than run around aimlessly in the dark."

Much manpower and man-hours went into building up Adak. When roads became impassible, supplies were often carried on GIs' backs.

The Garfield archive noted that in December 1942, "Seabees and engineers at Adak worked through the perpetual night under floodlights, building accommodations for 15,000 men and all the warehouses and facilities that went with them." Also, some of the Seabees were from Texas, and "their Mexicans had never seen snow."

Tech five Frederick Rust of the 18th Engineer Regiment wrote in 1944, "Since our arrival at Adak ... the men have worked seven days a week ... The regiment has had no fresh food of any kind for five weeks ... Due to no entertainment available, gambling became the entertainment of choice."

Somewhere else in the outer islands, SSgt. Delbert Morley helped create a dummy airfield with fake planes to fool the Japanese.

GIs at some of the more developed bases complained that the civilian workers who were exempt from the draft got paid more and often had better accommodations. Of course, GIs didn't mind if those employees were women.

A navy sonarman based on Adak, Eugene Babb, enjoyed picking up underwater whale sounds while listening for Japanese submarines.

A weather observer on Shemya, Bernard Mehren, noted that on April 10, 1945, he had his first day off in forty consecutive days.

Due to Japanese threats and awful weather, there was a lot of stress placed on certain individuals. Aviators depended upon accurate weather reports and predictions generated by men such as Paul Carrigan. Navigators on bombers were relied upon to bring aircraft back home to fogged-in small islands without the benefit of advanced navigational aids. There was a lot of stress placed on navy communications people such as James Doyle and my father to not make mistakes in receiving and sending important messages, and in encoding and decoding messages. Aircraft maintenance crews were under pressure to keep planes airworthy enough to fly many hundreds of miles without failing. Ships' officers had to avoid grounding their vessels. Mistakes in that part of the world could easily result in deaths and weren't often tolerated.

Medic Cecil Fuller on Kodiak Island was a Seventh-Day Adventist who wanted to have enough time off on Saturdays to celebrate the Sabbath, so he made an arrangement to work Saturday evening through Monday evening. Oftentimes he was the only medic on duty at the hospital then, and if there were no patients he could catch some sleep. But if there was a patient, Fuller would take his own shoes off and put them on the edge of the bed, so if the patient moved, falling shoes would wake him (Fuller) up.

In the military newsletter on Kiska in 1943 was the following lament: "A sailor is a guy who is worked too hard, gets too little sleep, takes verbal abuse no civilian would take, does every imaginable kind of a job at any imaginable hour, never seems to get paid, never knows where he's going, can seldom tell where he's been—yet accepts the worst with complete resignation."

Chapter 15
Male Call

Getting mail was more important than getting a good meal.

Before the internet there was regular mail.

Nowadays, military men and women overseas or on local bases most often have access to email, Skype, Zoom, and social media. It helps ease the pain of separation.

But in World War II, ordinary mail was the way people usually communicated over long distances. Mail was king. It was slow and usually required cursive handwriting, but it was very, very personal. In the hierarchy of things, getting mail was more important than getting a good meal.

During the war, I'm sure many loved ones and relatives in the States understood how important their letters were to GIs in the Aleutians, while perhaps others just saw letter writing as a chore.

Aleutian guys knew that getting letters usually required writing letters. It gave them something to do. Postage for them was free.

Some kindhearted GIs would share their letters with those who weren't so lucky.

Kiska's military newsletter, the *Overseas Chatter*, noted in 1944 that "lots of excitement was displayed when the mail came in [today]. It was a welcome sight only to be followed by a letdown feeling at the discovery it was nearly all [newspapers and magazines]. Oddly enough, however, the [microfilmed mail] fans did get some letters. What this mail can do to a fellow!! And what the lack of it can do!!!!"

There's the story of an isolated, nine-man military outpost on Ogliuga Island welcoming a flight carrying food. The air crew expected to be welcomed with open arms. However, when the island's residents learned there was no mail aboard, the crew was met with hostility.

The Brian Garfield archive included this from Dr. Walter Feinstein, serving somewhere in the Aleutians: "No mail again today. Three weeks have gone by and not a single letter … A transport plane landed [today] and we all had hopes [but]

"*I DON'T REALLY LIKE TO FISH, BUT IT'S SOMETHIN' TO WRITE HOME ABOUT.*"

Artist: Oliver Pedigo

all it was carrying was valuable airplane parts … " Three days later he added, "Still no mail. Three air force men landed here today from Anchorage and told us that the hangars there were loaded with mail but there [were] no available … planes."

Some girlfriends would send provocative kisses by blotting their lipstick on Kleenexes and including them with letters.

At Dutch Harbor, Marine corporal Earl Shalin was hated because he was the bugler who blew reveille early in the morning—and loved because he was the base postman.

Charles Fitzpatrick, a navy air navigator on Attu, summed up things nicely in his book *From Then 'Til Now, My Journal*:

> I was probably one of the possible dozen guys [in my outfit] who was blessed with a wife, my sweetheart, that wrote every day. There were a number of times when a letter didn't make it to keep my consecutive streak going, but that was because of weather. However, the next day or so, weather permitting, the mail plane brought in three or four delightfully scented letters for me.
>
> Once, and thank heaven it was only once, … twenty days went by, because … severe weather kept the mail plane from getting into Attu … All hands, both navy and the army, became so upset by the lack of outside communications it was agreed to let a volunteer try to [fly] to Adak for the mail. Our navy volunteer got off, made it about a third [of] the way to Adak but because of the severity of the weather turned back …
>
> [Later,] when [the Naval Air Transport Service] finally arrived, they buzzed the field, thereby advising all that the mail had arrived. Their touch of humor was appreciated.
>
> That afternoon I sorted my thirty letters and [news]papers by date of postmark, then [turned on] my radio to hear some of those romantic ballads from stateside, leaned back on my bunk with feet propped up, then spent the balance of the afternoon and evening reading Betty's [perfume]-scented letters. Each epistle was reread, missing nothing. The best part—most were very long. I read late into the night. I cherished every second of the reading and with every … letter written, loved [Betty] even more. Last but not least were the few newspapers and magazines. Such periodicals ultimately were passed on. They reached many hands before they were discarded.[1]

GI Walter Kellog said, "Because we moved so often, mail was a big problem. Often no mail came for five weeks, and then we got 18 or 20 letters all at once." Here's his record of mail received over a six-month period, in his words:

August 26, 1943 – one letter
August 30 – one letter written May 9 telling of Grandma's death. It had been forwarded six times …
September 4 – I got two letters …
November 28 – I got a new Elgin watch from home and 19 letters
December 22 – I got packages from [relatives, which took seven days to arrive]
January 18, 1944 – One letter from home …
February 22 – I received 23 letters …[2]

Here are excerpts from several letters sent by Samuel "Mack" McKay to his parents:

"Oh yes mom. I made sergeant the other day. Looks like I am going up in the ranks, doesn't it."

"It has been quite a long time since I have heard from you. I guess it has been a [long] time since you have heard from me too ... Mom, I wish you would cross your fingers and hope I get home soon. Last time it worked, so try it again, will you."

"Today was mail call and I got one little one-page letter; a small page at that. A girl in Seattle."

"I was listening to the war situation on the radio. So far it looks promising. I hope it ends pretty soon, so I can go back and start hunting for a job."

"Oh yes. We had beer the other day. Some [got] drunk and some sold theirs for a dollar [or] two dollars. I drank mine. I wished I had sold it. But it is too late to cry over spilt beer."[3]

An *Air Force Magazine* article from December, 1943 observed:

Men in the Aleutians receive strange gifts through the mail. As any soldier knows, Spam or luncheon meat appears on mess tables with disturbing frequency, and yet one officer received a can of it from his wife—as a birthday gift. Another man got a can of tuna fish, also on the menu far too frequently. A tough crew chief received, for no ascertainable reason, an application blank to join the [Women's Army Corps].

One day an intelligence officer, Captain Phil Orcutt, was sitting in his Quonset hut, going through his mail, while outside the rain fell and the wind blew. He opened a form letter from a well-known national magazine, which began as follows: "As this letter reaches you, you are, no doubt, sitting on the porch of your summer cottage, or perhaps you are seated on the deck of your yacht, thinking about the fine job our boys are doing overseas."[4]

Navy radio man James Doyle, who served on Adak, and I concluded that it was my father, the Adak naval postmaster, who backdated the postmark on a late anniversary card to my mother so she wouldn't think he'd forgotten the date. Another time, my mother sent my dad a box of nuts for Christmas. By the time they arrived, worms inside were gorging themselves.

Some GIs off the beaten track received Christmas presents several months late—even as late as April.

Mel Plate's son was born back in the States on December 2, but he didn't get the joyous news until after Christmas. Army man Frank Bosak's wife was pregnant when he left for the Aleutians, and she gave birth to a daughter while he was there, but he didn't find out until he later reached the Philippines.

Men serving at the remote weather station at Cape Wrangell on Attu patiently awaited their once-a-month mail delivery.

Serving on a ship, George Sinclair received mail only three times during April 1942. A year later, on Amchitka, he didn't receive any mail between March 14 and April 9. Then he "heard from Louise, Margie, and Margrett [and I] feel swell now."

Lt. George Reeder of the 7th Infantry on Attu said it would take three weeks to get a reply after mailing a letter home.

However, things did get better over time. As the war continued on into 1945, my mother's letters from Wisconsin to my dad on the headquarters island of Adak were being delivered after only three days.

William Chesney was temporarily assigned to Anchorage on the mainland, where he was able to telephone his wife and family down in the States for a half hour. No such luck out in the islands, although there was a navy man with a ham radio station at Dutch Harbor who was able to send GIs' radiograms to a ham operator in the lower forty-eight states, who then forwarded them to other hams around the country for delivery. The system also allowed the recipients to send return messages. (Amateur radio activity was forbidden during the war, but an exception may have been made for stations carrying GIs' messages.)

Not every letter contained placid news about cousin Joe, or mom trying a new pie recipe. Lt. Eliot Asinof received one of them:

I held her unopened letter, preparing myself for whatever it might contain … I opened the letter with a defiant smile. She would gratify my need for love. It will tell me how she missed me; that our marriage will be the ultimate reward for being the soldier I had desired to be.

"*Dear Elly.*"

Not "dearest," not "my darling."

It was like suddenly getting kicked in the gonads.

"*I never thought I'd ever write this to you. I never thought anything like this could possibly happen. I've got to be harsh. To be painfully blunt, I don't know how else to put it, but I've fallen in love with someone … An actor. He plays villains but he's really a pussy cat. I met him at a party in the Village.*"

There were two more pages. About [the actor], mostly, and I didn't read them. Whatever she had to say would feed my rage. I could barely breathe. Face it, [the] greatest affliction that the US mails ever imposed on an American soldier … was called "Dear John."

There was no one around, thank God. I must have turned a nasty pale. I had to sit before I fell, legs trembling, beaten by a force I couldn't cope with. I really couldn't believe it and then I could. We weren't meant to be married …

That this was happening to me on Adak, not at home, was the worst of it. On Adak I was left to suffer with no way out.

There was rage, like being slapped in the face, hard. I tore the letter into pieces, crushed the scraps in my fist. I went to my footlocker, found her letters [and] destroyed them all. I smashed her picture then stabbed the scarf she had sent me for my birthday with my pocket knife. I cried out, "Fuck you … " What could be worse than bellowing hate at someone who wasn't even there?

Noncombat Adak was a killer. I sat in my office and heard pool balls clacking behind the plywood walls. I couldn't stand anyone's pleasure. I got in my Jeep and drove to nowhere as the winds splattered the windshield with a driving rain, … barreling around curves I didn't recognize and roads one could get slaughtered on. Eventually I ended up at a bay where the road ended.

The winds were vicious; a williwaw, I guessed. I didn't care; I got out and worked my way down to the beach. In seconds I was thoroughly soaked. I didn't care about that either. Like a suicidal idiot [I] sat on a rock and took the punishment of howling nature as if I deserved it. It was so ferocious I began to scream … I'd never been so wet, so cold in my life. If I stayed there ten minutes longer I'd be dead. Above me I heard an animal cry. There was a huge sea lion, perched on a rock and I let out a yell, needing to show I was master. I had never made such a sound.

I got up, struggled to work my way back to my Jeep, crawling on hands and knees against the wind. The Jeep was shaking and I had to grapple with the door to get it open.

When I finally got back to my hut, the warmth of the kerosene stove made me laugh. And there was my friend Captain Kirby, the medic, sitting on my bed, a half-empty bottle of tequila in his hand. He looked at me, his mouth open in horror at what he saw.

"Jesus!" he said.

I got to the stove, where he gave me the bottle. I stood by the heat and drank. For minutes I could not talk. When I could, I made a feeble joke. "It's raining," I said.

I undressed with his help. He bundled me in blankets and I stayed by the stove shivering until the heat penetrated. He didn't ask me what had happened; he kept massaging me under the blankets.

"I went crazy," I said, summing up the day. The thought made me shudder. In time, I got over my chills. I could even feel my flesh again; I could talk.[5]

An equally poignant story was related in the book *Short Cut to Tokyo*, by Corey Ford. The author saw "one tow-headed kid from Tennessee … sitting alone at a table … He had a letter from his mother. He'd … reread it so many times it had finally come apart at the folds. He was rearranging the pieces on top of the table, so he could read it again."

Jerry Dubuque on Shemya related this lighter story:

Having to carry a camera case, gas mask and rifle wasn't too easy … I tried to get a .45-caliber pistol to carry instead of a rifle, but couldn't get one issued to me. Not being an officer, that is. So I wrote to Ginny and asked her to send me an item I had in the top drawer of our bureau. It was a .32-caliber pistol. I couldn't come right out and say what I wanted because our mail was censored. She understood, and not long afterward, I received a package and the pistol was in it. However, no bullets. Well, I wrote back and, again, my mail was checked out so I had to be careful what I wrote. I asked her for the .32 shorts that were next to the item I had just received from her. In the next mail [was] my package and there were the … shorts—boxer shorts, that is! Needless to say, I kept carrying the rifle.[6]

Joseph Sasser, an army combat engineer, said in an interview that he wrote love letters for a Chinese-American cook on Attu who couldn't write.

In ending, a poem written by Pvt. Robert Glassburn, from the book *Cheechako Don in Alaska and Aleutians: Collections of a GI*:

The Sad Saga of Pvt. McFudd

Hundreds of miles from civilization
Sat the saddest man in all creation,
Pvt. McFudd, homesick and dejected.
Letters to him his friends neglected.
At last, through the mist, a plane appeared.
When McFudd saw it, he shouted and cheered.
His heart thumped and his pulse beat madly,
His pay for a letter he'd give up gladly.
The moment arrived, the mail was passed out,
McFudd stood in front with his hand thrust out.

Into his hand one letter was thrust,
So excited he was, he thought that he'd bust.
Now here lies the body of Pvt. McFudd,
Stabbed to the heart—fell with a thud.
The letter he thought from his gal he'd get
Was merely a bill, reading "PLEASE REMIT!"[7]

Chapter 16
Censorship and Secrecy to an Extreme

Hi, folks. How are you? I'm fine.

"Loose lips sink ships" was a memorable wartime slogan. The idea was that if the Japanese and Germans learned where our ships were headed and what time they'd be there (due to sailors talking too much), they were vulnerable to submarine or other types of attack.

The military in World War II sometimes took secrecy to extremes, and yet our enemies often knew a lot about our movements and locations anyway.

Prior to the attack on Pearl Harbor, mail from GIs in Alaska wasn't censored. Afterwards, that all changed. Censorship involved designated officers blacking out or physically cutting out portions of letters deemed potentially harmful to the war effort. Even officers didn't escape the scrutiny. A letter from my father to his parents carried the rubber stamp "Passed by naval censor" on the envelope.

Aleutian GIs' personal letters to the States had to have an officer-censor's stamp on the envelope before being mailed. *Harry Paul Jr.*

Ostensibly, censorship was to prevent military information from being passed on to the enemy. But as navy radio man James Doyle told me, "Mostly [on Adak] they were looking [to censor] anybody that was complaining about the food … [or if someone] thought they were being overworked." So—the military was trying to convince the folks back home that everything was fine. I read accounts of Black GIs in other Pacific sectors having their comments about discriminatory and poor treatment being censored.

Censorship was so strict that letter writers couldn't give any hint about their location, including using the word Alaska. Men in the Aleutians with German last names had their incoming mail closely monitored, due to the wartime alliance between Germany and Japan.

If those at home sometimes wondered why their GIs were not inspired to write often, censorship may have had something to do with it. Donald Brydon, in the army air force, admitted that he "didn't write so often once we got on Attu and Shemya because there wasn't anything to say, because every letter was censored. If you said anything that amounted to anything, they'd cut it out of the letter, so we … couldn't even say what the weather was."

Another GI, Gaylord Tapp, said he saw some of his letters when he returned home. "They [were] just blanked out. Nothing. [They said,] 'Hi, folks. How are you. I'm fine.' That's all; the rest [was] all blanked out."

Some resorted to subterfuge. Navy Seabee Earl Long passed his spare time by reading books and writing his wife. To get around the censors, he hinted at his location by making references to an "Aunt Ada"—Ada hinting at "Adak."

Someone wrote to Pvt. Edward Thomas asking about what kind of work he did. Thomas replied, "I'd like to answer but do not believe it is permissible." That must have made it sound like he was involved in some super-secret operation. Also, he wrote his mother that "I'll have to leave questions about the weather unanswered." He was finally allowed to say that he was on one of the Aleutian Islands and that if he was on a high hill he could see both the Bering Sea and the Pacific Ocean.

On the other hand, sometimes GIs censored themselves—not wanting to worry relatives, girlfriends, or wives by telling them they'd been hospitalized, or that their mental state was awful. I came across a story about an American World War II pilot in Europe, Quentin Aanenson, who began a letter to his girlfriend, "I have purposely not told you much about my world over here, because I thought it might upset you. Perhaps that has been a mistake, so let me correct that right now. I still doubt if you will be able to comprehend it."

Photographs were also censored. On Kiska, privately owned cameras had to be kept under lock and key until checked out, and GIs could only send home photos of people—and even then, the photos couldn't show land forms such as volcanos.

Lt. Rudy Leach said it was against navy regulations to keep a diary. Thankfully for this book and others, many didn't abide by that rule.

During the war, and I believe to the present day, mail going to military locations overseas was and is addressed to army post offices (APOs) and fleet post offices (FPOs). This is a convenience, but it also camouflages military units' locations. My dad's mailing address (he was stationed on Adak) was his unit via the FPO at Seattle.

He only once expressed anger in a letter home—this one to his parents:

Just where did you cook up that address you put on that letter you sent? Do you know I could be court martialed if I even mention where I am? Let's get on the ball down there and wake up to the fact there is a war on. I'm just sweating blood waiting to see if I get called in to explain that address.

I sure got a knife in the back from [you] folks at home. Don't you ever try to make up an address of your own again.[1]

Apparently, his mother had mistakenly sent a letter addressed to his unit, with Adak, Alaska, as part of the address. My father was partly to blame, too, because he must have ignored orders by telling them which island he was going to before leaving the States. As far as I know, he wasn't called to task for this error.

Another concern about censorship was that outgoing mail was usually read and censored by a unit's officer who knew the letter writers, raising privacy concerns.

A naval officer censoring mail at Adak in 1943. *National Archives*

An anonymous poet somewhere along the chain added this delightful ditty to his letter home, which ended up being used by other GIs as well:

I hate the thought of these tender words
being read by a stranger's eyes
these soul-writ words for her alone
these lies and alibis.

So read my letters gently, sir
they are not meant for you
but for a girl in Arkansas
I write this silly goo.

And when you read this letter, sir
and chortle with delight
just think of another censor
who's reading each letter you write.[2]

Even Alaska's territorial governor, Ernest Gruening, said in 1942 that "censorship in Alaska has been and is … unduly repressive [and] wasteful … —[it's] wholly unnecessary."

Secrecy involving GIs had actually begun back in the States before they left for Alaska. Navy Seabee Earl Long, in an oral interview, recounted:

Here we were, a body of uniformed men marching through the streets of Seattle … with sheepskin coats on and rifles. We still didn't know where we were going, but we were damn sure it wasn't to an island in the South Pacific, and so did everyone else that saw us that day.

We shipped out on the SS *Yukon* early in the morning heading for what we were then told was Island X. For reasons of security, all destinations at the time were Island X.[3]

Dean Galles, a soldier being shipped to Alaska with his outfit, said he didn't know at the time that the Japanese occupied American soil in the Aleutian Islands. "We had no pre-information on that at all. It was so secretive," said Galles. He didn't learn until much later that he would fight the Japanese on Attu.

Paul Worley said, "We didn't even know who was winning the war."

GIs resorted to listening to Tokyo Rose on Radio Tokyo to get news, even though her reports were often false. MSgt. Frank Carnes wrote about sailing on the troopship *Ulysses S. Grant* to Alaska:

It was so crowded that I spent days in the radio room copying news from the USA in Morse code. And, also listening to [Radio Tokyo] and the news there by … Tokyo Rose. One day she had a message addressed to the *US Grant* in the North Pacific waters. The news was that their navy would sink [our ship] and being thrown into the cold water, a soldier would live for only a few minutes.[4]

Wilkins Dixon on Umnak said, "[Radio Tokyo] knew more about what was going on here than we did." In the Brian Garfield archive was this note: "Radio Tokyo came in more clearly on sets in the Aleutians than any other overseas station."

The result was that targeted Radio Tokyo "news" could start unfounded rumors and damage morale. It's interesting that the station wasn't jammed by American transmitters.

A psychiatrist who served on Adak advised that "the barriers of military secrecy are usually not so great that the men cannot be told the following before embarkation: their mission, the probable duration of their tour of duty, the climate [and] housing conditions."

The navy had downplayed damage done to Dutch Harbor when the Japanese attacked there early in the war, wanting to emphasize positive stories to rally Americans at home. As the war in the Aleutians heated up, journalists were either sent home or their dispatches were delayed and tightly limited by censors.

An example is a *Life* magazine dated October 19, 1942, when that magazine was at the zenith of its popularity and influence. This issue had a two-page photographic article headlined "Aleutian Attack." First of all, the story was only allowed to state that a landing was made on one of the Andreanof Islands, when the island was actually Adak. Also the story didn't succinctly state that the Japanese had captured two of the outermost American Aleutian Islands. Finally, although the landing had taken place around August 30, the story wasn't published until more than a month later, due to a military hold. *Life* complained that interference made coverage of military events in the Aleutians difficult.

Col. James Hammond Jr. admitted that "news was delayed, censored and incomplete, while Americans [back home] knew comparatively little of what really happened during fighting on their own soil [in the Aleutians]."

For example, journalists representing wire services and newspapers accompanied the armada of Allied ships headed for the landing on Attu. Once there, the reporters weren't allowed to go ashore. Eventually they were able to piece together what was happening, but even then they weren't allowed to submit their reports to their home offices. Americans back in the States were kept in the dark.

Perhaps one of the reasons little news got out about the battle for Attu was that commanders originally expected the battle to take three or four days, but took nineteen instead; American deaths were high (580); and the troops were ill-prepared for the cold and windy weather.

Navy radio intercept man James Doyle and many other GIs who'd been sworn to secrecy about their work during the war kept their secrets for many years. Doyle waited until the 1990s to tell his family that he listened in on Japanese military Morse code. I don't think my own father ever told us everything he did working in the same operation.

Chapter 17
Taking the War to the Japanese Northern Islands

Well, you know, we were all young bucks and we were indestructible—everybody felt that way ... Somebody else [might die, but] it won't be me, you know.

After forcibly taking back the island of Attu from Japan and building an airfield there, American air forces in the area were left with three main missions: patrolling the waters around the western Aleutian Islands, helping take back Kiska, and eventually, taking the air war to the Japanese northern home islands, the Kuriles.

Taking back Kiska was the easy part. The Japanese had already left.

The bombing flights from Attu to the Kuriles and back were the longest overwater attack runs of World War II. The flights typically lasted, according to pilot Milt Zack, about nine hours over 1,500 miles of cold ocean. That was a lot of time for boredom to develop. Also, there was the task of staying warm and fed.

If American planes were shot up over the Kuriles or had mechanical problems far into the flights, returning 750 miles to home base could be challenging.

Early on, when the attack (and reconnaissance) missions began, radio-based navigational aids were minimal. So, returning to one's home island—a relatively tiny dot of land in a big sea, often obscured by clouds or fog—could be difficult. Navigators' skills were highly depended upon. As stated before, more men and planes were lost to the weather than to enemy guns.

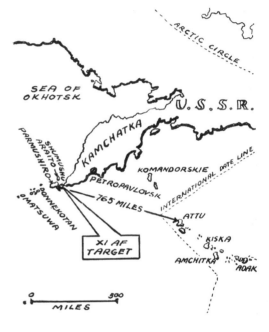

A map from *The Adakian* military newspaper on Adak illustrated the long-distance American bombing run from Attu to the northern Japanese islands, including Paramushiro (which is misspelled on the map). Enemy airfields and naval installations dotted the area. The Russian airfield at Petropavlovsk was an alternative landing point for shot-up or mechanically malfunctioning planes, but once in Russia the crews became the unwilling "guests" of Russia.

Later on, LORAN and other navigational aids made getting home easier. But they didn't always work as advertised.

American military strategy concerning the Japanese Kurile islands was a bit fuzzy. On one hand, attacking them could help prevent future Japanese excursions into the Aleutians.

More importantly, it was thought that shelling and bombing the Kuriles—and making the Japanese think that that the Americans were getting ready to invade them (en route to the Japanese main islands)—would force the Japanese to base valuable troops, ships, and planes there, removing them from other theaters of the Pacific war. That strategy worked.

Apparently, early bomber raids against the northern Kurile Islands (Paramushiro and Shimushu) lacked fighter-plane escort, making them more vulnerable to Japanese planes. After August 1943, planners decided to add escorts. The P-38 fighter, for example, had enough range to make the long trip.

I don't know the percentage of Kurile attacks which had fighter escort, nor have I read about a mission with fighter escort.

Army air pilot Milt Zack wrote:

> Many of our missions [to the Kurile islands] were pretty easy, since we had to turn back quite often, sometimes even after 2–3 hours out, because of weather conditions … One day, meteorology told us weather would be clear over Attu and decent along the route and over the Kuriles. So eight crews got ready and eight planes headed out the runway where they sat with engines running for over half an hour in a complete fog. The pilots were complaining about using up so much gasoline and begged to be able to shut down the engines, which they were eventually allowed to do … We did eventually take off and wound up in one of the biggest snafus you ever saw. The weather was so bad we could not get above it, so there we were with eight planes flying around the same area trying to find their way back to the field, unable to see their wingtips … By some miracle all eight planes did manage to land safely.[1]

Airmen prepare to fly their Ventura medium bomber on a Kurile Islands run. *National Archives at Seattle*

Navy air navigator Charles Fitzpatrick in his book *From Then 'Til Now, My Journal* wrote about preparing for a Kurile attack run:

Preparations for our first daylight mission had been completed for some time ... That morning we were awaked about 0430 by the master of arms who made certain we were awake, wide-eyed and bushy tailed ... A little fresh up, step out into the black cold and head for chow ... Breakfast before a mission was similar to the condemned man's last meal.

Briefing completed, we'd pile into the back of a truck with a canvas top, sitting on slatted wooden benches along either side. The driver would drop us off at the revetment where [our bomber] was getting an early morning treatment of deicing. [The plane's] cold engines coughing and sputtering would, with a little coaching, finally catch. Oh! That beautiful sound, even at that early hour of the morning ... Satisfied all was in order we taxied to the end of the runway ... and shut down the engines. Immediately, [a] large gas truck pulled up and topped off our tanks. Gas was that critical to the mission's success, and our own necks.[2]

The Ventura medium bomber they were flying was supposed to weigh no more than 31,000 pounds for safe takeoffs under ideal conditions. However, they typically took off weighing 34,000 pounds because of the bomb load. The lumbering planes would only reluctantly lift into the air.

Fitzpatrick wrote:

Immediately, after we [took off] over the Cove's cold waters I was sure, on more than a few occasions [that our plane dropped] a foot or so. None could verify it since those in the [cockpit] were too busy holding their breath ... This was no fighter jockey takeoff ... Each and every one was in itself a very scary and frightful event ... no matter whether it was the fifth ... or fifteenth.

So we were off on our first trip that would take us over Russia and to Japan. Here I was in a plane flying over the Pacific with water as far as you could see on any point of the compass ... Me, accountable for navigation. Responsible for getting the bunch of us to the target and back to Attu safely. It was tough to quite fathom it all.

I learned in a few trips flying across the ocean that no matter how savagely beautiful or serene and calm its appearance, a certain unending hesitation and trepidation rode silently with every crew member—no matter his background, experience, age, rank or rate. Even though none mentioned the ... thought, if you ever [ditched in] the sea, hope wasn't yours ... Life expectancy in the water was twelve, maybe fourteen minutes.

For the up-to-ten-hour flight, sandwiches were stowed on board ... If [they] weren't eaten in the first hour it was doubtful if they'd be eaten at all. They were frozen rock solid.[3]

Pilot Thomas Erickson wrote: "Usually we took off around midnight to put us on target by dawn. We carried three 500-pound bombs ... On these trips I had on seven layers of clothing. In an eight- or nine-hour trip a certain bodily function had to be performed more than once. The main problem was not so much getting back to the funnel-headed metal tube at the plane's rear but rather how to locate that part of a man's anatomy vital to the act." (From his partial memoir on file at the National Park Service, Alaska Regional Office, Archives, Unprocessed Collections, Alaska Veterans Files.)

In an oral interview, army air force veteran John Pletcher mentioned the concerns about frostbite on flights: "They said, 'Watch out for other people ... and if their cheekbones and cheeks begin to look pale, or ... [the] top of their ears begin to look pale, make them get in where it's warmer ... because they're beginning to get frostbite.' And they warned us ... [that] if your fingers got frozen ... don't try to bend them ... The frozen flesh, you'll damage it."

Navy navigator Charles Fitzpatrick in his book *From Then 'Til Now, My Journal* endured a near-catastrophe when his pilot, Jim Moorehead,

> decided to attempt to cross through a heretofore-unknown ... valley ... on the [Kamchatka] Peninsula, thinking we might [create] more of a surprise attack on the Japs. It wasn't the day for such an experiment ... [We] were flying at maybe 100 feet above the ground and about the same beneath the overcast, twisting and turning, wending our way at ... 160 mph when suddenly there was no more valley ... There was no choice—within [a] minute, either hit the fog-shrouded hill or hope to execute and complete a 180-degree turn, retracing our entrance flight.[4]

But that didn't quite work as planned, and Moorehead was forced to make tight 360-degree corkscrew turns in a desperate attempt to gain altitude and escape. Crew members would yell sightings of mountainsides emerging from clouds. Fitzgerald remembered:

> Jim was frozen at the controls, his knuckles white as the clouds we were in ... Drift kept crossing my mind—are we drifting closer to one of these slopes on each revolution? Would we hit head on or pancake against the mountain's side? ... Then I'd think, where is our first aid kit? Like it would help if we flew into the Kamchatka mountain.
>   [We could only] continue tight spiraling turns climbing upwards, barely above the plane's stalling speed.[5]

They eventually emerged unscathed and relieved. Fitzgerald concluded: "Our ordeal was tougher on [our pilot] and it showed. He sweated through his T-shirt, long johns, two wool shirts and clear through his leather flight jacket ... It was indeed a gut-wrenching time."

Undaunted, and despite having wasted fuel, they went on to drop their bomb load on the island of Shimushu.

Sgt. Ray Duncan, writing for *Yank* magazine, described a bombing run on the Kuriles:

> The monotonous sea, and the pound of propellers, became hypnotic after an hour ... Nobody attempted conversation anymore, and the few necessary scraps of interphone talk sounded far-off and listless.
>   [As we approached our targets] the plane coughed and trembled. The pilot had tested his guns in the wings ... A far-off burst from the tail [gun] ... made the plane seem to jump forward.

"Flak suits!" said the pilot. We crawled into our heavy metal vests. We dived through the overcast. In the middle of the bay, a big freighter was burning, set [afire by] the flight just ahead of us. Thick crimson flames oozed from it … We dived through its smoke … down and sideways [past] Jap guns that flashed bitterly up from the ground. We felt the combination of excitement and resentment that comes from being shot at. Our tracers raced ahead of us toward the docks.

This island looked like [one of our own, with the] same huts, same roads, same barren, ugly hills.

Far to our right a B-25 had gone down … It streamed red flame like a scarf as it hit the water [making] … a huge wave.

We dropped down and streaked for home, belly skimming the water … The crew began to talk. Worst flak anyone had seen; toughest mission our crew had flown.[6]

Joe Baldeschi in an oral interview described another bombing run:

Some of that ack-ack started coming up … You knew you had bullets coming because you could hear them coming through the aircraft … You hear that noise penetrating through the sheet metal like you wouldn't believe.

What happened to me is that one round came through my radio compartment and hit one of my electrical … boxes … The box … fragmented in small pieces and they got stuck all over my legs. And by the time I looked up I saw two wires … and they were burning. And about three feet to my left … was a 150-gallon … fuel tank [with the possibility of] fumes … And I just . . .forgot that I was hit and I … grabbed those wires and I didn't give up; I twisted and twisted until they broke, because if that fire went close to that fuel tank you never know what could happen … There could have been an explosion and the airplane would have been in pieces.[7]

The Japanese, realizing their vulnerability in the Kuriles, had numerous defensive aircraft and some early-warning radar sites. Incoming American bombers and reconnaissance aircraft tried to catch the defenders by surprise, but typically, Japanese aircraft rose to attack them with machine gun and cannon fire. Bombers could return potent machine gun fire, and in some cases, they simply tried to outrun enemy fighters.

Pulling defensive gun turret duty on a bomber was no piece of cake, said Robert Brown during an oral interview. "You had to be about 5 feet tall and as thin as Don Knotts to really get in one of those things," he related. "On [a mission where we had Japanese planes attacking us] … the nose turret gunner—who's a little Jewish kid, Dave Struckman from Brooklyn—he got into his turret, just prior to going over the target, and he was testing all of the actions. And that turret got stuck … pointing to the left. He could not swing it around in the horizontal … so he had to wait until the fighter came into position for him to hit them. And boy, he was very nervous … I didn't envy him."

Following are some descriptions of Japanese aircraft attacks on American bombers on various Kurile runs, from norpacwar.com:

Japanese fighter pilots made multiple passes on [a] damaged [F7-A reconnaissance plane] ... A 20-millimeter cannon round hit the oil cooler of the number one engine, causing immediate loss of oil. With one engine shut down [the pilot] broke free from the fighters and began jettisoning equipment ... While en route back to Shemya, the [plane] encountered [a] Japanese Mitsubishi G4M "Betty" twin engine medium bomber, which made three [unsuccessful] passes attempting to shoot down the bomber with its tail-mounted 20 mm cannon.

[In another encounter,] six Japanese fighters attacked [two] Venturas ... as they were leaving Miyoshino [airfield] after dropping ... bombs. Divided into two groups of three planes each, the Japanese chased the bombers. The high speed capabilities of the [Ventura] came in very handy; after each attempt to gain an altitude for the attack, Japanese fighters found themselves behind. The "Zeros" finally broke off ... None of the American crew members were wounded, but both aircraft were riddled with 7.7 mm machine gun bullets and 20 mm cannon shells [from] the "Zeros," as well as fragments of antiaircraft shells.

[In a third encounter,] as Lieutenant William Lee Sparks came over Shimushu, he saw four enemy fighters heading north above his plane off to his starboard. In an attempt to intercept, three of these planes cut around behind the Ventura ... Bombs from Lieutenant Sparks' plane hit the [Miyoshino] runway ... It appears that Japanese pilots spent too much time getting into position for an attack; only one of them made a high-side approach, diving from above and ahead, but passed below the Ventura as it left the target. The other three fighters did not close and Lieutenant Sparks made it safely back to base.

[And in a fourth encounter, from an account written by Lieutenant Lewis Patteson:] Flying over Kashiwabara, my crew shouted that they could see planes taking off below. We continued south when two [Japanese planes] appeared ahead of us and went by before they apparently knew who we were ... The "Zeros" turned around and gradually began overtaking us. When they got in close I yelled at Jacobsen to fire. They had a very healthy respect for the twin 50s and quickly [dodged] out of range. After a few minutes they climbed above us to make the typical fighter passes ... My navigator ... was watching from the navigator's dome, and warned me when one began his run. All I had to do was cut into the direction of the fighter's pass and this shortened the angle so steeply that their fire always went behind us. The "Zeros" were faster and far better maneuverers at this altitude than we were, but our relative speed was the big equalizing factor. [8]

Majors Louis Blau and Frank Gash, writing in *Air Force Magazine*, described their bombing mission:

While the anti-aircraft fire did not bother us a great deal, despite its intensity, the Jap planes did. There were about forty in all ... armed with two or three machine guns and some with cannon ... The attacks lacked coordination and were not always pressed determinedly but they kept after us until we were well on our way home, a few of them for forty or forty-five minutes.

Most of our gunners had come up from the States as replacements only a few months before and had never had an opportunity to fire at a Jap plane until that day. Nonetheless, they worked like veterans.

[The navigator gave a Japanese plane] coming in at 11 [o'clock] a [gun] burst at about 500 yards. The Zeke broke off and trailed smoke as it went into a dive and exploded after diving about 2,000 feet. [Our] tail gunner and … belly gunner got the other one from about 900 yards. The Zeke pulled up into a stall and fell off on the right wing with flames coming from the engine. It dropped into the ocean.[9]

Milt Zack's plane wasn't so lucky:

I looked out to the right and did a double take. There was no propeller on the right engine. I hit the salvo button for the bombs, hoping that the loss of weight would allow us to gain altitude and keep flying … I made it into the pilot's compartment and remember the co-pilot turning and giving me a sick grin, and the next thing I knew we were on the ground skidding in a crash landing [on a Japanese island].

Fortunately, there were two or three feet of snow on the beach, and no rocks, so we seemed to go on skidding on our belly forever … Other than some bumps and bruises, no one was seriously injured in the crash.

Our first instinct was to move away from the plane, but every time we tried, a Japanese fighter plane flying overhead would point his nose at us as if to say "get back or I'll shoot." Then we decided it would be a good idea to burn the plane so the enemy couldn't learn anything from it [but we couldn't find anything to ignite it] … We did come up with the crazy idea of walking to the northern coast of the island, then stealing a boat and rowing to Kamchatka in Russia … After a while we saw off in the distance a company of Japanese coming toward us. When they were about 100 yards away or so they started shooting in our direction, and there was nothing left to do but raise our hands and surrender … As they neared us, they stopped shooting and surrounded us, and stripped us of everything we had, including watches and all personal items; everything except our clothing.[10]

Zack was flown to and imprisoned on the island of Hokkaido along with two other crew members, where he endured dysentery and beriberi, solitary confinement, little food, and no medical attention for the duration of the war. They survived, but three other crew members died when a ship carrying them to Hokkaido was sunk.

Not all missions were bombing missions. Photo reconnaissance missions were initially attempted at night, using magnesium flash bombs to illuminate enemy bases. The photographs were often overexposed and didn't provide the amount of detail required. However, they undoubtedly ruined the sleep of Japanese down below.

However, one daytime flight accidently provided great results. Lieutenant John Vivian, flying a Ventura medium bomber on a weather observation flight north of the Kuriles, found unexpectedly clear weather over the islands. "About 200 miles from the target," he later wrote, "I found this going through my head: Why not dash in and get a picture of that airfield? One plane could probably get in and out before the fighters could be alerted … I voiced this to the crew and found them willing to a man. I put my request on the circuit and received a flat 'no' from the base. I reworded the request stating that I had a camera aboard and wished to continue to the target. Before we received our answer we arrived at our turning point. We elected to continue."

Commentary from norpacwar.com, referring to Vivian's flight: "Shimushu Island was below them, visibility unlimited in all directions … Soon they found the new airfield in the southern part of the island. Vivian descended to 7,000 feet … They flew directly over the brand-new concrete runway and took a series of photos before turning in the direction of Attu … Despite the fact that the pictures were taken with a smaller, hand-held K-20 camera, they were so much better than photos taken at night that the command decided to approve another daylight photo mission to the northern and central Kuriles."

Pilot Thomas Erickson ran into weather problems while returning from a Kuriles bombing mission:

It was smooth flying—an eerie calm with no visibility. Our navigator could only go by earlier estimates of wind direction. Quite abruptly our air speed indicator went … to zero; the only explanation we could think of [was] icing … Before long we could see ice slowly building up on the leading edges of the wings. [The copilot] found he had to apply more power, little by little, to maintain altitude … To preserve precious gas, and in the hopes that lower altitudes would help, we slowly descended.

Then with almost full power on, we suddenly broke free from the ice-mist at less than 1,000-foot altitude, and just ahead on our left was a huge rock formation with waves breaking on it. We were supposed to be about halfway home … and 150 miles south of the nearest land—[the Russian Komandorski islands. Instead, we discovered that's where we were.]

After a quick huddle with our navigator, [the other pilot] and I agreed with him that the only explanation was that we were 150 miles off course, driven by [unusual] south-to-north winds … That big rock had to be believed.

As we changed course and as the ice disappeared from our wings we had major decisions still to be made, mainly [how we could preserve] enough gas to get us back "home." We knew it was going to be close.

High on my list of "the most beautiful sights I've ever seen" is that first little black spot on the horizon … then the close-up view of that jagged, mountainous rock [with] ice called Attu. After nine and one-half hours in the air we landed with enough gas for, we were told, about five more minutes of flying.[11]

As related elsewhere in this book, ditching a bomber in the cold ocean was usually a death sentence. Joe Baldeschi talked about the procedure:

They used to tell us in briefing that if you get in trouble you have to ditch the aircraft, [advising,] "Be mindful that you have an eight-man life raft inside … in a package in the side of the main door of the aircraft. So, you [pull a] chain and the door flies out and hits the water … and an eight-man life raft will deploy. Now you swim to that life raft, get in, take off your wet clothes and put on dry clothes."

They gave us seven minutes to do that … [Well,] when you ditch an aircraft you're gonna deploy the door probably at 100 or 150 miles an hour, right? How do you know where that door [and raft] is gonna end up?

And you get in the water … [and the raft] could be 100 feet or it could be a mile [or more away]. And you're gonna swim that far [in very cold water]?[12]

John Pletcher said, "Well, you know, we were all young bucks and we were indestructible—everybody felt that way … Somebody else [might die, but] it won't be me, you know … I was always confident that I could handle anything that happened."

Bill Hutchison, in an oral interview, recalled returning from a Kurile mission alongside another Ventura bomber that had only one engine working: "They made it back [but missed the first landing attempt and] had to make a go-around," said Hutchison. "So [the pilot] had to pour the coal on [with] a one-engine plane that had just flown 800 miles, … stress[ing] the engine to the point that it could have been fatal … and [finally] land successfully. Then we cheered. That was a happy time for everybody."

Planes returning from photo reconnaissance missions had to quickly remove film from cameras and have it developed and printed in time for debriefing sessions, said army sergeant Paul Kastor, who served on Shemya. Some photographers were lost on missions, so it could be a dangerous occupation. Also, photographers could find themselves in the doghouse if they messed up taking pictures after crews risked their lives to get them to the Kuriles and back. Some of the cameras were handheld and others were mounted within planes and operated remotely.

Shemya, close to Attu, was an alternate landing site in case Attu's airfield was socked in with fog. Pilot Thomas Erickson wrote, "I remember one time when we luckily found a hole in the overcast and made it into Shemya … There was a landing strip plus a few Quonset houses and almost no personnel … We slept on the floor in a circle around an oil heater, grateful that we always took along our sleeping bags for just such needs."

When planes couldn't make it back to home base due to Japanese battle damage or mechanical difficulties, there was the Russian option. About 200 miles up the Russian Kamchatka Peninsula from the northern Japanese islands was the Russian Petropavlovsk air base, where ailing American planes could land—or planes could crash-land along the way there. Because Russia was not at war with Japan yet, any American planes landing at the airbase were impounded and the crews sequestered. This was despite all the lend-lease aircraft and supplies the United States was providing to Russia. Mainly, Russia didn't want to risk having to fight on another front with Japan; it was too preoccupied with defeating Germany.

According to norpacwar.com, before the war ended, a total of twelve Ventura medium bombers, twelve B-25s, and nine B-24 bombers made crash or emergency landings on the peninsula. Approximately 242 crew members were interned.

One of the flights was described on norpacwar.com:

[After being shot up by Japanese planes,] an oil leak developed in Lieutenant Schuette's right engine [and there was a fuel leak]. Despite the best efforts of the pilot, his aircraft started losing speed and altitude … The pilot knew it was impossible to reach Attu on the remaining gasoline. Lieutenant Vivian, [flying alongside,] later wrote in his diary, "Schuette opened up on his radio and we talked as he limped up the [Russian] coast. I said I would write to his wife and tell her all that I could." ... Lieutenant Schuette landed in Petropavlovsk escorted by Soviet I-16 fighters.

After another bombing mission, a B-24 was shot up by Japanese aircraft. Both the pilot and navigator were wounded, but managed to start heading for Petropavlovsk during a snowstorm. With their plane failing, they were forced to crash-land on a beach on Russia's Kamchatka Peninsula. Russia was notified about their location and eventually sent out a rescue party on horseback. The crew spent that Christmas drinking vodka with their Russian hosts at Petropavlovsk.

Navy air navigator Charles Fitzpatrick in his book, *From Then 'Til Now, My Journal*, wrote about a trip that pitted military obedience against common sense. Apparently upon returning from a Kurile raid, four Ventura bombers were led by Cmdr. Charles Wayne. In the rear of the formation, Fitzpatrick informed his own pilot that the planes in formation were headed straight west for Petropavlovsk instead of Attu. He and his pilot found it hard to believe, and had no desire to give up their planes and freedom. But they were also reluctant to disobey standing orders to always follow their skipper. Unfortunately, they were operating under radio silence.

Using a signal lamp, Fitzpatrick's plane communicated with another plane alongside, saying: "It's [Petropavlovsk] or Attu tonight. Suggest return Attu." The other plane responded, "Return and hell will break lose." Finally, they broke radio silence, and in the end, all three planes returned to base with only Cmdr. Wayne flying on to Russia.

Fitzpatrick wrote that indeed all hell did break loose upon return to Attu, but gradually subsided when all the pilots reported the same story. "Nevertheless," wrote Fitzpatrick, "there were many tongues wagging in the officer's mess that evening and into the night, ... all wondering about Cmdr. Wayne. Did he go to Russia because he was really shot up? Or was it because he didn't have the petrol to make it home?

"No matter what or how, rumors were rumors and the skipper was out of our lives," wrote Fitzpatrick. "Out of gas? Really! He won't be back, you say, how devastating! That night on Attu [our aviation unit and our] many friends savored the biggest, wildest, raucous hell-raising soiree ever held on Attu ... Sorry skipper ... there wasn't a tear shed ... [It was] the greatest Attu party ever."

They later learned that Cmdr. Wayne did indeed fly to the Russian airbase because of battle damage or mechanical difficulties.

Robert Brown, in an oral interview, recalled seeing another bomber on a Kuriles run "on fire from the front to the back. He slipped out of formation, and I'm trying to keep an eye on him and keep something in the log ... When the plane got way down there it looked like it had burst and flaming parts were going down there. What I actually saw apparently was parachutes because [the] crew got back to the United States by way of Kamchatka. The Russians were kind enough to intern our people and then gradually move them around ... The Russians fed them, but they weren't gourmet meals."

Joe Baldeschi was on a flight where crew members were given the choice of flying to Russia or trying to make it back to Attu. "We sort of voted to go to Petropavlovsk and then we all changed our minds," he wrote, "[thinking, let's give our pilot] all the confidence in the world that he can fly this aircraft on one engine and get us back. And thank God he did."

Maybe a factor in their decision was a rumor that the Russians fed interned Americans their garbage.

Interned American airmen generally weren't treated as prisoners, but they were discouraged from straying from their accommodations. At their first point of internment, Petropavlovsk, living conditions and food were meager, and the weather, especially in the winter, could be harsh. Limited medical treatment was available for the wounded. The Americans had the feeling of being warehoused, with little to do, and with little news about their fate. Eventually, they were transported by plane or train to points west and southwest across the Soviet Union, and housed in other camps. The men wondered if the American embassy in Moscow was working on their behalf, and wondered if wives and relatives in the US knew they were alive.

Because the Russians didn't want to appear to violate their neutrality toward Japan, Russia eventually secretly arranged to transfer groups of the airmen across the border into Iran. There, Americans had a wartime presence, and the men could be clothed and fed, and sent back to the US. When Japan finally capitulated and surrendered, there were still American airmen in Russia waiting for repatriation.

There's a story told by pilot Thomas Erickson about bomber pilot Walt Whitman, ordered to make a night flight toward the Kuriles from Attu. Whitman became agitated, fell to his knees, and grabbed the legs of his skipper, who was standing next to Commodore Gehres, the officer in charge of Aleutian navy aviation. "I saw Gehres suddenly and strongly point at the plane," wrote Erickson, "of course ordering Walt to take off. Walt got aboard. Soon the plane roared down the runway, disappearing from our sight in a flurry of snow."

"The next morning, after the time limit for the plane to return had passed, we heard Tokyo Rose say on a radio report, 'Well … we got Whitman … last night. Why don't the rest of you save yourselves and go home?' Yes, I heard it clearly."

The fate of Whitman's plane and crew was unknown until 1962 when a Russian geologist came upon the plane's wreckage on the side of a Kamchatka Peninsula volcano. The Ventura plane had likely been trying to fly to Petropavlovsk.

American fliers weren't always good neighbors to the Russians. Charles Fitzpatrick wrote:

There were a number of occasions when [our pilot] flew across the [Russian] peninsula farm land when our … altimeter read around 15 feet. He flew so close to the ground our props literally cut through haystacks. As we passed over, props biting into them, Russian hay stacks literally exploded … Viewing it all from the astrodome bubbles I saw hay belch thirty feet into the air, leaving a trail more than 60 feet and every bit 40 feet wide … Several farmers were seen once and from their gestures it was a certainty [our] action did nothing to please them.[13]

Pilots on Kurile Islands runs generally liked to fly low to avoid appearing on Japanese early-warning radar screens.

Bill Hutcherson reported watching "A Russian woman flying a Russian Yak fly alongside of us and fire a stream of tracers and motion us out to sea … We had made landfall on Russian territory and were being told to get out to sea. She had a wonderful smile as she sat on our wingtip and smiled broadly and she had a wonderful gold tooth."

Robert Buchanan remembered flying a patrol flight when "We decided ... to take a little ride over the top of Kamchatka Peninsula. All we could see was woods down there. Of course, [on our home island, Attu, there were no trees]. So we decided to take a ride up to there and then all of a sudden I saw ack-ack coming up ... It was just a warning. Of course, we were supposed to be ... 3 miles from the shoreline of Russia ... Then ... Russian fighters [came] up and followed us back out to sea. And I don't think they even shot at us."

A mysterious bombing run was described in the army's Missing Air Crew Report 14612. Four B-25s from the 28th Bomb Group left Attu for the Kuriles just two months before the end of the war. Led by pilot Edward J. Irving, the target was Araido Island, near Paramushiro Island. After the bombing run, being pursued by six Japanese fighters, the planes were flying over water near the west side of Russia's Kamchatka Peninsula, an area that was technically off limits to American planes. A fellow pilot said he observed Irving's plane being hit by Russian antiaircraft fire from the ground. Another said he saw two Russian planes approaching and possibly firing. Irving's bomber headed down toward the coast, apparently to try to make a water landing or crash landing, but it exploded in a huge ball of flame. The other planes made it back to Attu safely. The United States, through diplomatic channels, asked about the men lost in the crash, and the Russians replied that they had recovered and buried them. The US did not dispute the Russian statement that Japanese planes were responsible for downing the bomber.

Pilots were supposed to have limited tours of combat flying. Charles Fitzpatrick, the navy navigator, wrote that his unit was scheduled for six months' flight duty on Attu, but were there for ten. He estimated his total air time as between three and four hundred hours, the result of forty-five combat flights. Milt Zack wrote that army pilots' tour of duty was one year.

Pilot Howard Bernstein was asked in an oral interview why he never saved money while serving on Attu. He essentially answered that he didn't know how much longer he'd live, so he tried to enjoy life to the fullest.

Chapter 18
Friendships and Pinups Substituted for the Genuine Article

The only females on the island were eleven nurses who were quartered in a large Quonset hut that was completely enclosed by two concentric circles of barbed wire fencing.

Many thousands of young men in the Aleutians—35 percent of navy personnel in the war were in their teens—were in their physical prime. If the war hadn't happened, they'd have remained in the States, most of them eventually dating, having sex, falling in love, and getting married. Sent to the Aleutians, they were emotionally and physically primed to engage the opposite sex (or for some, their own sex). They could be hot … but they were shipped to the cold.

Weather observer and officer Bernard Mehren wrote in his diary upon leaving for Alaska, "A few short hours behind us there [were] bright lights and movies, crowded streets and smoky bars … and sex. Ahead of us lies the cold North … and long months."

Already there, navy man George Sinclair wrote, "Our abnormal life, led without female companionship, is beginning to tell on most of us."

One twenty-four-year-old GI said every time he looked at a picture of his girlfriend, he had a burning desire to hold her again.

In an Aleutian army newspaper cartoon, a water-soaked soldier walking through mud says to another, "All I want is to hear is high heels clicking on a cement sidewalk."

In another such cartoon, a burly GI in a T-shirt dances with a broomstick adorned with an army uniform, while holding a picture of a pretty woman just above it, saying, "You send me right out of this world."

At Elmendorf Air Force Base on the Alaskan mainland in 1942, according to the Brian Garfield archive, "the 11th Pursuit Squadron had typhus shots and sex morale lectures."

Military recruits in boot camps were shown films to try to keep them away from women by playing up the possibility of catching horrible diseases. That may have been effective for a few months. A wartime army pamphlet quoted in *Wikipedia* stated that "most prostitutes have venereal disease" and that "will power and self-control help to keep a man's mind and body healthy. A healthy body and a healthy mind lead to happiness."

In his book *Coming Out under Fire: The History of Gay Men and Women in World War II*, Allan Berube noted that:

> psychiatrists … were able to give recruits standardized lectures on "mental hygiene" and "personal adjustment" that were designed to help them cope with the many emotional problems of military life … Lecturers encouraged male recruits … [to] be tough, "take it," and "develop guts"; to … take part in exhausting physical exercise so that they were "too dog-tired to think"; and to rely on each other for support.[1]

From the same book, Berube mentions *Psychology for the Fighting Man*, a privately published paperback book meant for GIs, which advised taking up athletics and dancing, attending band concerts, and singing or practicing religion as substitutes for sex. It said the "only permanent relief" for sexual yearnings was for a GI to put "his whole heart into the business of training for war and destroying the enemy." That may have worked for some men, if only temporarily, but they wouldn't stop surging hormones and the steady production of semen.

It was probably author Dashiell Hammett who added this caption to a cartoon in his army newspaper: "Strictly speaking, there are no real substitutes for sexual satisfaction."

Paul Carrigan, in his excellent memoir, addressed the issue:

The animal-strong male sex drive of young men in the prime of life, in good health and 1,000 miles from the nearest female companionship, found relief from tension in two primary ways. "Wet dreams" are nature's built-in safety value. Many a man, it was said with great truth, falls asleep with a problem on his mind and wakes up with the solution. Masturbation was the most widespread form of relief. Relief in this manner, without getting caught, was a far more difficult pursuit than one might imagine because there is scant privacy about a crowded warship.[2]

Carrigan told the story of a young communications officer, who he called "Derkin"

… [who] found himself temporarily alone one night in [a ship's] radio shack. He became aroused while thumbing through a girlie magazine. He decided his self-gratification could not wait until he was in the semi-privacy of his bunk in a darkened compartment. He locked the door to the radio shack.

A passing sailor slowed his walk and stopped in front of the radio room … He could hear the faint strains of his favorite tune being played over a stateside frequency. He tried the knob but found the door locked. He thought this odd but instead of knocking, he … put his eye to [a] half-inch diameter hole and saw the communicator playing with himself. Other men coming through the passageway were given a look.

I'd come off watch at midnight and … was asleep … when raucous laughter … woke me two hours [early] … One [man] would start to laugh so uncontrollably it was infectious. When I grouchily asked what was so funny … the spontaneous laughter erupted again. It did not end until both men were sobbing with side aches.

"I GOTTA GET ME A BOOK WITHOUT KISSIN' IN IT."

Artist: Donald Miller

Finally, between gasps for breath, [one of the men] choked out, "Someone caught 'Derkin' flogging his bishop."

I asked why this was so hilarious.

"I don't want to spoil it for you by telling more. Swing past the mess deck bulletin board on your way back from the head," [the man] said, "and you'll see why."

A dozen men were gathered around the bulletin board. They too were laughing uproariously and I learned why ... In bold black print were the words of a crude but quick-witted poet which proclaimed:

THAT THING'S FOR FERKIN, DERKIN, NOT JERKIN[3]

Carrigan speculated that "as long as 'Derkin' stayed in the navy he could travel to duty stations at the four corners of the earth but the story would always precede his arrival" and noted that "Derkin" received transfer orders three days after his unwanted exposure.

I suppose what made the episode so funny is that men went to great lengths to conceal their masturbation, fearing being discovered, so that when "Derkin" was so publicly seen—and he was an officer to boot!—they could laugh at another's vulnerability.

I doubt if any girly magazines were thrown away, but were passed around until they literally fell apart.

I note in many photographs of enlisted men in the wartime Aleutians that they naturally put their arms around each other, more so than is done today. Whether or not that was common for men in that era, I don't know.

My navy officer father saved a photo of another officer picking wildflowers on Adak; and he (my father) had some pressed into a book. I can only assume they were buddies.

An Aleutian army newspaper cartoon shows two GIs lounging in a Quonset hut, with one saying in a pique: "Awright, read y'r damn book, but just wait till YOU wanna talk."

I was interested in incidence of homosexuality in the Aleutians during the war. Interestingly, in all-male environments, references to gay sex can flourish.

In his book *Coming Out under Fire: The History of Gay Men and Women in World War II*, Allan Berube talked about the World War II military environment in general:

[The word] *cocksucker* became a favorite putdown among GIs during the war. When a GI was reprimanded by superiors, he was said to have "had his ass reamed."

Much of the male sexual culture of basic training revolved around joking and teasing ... Wartime observers of trainees found "continual joking about homosexual practices" in the barracks ... "One soldier," [observed an army psychologist], "returning from the shower room in the nude, will be greeted with cat-calls, salacious whistling, and comments like, 'Hey Joe, you shouldn't go around like that—you don't know what that does to me.'"[4]

Drag shows were quite popular during the war, usually with men crudely imitating and satirizing the missing element in their lives. In a photograph of such a show somewhere in the wartime Aleutians, there are eleven men in drag, a violinist, and what looks like a barbershop quartet, along with other performers. Herb Gedney, an army air corps mechanic in the Aleutians, wrote, "We would have plays where some of the guys would dress the parts of women."

GI Sascha Brastoff performs as Carmen Miranda at the Ft. Mears Theatre in one of the more accomplished female impersonations on the islands. Drag performances were a common element in amateur shows. *Alaska State Library, H. Marion Thornton Photo Collection. ASL-P338-0901*

According to one Aleutian psychiatrist, some men feared they'd become gay because of a lack of sexual intercourse and guilt about masturbating. Some questioned their sexuality after noticing undercurrents of homosexuality in their environment.

Due to the need for as many healthy male recruits as possible during the war, military screeners of enlistees and draftees were willing to admit into the services men who exhibited effeminate or stereotypically gay tendencies. (The Kinsey Report of 1948 published in the book *Sexual Behavior in the Human Male* found that 4 percent of the American male population acknowledged being exclusively homosexual throughout adulthood and that about 10 percent of men aged twenty to thirty-five said they were bisexual.)

There has been speculation that more homosexuals were sent to the Aleutians during the war years than to other war zones because it was an out-of-the-way, mostly noncombat area. At any rate, there were homosexuals on the islands. They coexisted with straight men, and weren't much bothered unless they were discovered having actual gay sex (or aggressively sexually approaching straight men).

I couldn't find any court-martial records in the National Archives unmistakably relating to such cases, but one possibly did. Two submariners—talk about being in a tight environment—in 1945 were charged with "scandalous conduct tending to the destruction of good morals." Due to their serving on dangerous missions to the northern Japanese islands, one was sentenced to four months confinement and a bad-conduct discharge and the other to six months and a similar discharge.

In another court-martial—just to show how squirrelly Aleutian GIs could be regarding sex—a man on a transfer boat had his penis exposed "and in contact with the mouth and tongue of one female dog." It was argued that because he did it in front of seventy-five men, he wasn't a homosexual. Of three men involved, only one was charged and convicted of a crime. In a different case, aboard a ship docked at Adak, two sailors put a man over a barrel and pulled down his pants while one held a hammer handle next to the victim's anus. Another nearby sailor was holding his own penis. The conclusion? They were "skylarking" and there was "no intent to commit sodomy." Apparently, the punishment was very light.

In some quarters, there was an enlightened approach to gay GIs. Writer Allan Berube in *Coming Out under Fire: The History of Gay Men and Women in World War II* described:

One pragmatic commanding officer stationed at a post near Atka Island … found that he could best utilize known homosexual personnel by keeping them under his close supervision. This … colonel … became aware, unofficially, of a number of homosexuals in the troops under his command. No difficulties had been reported in connection with these men. By careful assignment and by attention to problems before they became serious, these men were kept on effective duty over a long period of time. Some of them were gradually moved to a somewhat isolated area of the post where they would not be disturbing to other men on the post.[5]

In another Adak army newspaper cartoon, a soldier striking a somewhat effeminate pose and holding a Coke, says to another GI, also holding a Coke, "Well, you don't look like a Coke ad to me either."

And in still another such cartoon, a bulky GI sits, sewing a piece of clothing by hand, blithely saying to his companion, "I used to wish my wife were here to do it, but now it kinda fascinates me."

Paul Carrigan wrote about meeting an effeminate fellow weatherman who fell ill on a voyage:

Mortified by his [own extreme seasickness while at sea, the effeminate officer had refused an] offer to help him … When [his ship] reached Adak this "tender" passenger came out of seclusion. He stopped by the weather office to say goodbye.

"I hope you had a nice trip," [a sailor] said.

With a limp wrist gesture the little doll replied, "Oh, I hope I never see your old boat again."

[Another sailor] was also in the office. He cracked up with laughter in spite of his Herculean effort at self-control.[6]

Some men expressed a dislike for USO show performers they thought were gay.

The war resulted in men thrown together helter skelter, without much consideration of their sexual or personality orientation, or if they were from rural or big-city environments. In the United States, gay men often gravitated toward big-city enclaves, but in the Aleutians the best they could do was join small groups of like-minded individuals at the larger posts.

Psychiatrists' reports downplayed the presence of homosexuals in the Aleutians, but I feel gay men stayed away from shrinks' offices unless they had serious mental issues. I feel that most gay GIs didn't want to stand out and be forced out of the service with a bad-conduct discharge (called a Section 8) because it could hurt their postwar employment chances.

Also, psychiatrists were reluctant to send gay men back to the States because other men might see that as a reward. Some men were so desperate to leave they would fake being gay. Psychiatrist Maj. Frank Gelbman said in an interview with Allan Berube that he devised ways in the Aleutians to determine if a patient was actually a homosexual, including having the person write out his complete sexual history.

Navy nurses on their way to assist in the upcoming battle for Attu. *Alaska State Library, Aleutian/Pribilof Project Photo Collection. ASL-P233-V116*

There were a few military women in the islands, mostly nurses, who held an officer's rank. However, enlisted men didn't have to salute them and they received less pay than equivalent-rank male officers. Army pilot Thomas Erickson on Attu wrote, "The only females on the island were eleven nurses who were quartered in a large Quonset hut that was completely enclosed by two concentric circles of barbed wire fencing about ten feet high. One [male] lieutenant commander, not in our squadron, had returned from a tough flight, got thoroughly soused and was caught trying to claw his way through or over the inner fence. Getting over the other fence had made a bloody mess of him."

Fort Mears at Dutch Harbor received a contingent of seventeen army nurses.

Pilot Thomas Erickson recalled:

One of our pilots ... was badly hurt in a takeoff crash. Fortunately he recovered, thanks in great part to the nurses. When he was well enough to be released, the nurses got permission to have a special party for him at the large common room in their quarters.

It was a juke-box, dancing, cake and cookies kind of thing … [He] invited 10 of us to attend. Eleven guys, eleven nurses. Shortly after this evening party started, the nurse with whom I was paired off said she wasn't feeling well and disappeared. My buddies seemed to be having a good time and I did too, cutting in on dances and conversations.

At one point the door opened and in walked [famous actress] Olivia DeHavilland, having just finished a USO visit to those in the island hospital. Everyone clapped. She of course was spending the night with the nurses, and she accepted the head nurse's invitation to join the party. I was the only "unattached male," making me the lucky one to have a date after all—and what a date! We talked, we danced, we ate cookies and drank lemonade and we smoked! She asked about what our squadron was doing, and when I told her we were scheduled for a flight the next night she stated flatly that she was going along with us. [But she didn't.][7]

Lola Engler of the Navy Nurse Corps wrote about helping to staff a secret radar installation on a small Aleutian island for three months during the war. There were two doctors, five nurses, and no mail service, and there wasn't much for her to do when off the job. "You learned how to live with yourself," she said in an interview, "[and] I can [still] hear that wind now."

GI Dix Fetzer, wounded during the battle of Attu, recalled a nurse named Mabel Jorgensen who brought him a beer and a puppy during his hospital stay on Adak. He was nineteen and she was twenty-three.

Three nurses died in a plane crash on Umnak Island in 1944. It was thought they were on their way to inspect a hospital.

An incident involving nurses on Adak resulted in a court-martial: A ship's captain entered nurses' quarters with a bottle of beer, insisting on seeing one or more of the nurses, but was told they were away or not available. He pulled rank and refused to leave, telling the nurse in charge she wasn't fit to be a nurse, and saying that other nurses should be ashamed to serve under her. At his court-martial, the nurse was cross-examined by him, and he received only a private reprimand and the recommendation that no other disciplinary action be taken.

Sometimes nurses were invited by officers to have dinner on their ships. However, an army psychiatrist serving on Adak wrote that some nurses complained that their primary function seemed to be entertaining officers.

A brief exposure to women happened when Russian ships docked in the Aleutians. Their ships had some women crew members, but they generally weren't considered attractive.

During 1940 at Dutch Harbor, civilian contractors and military men engaged in some extracurricular activity at a cathouse located on what was appropriately called Pecker Point. The place was eventually closed after too many men turned up AWOL.

On the mainland, Fairbanks had a red-light district.

Army air force sergeant Hale Burge on Adak took advantage of an offer to go on R&R to Anchorage for a couple weeks. He left town to visit Mount McKinley (now renamed Denali) where he luckily met, in his words, "a young girl by the name of Mary Evans, from down in Tennessee—she worked as a secretary … in Anchorage … We had a lot of fun up there dog-sled riding and what have you."

GIs sometimes went to great lengths to see a real woman. One day, three of them with some time off got in a Jeep and drove a good distance, including crossing several rivers, to check out a woman reportedly living with a trapper in the boonies. Upon being invited into the trapper's shanty, they were mightily disappointed in her appearance. Also, her trapper partner made it clear via bone-crunching handshakes that this would be a short, one-time visit. Another turnoff was the couple's urine-cured clothing!

Pinups were to be found in most nontent living quarters, whether they were of actual wives or girlfriends, or movie stars. Navy man James Doyle said, "I had a leggy picture of Rita Hayworth. She had nice-looking legs and she [had said], 'These are all mine. These are not retouched.'"

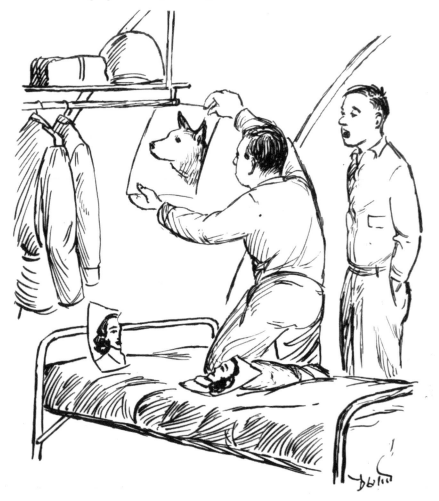

"DISAPPOINTING FURLOUGH, HUH?"

Artist: Donald Miller

An army private wrote about the walls of his hut being plastered with pinups from *Esquire* and movie magazines. Mentioning that across the way from his bunk were photos of actress Paulette Goddard, he somewhat humorously wondered what she thought about seeing him go to bed in his long johns.

Sometimes all it took was a woman's voice to enthrall the lonely men. Men often tuned in to listen to Toyko Rose on Tokyo's propaganda radio station, which could be easily received on men's personal radios in the Aleutians. ("Rose" was actually several different women.)

Paul Carrigan wrote affectionately:

Tokyo Rose, strange as it may seem, was a sex symbol to us. In the barracks hut we discussed her personally much more frequently than her propaganda. There was … the question of her nationality. Was she Japanese? English? American? … There was unanimous agreement that her voice, the only female voice we heard nightly, was the sexiest, most seductive sound to caress our ears in endless months. We were also certain that God, the master creator of perfection, had blessed her with face and form to match.

Because the mystery surrounding her left so much to the imagination, Tokyo Rose was an even greater sex symbol to our active young minds than the Hollywood starlets whose leggy pin-ups adorned hut walls.

One night, for example, she was detailing how the imperial Japanese paratroopers would slip silently into our huts and slit our throats while we slept. In the midst of her talk, one [man] announced in a loud, longing voice, "Boy, I'll bet she's got luscious knockers and great legs."[8]

Of course there were girlfriends back home, some loyal during months apart, and some fickle.

Walter Stohler in an interview mentioned his "high school girlfriend [who had] wanted to get married, so she met me in Seattle just before we shipped out. And we got married and I got shipped out the next day. And after I was at the Aleutians for about a year I got one of those 'Dear John' letters."

An anonymous poet on Kiska wrote in the island's newsletter:

She took my hand in sheltered nooks,
she took my candy and my books,
she took that lustrous wrap of fur,
she took those gloves I bought for her,
she took my words of love and care…
she took, I must confess, my eye,
she took whatever I would buy,
and then she took another guy.[9]

For a more favorable story, in an oral interview, Charles Donovan spoke about beginning to write to a young woman he selected from a photo shown him by an Aleutian friend. Three of the four women in the photo were sisters in Waltham, Massachusetts. "We're writing back and forth for two and a half years," said Donovan, "and finally I got … home on leave. I … picked up the phone and asked her to marry me. She accepted, and her father and mother and one of her sisters drove her … to Buffalo, New York, and we got married there."

Afterwards he had to return to duty on the islands for a time, but by the time of his interview in 2010, their marriage had lasted sixty-four years.

For a tender and almost childlike ending to this chapter, navy man James McCrary wrote:

I think of you and the folks back home,
each night as I nestle in.
And I wonder how long the time will be
before we meet again.

I see your hair of golden hue,
and your eyes of sparkling brown.
I see your tiny freckled nose,
that is slightly powdered down.
I feel your arms around me fold,
your lips upon my brow,
then I go quickly ... to sleep
cause I feel much safer now.[10]

Chapter 19
For Some, the Aleutian Stare

I get terribly depressed for several days at a time. I don't particularly give a damn. It's strange—I find it very difficult to write letters anymore.

"Desolate and bare" would have been the first impression many GIs had when first seeing the Aleutian islands. Most noticed (and perhaps *felt*) the absence of trees. During their training back in the states, GIs may have assumed they were going to Hawaii or the south Pacific. Instead, their ships turned north and dropped them off in the land of snow, sleet, rain, fog, and wind.

These men in the wartime Aleutians, it seems to me, ended up in one of three existences: in active, dangerous warfare against the Japanese (and the weather); or in remote, inhospitable locations; or in built-up bases with amenities and possible boredom. Some would've passed from one phase to another.

How the men responded to these conditions is interesting.

There were a few military psychiatrists in Alaska. One of them, in analyzing several hundred mental cases on Adak, found that instead of most men being brought down entirely by the isolation, depressing weather and homesickness, around 80 percent of them had psychiatric problems before they entered the military. He calculated that two-thirds of his patients were returned to duty while the others were evacuated.

Anxiety was the most common symptom. The army men being treated, it needs to be noted, had not been in combat, and yet the tenseness of being in a combat zone had its effect.

A classic depiction of sanity versus insanity in war is the novel *Catch-22*, about World War II combat pilots in the European theater, some of whom were "losing it" while continually flying dangerous missions. If they were genuinely crazy and yet had the wherewithal to request grounding for that reason, they were deemed sane and good to fly. The term "Catch-22" is still alive and well today.

A lighter example was the character Max Klinger in the TV series *M*A*S*H*. An enlisted man in a medical outfit in the Korean War, Klinger took to wearing women's clothing in hopes of being found crazy and sent home. It didn't work.

Van Vechten, an Aleutian vet, wrote:

As long as the Japanese occupied [the American Aleutian islands of] Attu and Kiska, the morale at the Cape [on the island of Amchitka] was very high and gung-ho, and we were all busy with our various jobs … Once the islands were taken, and our only duty was one of patrol and radar watchdog over the area, we and our support units began to be bored, lazy, argumentative, and generally and unpleasantly displeased with our isolation and one another. We missed the constant threat of air attack, the roar of our bombers and P-40s slicing the air toward battle, and the general feeling that we were doing something vital … and so a general letdown became prevalent … There was little to spend money on, so there was heavy gambling, betting and quarreling.[1]

Poet Fred Ellis wrote:

Disgusted at night on our pillows,
With an ill no doctor can cure,
No, we are not convicts,
Just Marines on a forgotten tour.[2]

There were quite a few stories about suicides. Some may have been unsubstantiated rumors or exaggerations. At minimum, circulating rumors or reports of suicides reflected the strain men were under.

Navy Cmdr. Oliver Glenn, a pilot, wrote that "a number of guys got despondent and blew the tops of their heads off." An army band member at Dutch Harbor, Robert Boon, said "There were a fair number of suicides."

A researcher named Pete Fineo checked graves on Amchitka Island. Of the forty-one graves he found records for, five were suicides. One was murdered by his bunkmates.

In the National Archives in Seattle, I found notes about a marine who was killed ostensibly by accident when a .45 pistol fired through his brain. I suspect this was instead a suicide.

Then there were those who'd had enough and tried to leave. Paul Carrigan heard a rumor about a weatherman who became "rock happy" (referring to the rocky islands), hooked himself in a parachute harness to a dozen big weather balloons, and was about to leave his island courtesy of the wind when stopped.

My navy officer father wrote his parents to say, "We have one officer here who doesn't like it and (we think) is deliberately trying to get out. He doesn't eat, drinks a lot, and is just generally making a fool of himself. This not-eating business he has just started. I don't think he will like it any place but home."

Brain Garfied noted in his archive that a lieutenant in a fighter squadron was evacuated to the States after shooting himself in the leg with a .45. It was written up as a pistol-cleaning accident.

There's the story of a Dutch Harbor military dentist who lopped off his trigger finger in a footlocker. The event was declared an accident because there was no evidence to the contrary, but some thought it was a deliberate "million-dollar wound"—one that would get him sent back home.

The seasons of the year contributed to the malaise. Being as far north as they were, the Aleutians' nighttime darkness in June only lasted five hours, while in the depths of winter, daylight was just as short-lived. Paul Polink wrote that "in the wintertime, it was dark, dark, dark."

Also, unremitting foggy or overcast weather was the norm while clear, sunny days were rare. Polink said that "some of our planes used to take personnel up to see the sun … The sun was [up above the clouds] but it wouldn't burn through [them] … I thought it was rather funny at the time."

The *Kodiak Bear* newspaper ran a column titled "What to Do in Case the Sun Shines."

GIs from the southern states weren't used to nearly constant cool-to-cold winds, and snow in the winter. These unwelcome environments could make them want to retreat into their tent or hut, where boredom or friction with others could develop.

Because of the adverse conditions and isolation, dress codes and personal hygiene often weren't possible, or enforced. Van Vechten wrote:

We finally made landfall at the northwestern tip of [Amchitka] Island … We dropped anchor offshore as there were no docks, and I raised my bleary eyes to see a fleet of amphibious trucks heading our way through the surf. On the cliff above the beach I saw a frieze of animated figures that looked prehistoric to my jaded eyes … We boarded the bobbing amphibians and sailed toward the beach.

We were herded into the Jamesway hut that served as the orderly room and command post, and enroute the … men we saw had little resemblance to soldiers. They were bearded, unwashed (there were no bathing facilities), smelled bad and their fatigues and parkas seemed able to stand alone, whether the occupant was inside or outside of them! We were the source of some amusement in our clean dress uniforms and shaven faces. Their long hair was a herald of what was to come later in the hip [1960s]. There seemed to be little of formal military protocol or discipline, but our [commanding officer] was cordial, if scruffy.[3]

From time to time, things could boil over. Some men are more inclined to use their fists than mouths. Otis Littlejohn, in an oral history recording, said, "This one man in particular always had a chip on his shoulder and he got into several different fights, including with me." It all began when Littlejohn kept trying the rouse the man for watch duty, and the fellow "would just grunt and groan … so I lit into him pretty good about it and … he wanted to fight about it and he called me some dirty name that I didn't like, so I hit him right in the nose as hard as I could. I think that's the only lick I got in … He beat the heck out of me, so that's the last time I tried to fight anybody."

In his memoir, Paul Carrigan mentioned some altercations:

Under crowded living conditions a person's habits can become increasingly irritating to others. Short-fused tempers were sometimes on display but generally resulted in no more than a sharp exchange of words. Most of these flareups were brief and soon forgotten. Two were not.

Both incidents involved Jesse Vowell and Sandor Podmanski. They were [usually] good friends.

Vowell was from Tennessee. Well-built on the lean side, he could also get a little mean when his violent temper got the best of him. He did not … take kindly to his sometimes nickname "Hillbilly." Podmanski seemed to delight in calling Vowell "that crazy hillbilly."

Podmanski, called "[the] Count," … was a blond, blue-eyed young giant standing six foot five … In contrast to his imposing size, his temperament was meek and mild … He often recounted his blue-blood Polish lineage and espoused his thoughts on operas, classical music, literary classics, etc. … After listening to the persistent Podmanski for two years Vowell had … been telling the Count to "shut up. My ears need a rest."

Podmanski solemnly replied, "Unless you take an interest in the finer things of life, you'll always remain just a dumb hillbilly." [Vowell] invited the Count to step outside [but] Podmanski would not fight even though he was almost twice Vowell's size … [Vowell] would not slug a man who would not defend himself. Livid, he stomped out of the hut to cool off.

The second incident a week later was deadly serious and could have been extremely messy … Vowell cannot recall what started the argument … but he does remember throwing a knife that missed Podmanski … Podmanski picked up the knife and started toward Vowell. Vowell grabbed his rifle, worked the bolt and slammed a live round into the chamber. In a panic, Podmanski dropped the knife, turned and ran pell-mell out of the hut.

[Carrigan:] I was climbing the hill … and was fifty feet from the hut. When I heard a commotion and looked up, Podmanski was charging downhill toward me. [Vowell had a rifle] and was hot on his heels … Podmanski knew he couldn't outrun a bullet no matter how long his legs were. He reached me and in terror pleaded, "Save me." He then leaped behind me and wrapped his huge arms around my chest, thereby pinning my arms at my sides.

"Get out of the way," Vowell ordered in a strained, shaking voice. "I'm going to kill that big, dumb, phony sonofabitch."

"Put the gun down, [Vowell], you're not going to shoot anybody," [Carrigan said].

"For the last time, get outa the way."

"You'll hang. Look at all the witnesses behind you. You going to shoot them, too?"[4]

SAY — I THINK THERE'S A RHINOCEROS IN THERE."

Some men began to lose it. *Artist: Donald Miller*

Vowell began to reconsider, and Carrigan talked him into giving up his gun. Carrigan was furious at Podmanski, so furious that when Vowell handed him the rifle, Carrigan was tempted to shoot Podmanski himself. Later, when Podmanski tried to thank him with a bear hug, Carrigan pushed him away, saying, "Don't ever touch me again."

"Vowell and Podmanski were equally frightened by the experience and some soul searching took place," wrote Carrigan. "Vowell had always been a little on the quiet side and Podmanski became so."

There were some breakdowns, or at least changes in personality.

Murray Hanson, writing in the *Military Journal Online*, tells the story of a PBY pilot who reported seeing an entire enemy naval task force, then losing sight of it. Neither his crew nor other searchers verified his sighting. As a result,

the consensus was that, precipitated by the stress of the Aleutian environment and the ... preoccupation with [an] offer of Christmas leave [for an enemy task force sighting], the pilot had suffered a hallucination or else he had deliberately fabricated the incident in order to win the prize. In any event he was judged to be abnormal, ... was banished from the Alaskan Command to undergo psychiatric examination on the mainland and quickly left Dutch Harbor. But he had the last laugh. He got his Christmas leave in Seattle and never returned to the Aleutians.[5]

"I get terribly depressed for several days at a time," wrote Paul Carrigan at one point. "I don't particularly give a damn. It's strange—I find it very difficult to write letters anymore."

Severely distressed men could sometimes develop what came to be called the Aleutian Stare—a blank, fixed gaze and the loss of any zest for life. Numbed, they would find it difficult to perform ordinary daily routines such as keeping clean.

Dr. Nathan Davis, quoted in the Garfield archive: "I was on a plane once with six GIs in strait jackets—'mentals.' One of them kept yelling at the nurse, embarrassing the poor girl; he kept shouting defiantly, 'So what if I masturbate?' All six of them had the Aleutian Stare. They'd been on these islands too long."

Eliot Asinof, a lieutenant whose job it was to keep troops entertained and occupied on Adak, heard professional jazz saxophone musician Bud Freeman and his Aleutian military band play one evening in a mess hall:

Freeman had put together sounds I'd never heard. [One number] made me sing for joy. When it ended, I had to thank him. "It was great, it was really great!"

He turned to look at me, and suddenly there it was. The Stare. Eyes clouded in tears, mouth curled in pain, his face colorless. He saw my lieutenant bars and tried to be pleasant.

Then it began: "I'm dying, lieutenant. I'm dying."

The army stifled him. Adak crushed him. He couldn't hold up in its ugliness. He

"SOMETIMES I THINK I JUST CAN'T GO ANOTHER DAY WITHOUT A BANANA."

Things taken for granted back home could attain an outsized importance in the islands. *Artist: Oliver Pedigo*

shouldn't be a soldier. He wanted me to get him sent back to the States. As he spoke, The Stare became terrifying. His asking me to do this was, of course, preposterous. It was said he was too important to be discharged. I could understand that. I told him I was sympathetic but couldn't help him. He followed me across the room as though I was his only chance. He had gone crazy.

Months later, I saw him again. The Stare seemed imbedded as if it had become a permanent feature of his face. Weeks later I heard he'd been discharged with a Section Eight.[6]

Some GIs were simply quite different, but they weren't disturbed enough to remove from duty. Roald Forseth, in an article in the *Baltimore Post-Examiner*, described

a guy we all called "Whips and Jingles." He wasn't too smart to start with, and he had all these little tics and oddities. When he walked, talked, sat or slept, he was always jerking in funny little ways. "Whips" had a habit of shouting until a crowd gathered, and then throwing a handful of nickels, dimes and quarters into the air just to see everyone scramble.

When "Whips" was [drunk], he talked so fast that half the words were omitted … He never bothered with trivial words, and often was so anxious to get to the next sentence that he didn't bother to finish the sentence he had already started. One night he came in about ten o'clock and started jabbering. Everyone went to sleep, but he kept at it. About one o'clock, one of the boys woke up and heard him still jabbering all to himself. Three o'clock—the same thing; more speed, less volume. What a man! Yet, it's guys like him who kept all the others from getting too bored with the place.[7]

Some of the men, as covered in another chapter, weren't careful about the source of the alcohol they drank. Navy man Walter Stohler described one "guy [who] was a postal carrier and … a nice guy. He lived in the same barracks with us. But he went nuttier than a fruitcake. They sent him back, of course. But he was taking some of that Sneaky Pete [hut-brewed liquor]."

The book *War Psychiatry* concluded that homesickness was a factor in twenty percent of mental casualties during World War II.

Navy air navigator Charles Fitzpatrick remembered that "Thanksgiving, Christmas, and New Years were extremely hard. I'd guess there was more drinking of the hard stuff during those periods than at any other time. Hearing the Christmas carols and seasonal songs such as "I'll Be Home for Christmas" and "White Christmas" brought tears to the eyes of even the most stouthearted of Attu's stalwarts."

Donald Brydon, with the army air force on Shemya, felt much the same: "Keep in mind, this was the first time I had ever been away from home more than overnight. And I can remember listenin' to Bing Crosby on the radio singin' "White Christmas" and being so homesick I could hardly stand it. But, somehow I got through it."

Earl Long, a navy Seabee who had just arrived in the Aleutians, remembered that on Christmas Eve 1943:

I was sitting on the ship's rail just under the bridge. The bay was as calm as a mill pond and the sound of Christmas carols drifted across the water. I guessed the music was coming from a church or recreation hall somewhere off in the distance. The sound of that music had a melancholic effect on me, bringing forth thoughts of my wife and home, a place I now felt so far away from. Up to this time in life I felt I could handle most situations, but I was quite nostalgic and I felt very much alone.[8]

In the 36th Squadron war diary, Billy Wheeler noted that "Christmas was celebrated in a satisfactory fashion because a few men had hoarded precious cases of whiskey for that day. New Year's Day meant little other than the fact it elicited many wishes that the following New Years would not 'still see me in this hell hole.'"

My dad wrote in a letter, "It was an awful lonely spot here Xmas eve. If you can imagine that, you can imagine what I felt like and what the other men here felt like—some of whom haven't been home for Xmas for three or four years. So make the best of it. It could have been worse and better times are coming."

Gen. Buckner advised his Aleutian troops that "Ample evidence exists that the enemies of our country are … conducting an insidious campaign of propaganda calculated to undermine morale by attempting to make our soldiers feel sorry for themselves, become disgruntled and complain of mistreatment. Our [news]papers, our magazines and some of our associates are full of subtle propaganda of this nature. If we are not on guard against it, we are likely to play into the hands of our enemies … Let your letters home be cheerful [and] harden yourselves against minor discomforts."

An unattributed quote about the wartime Aleutians: "There comes a time when monotony gets damned monotonous."

GIs called the island of Atka "Alcatraz." There were magazines to read and laundry service, but very little to do. Tech Five Frederick Rust complained, "The Fourth of July was exactly like any other day. We worked as usual and anyway a soldier doesn't go around making a lot of noise about being independent."

Researcher Pete Fineo, quoted in the *Alaska Dispatch News* Issue of May 24, 2014, reasoned that "Most of these [GIs] were a product of the Depression. Most didn't have more than a fifth-grade education, because that's the age they can be productive [on] the farm, so they dropped out of school. They were plucked from farm life, given not a lot of training, and sent to the Aleutian Islands to be bored to death, have lots and lots of accidents and get into trouble."

Aviators, especially patrol and attack-mission people, had to deal with down time. Jim Schroeder of the army air force on Shemya said, "You just didn't fly that much when the weather was bad. You maybe [had] three missions a month, you know. And then, you just sit there and do nothing … I'm lucky, I didn't have to pull KP … [We] played cards and stuff like that, you know. And when you didn't have anything to do, you'd try to find something. But you got by, you know—you just had to find something to do."

In Billy Wheeler's 36th Squadron war diary, he observed that "no single factor has as great an effect on the morale of the flight personnel as being grounded and at the same time being kept on a continual readiness status. Patience is a virtue that is rarely present … in the makeup of a flier—and, [unable to exercise his skills], he is lost."

Murray Hanson, in the *Military Journal Online*, tells of naval airmen who "each read their own collections of paperbacks through and through, then swapped and read each others'—then swapped back again. They played pinochle, listened to the radio, and played chess and checkers until they hated the games. This was air warfare?"

A common military refrain from all wars is the admonition, "Hurry up and wait."

Paul Carrigan generalized: "All wars have one basic pattern that never seems to change. Combatants must endure long periods of intense boredom punctuated by relatively few short bursts of violent, chaotic action. It is often more difficult to suffer through the periods of inactivity. Any small sidelight which altered the humdrum daily routine was a welcomed change ... eagerly pounced upon."

Not the least of problems was not knowing when one could return home. GIs were "owned" by the military for the duration of the war. There was no light at the end of the tunnel, no hint that atomic bombs would soon shorten the war.

Tech Five Frederick Rust wrote, "The one great hope of the men for 1944 is the possibility of reaching home; this amounts to an obsession and is a constant topic of conversation. [I have heard] many men say, 'If I could only get home for a few days, I wouldn't care after that.'" Rust noted that one fellow in his engineer outfit served on the islands without a break for three and a half years, not even leaving for his mother's and father's funerals. In navy radioman James Doyle's unit on Adak, only one man ever received an emergency leave, and that was for his wife's funeral—afterward, he returned. In an oral interview, Donald Brydon remembered his three years in military service, saying, "I never got a leave in that time. I don't think I ever got an overnight pass."

It was easy to become jaded and disdainful. In the 18th Engineers Regimental diary, Frederick Rust told about men watching an instructional film on Shemya Island: "The Hollywood influence evident in these signal corps films raised derisive laughter. In the tank [film] a professional actor, dressed as a soldier, with a mug of beer in his hand, was the narrator. He frequently employed the words 'damn' and 'brother,' twice mentioned the 'hell of a tough outfit' he was in [and] managed to give a wholly artificial and phony tone to the otherwise excellent film."

Film narrators and instructors of the time were often selected for their tough-guy voices, often with machine-gun-like word delivery.

The specter of death often lurked in the background. Wilkins Dixon on Umnak sometimes had the duty of picking apart crashed planes with human remains.

Bill Grigsby, in his book *Grigs! A Beauuutiful Life*, also mentioned death:

One day when I was out walking on the tundra in the early spring ... I came across seven crude crosses ... and on them were the names of seven women nurses. They had been killed in an airplane crash on their way to serve in the Aleutians. I think it was at that point that I realized what war and death were. Here were seven young women who had left home at about the same age that I had. But they were buried in a god-forsaken area that no one could ever find or visit.

Seeing that was very depressing, because there was no one with them when they died ... I almost cry today when I think about it, and that was sixty years ago.[9]

"Adak was more than a desolate island," wrote Eliot Asinof, "it was a state of mind that could crush any attempt to overcome its power over us. Whenever possible I took to taking mid-day naps, always with the Adak radio [station] on to remind me I was still alive."

A Brian Garfield archive notecard describes: "Four signal corps privates [were sent to the Pribilof Islands] to set up two outpost radio warning stations. They kept a twenty-four-hour watch but had little to do except monitor aviation frequencies. The four young soldiers—two on St. Paul Island and two on St. George—were not relieved until October." That meant the two pairs of men spent three or four months virtually alone, testing their mettle.

It wouldn't be right to paint service in the Aleutians as an insanity pit. If you'd been there yourself, you wouldn't have seen plane after plane of men in straitjackets leaving, or endless graves of suicides, or men brawling outside every Quonset hut. The stresses and depression would have been more hidden.

Sometimes, men actually had uplifting experiences.

Army SSgt. James Liccione Sr. said, "I would stand outside my tent looking at the sky, ocean, and land for inner feelings of strength."

Bill Fry, also an army man, recalled that "after one ... storm where Kiska [Island and the] surrounding ... volcanic peaks were all covered [with snow, at night] ... there was the most beautiful sight. There was no moon, but the white peaks were rising out of the ink-black ocean. There wasn't a sound and the stillness left a feeling of peace and calm. The thoughts of a world at war could not invade the moment."

Van Vechten realized that in the Aleutians, "I grew up and matured fast and learned things about myself and [my] fellow man that no college could have done. I ... always lived in a private world of fantasy, and to this day I am often accused of painting the picture of life a little brighter than it really is, so it should surprise no one ... that I and my mates lived in La Casa Williwaw, at number 10 Lava Lane, and our mess hall was known as Café Ptomaine."

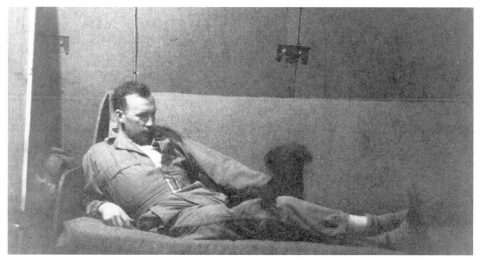

Warrant Officer Riley in a private moment on Kiska with a pet. *Courtesy of Katie and Robert Dougal via National Park Service. WC7335020*

Dr. Norman Reitman, quoted on a Brian Garfield note, spoke of "one officer I knew [who] spent an entire year maintaining his sanity by compiling an atlas of all the plants and flowers on Amchitka … Most of the men didn't have that kind of ingenuity."

Joseph Hutchison, in an oral interview, fondly recalled that when "the sun did come out, all of a sudden there would be these little wild flowers all over the place: pretty, different colors and so forth. I picked a bunch of them and put them in a book and brought them back for the wife."

The author's father on Adak also pressed Aleutian wildflowers within the pages of a book which the author still has today.

Other GIs took interest in the great profusion of waterfowl in the islands. There were kittiwakes, murres, cormorants, terns, albatrosses, puffins, petrels, fulmars, auklets, and shearwaters—with many variants. Nesting spots, when disturbed, could erupt with thousands of birds in flight.

One pilot, after dissing the Aleutians, conceded that the islands could also present an intense beauty. Flying along the chain on days when the views were clear, he enjoyed flying low over volcanic ridges, admiring the green carpet and the wild valleys and shores below.

Others were mesmerized by the colorful ribbons of the northern lights at night.

Joe Baldeschi had good memories of his stay: "You know, [my hut mates and I] got along. There were never any fights among anybody in that hut, or negative words. We got along like brothers—better than brothers."

When GIs returned home after the war, probably few who welcomed them realized what the veterans had dealt with: resentments, tough weather, uncertain tomorrows, loneliness, and boredom, with a few slivers of awesome beauty. And, for some, mental trauma from the brutal fighting on Attu.

Chapter 20
Blacks and Jews Apart

Ain't that something. Well, Mr. Fitz, that kind of makes us friends.

The status of African American GIs during the war years of the 1940s can be described in two major ways: they were usually segregated and often treated as inferior. As the war ramped up, several large all-Black units helped build the Alcan Highway through Canada to Alaska. Some Black units served in demanding work categories in the Aleutians such as construction and ship unloading. Other common jobs were serving as stewards and cooks in navy officers' mess halls.

A Black labor battalion unloaded boats and carried the wounded on stretchers at Massacre Bay during the battle of Attu, and a Black infantry unit was defending the island of Amchitka about the time the war ended. These units were almost always led by white officers, something many Black enlisted men resented.

Gen. Buckner, generally a popular officer in Alaska, nonetheless carried racial baggage from his upbringing in America's South: he didn't want Black and white troops mixing and didn't want Black troops mingling with natives.

Little thought was given to racial sensitivities: The author has seen a photograph of an Attu GI in blackface, in a dress and wearing a frizzy wig. Alongside, another GI plays a trombone. Some GIs called clumps of muskeg "niggerheads."

African American GI Jerome Jenkins was at Dutch Harbor when the Japanese attacked, and recalled, "I tried to get in a foxhole, but the guy who was in there told me I couldn't get in because he was from Alabama. Well, the Zeros were strafing the area, and I wasn't about to go anywhere and I told him so. We got along fine after that and he invited me back the next day, but I told him I'd make other arrangements."

On a former banana ship taking GIs home from the Aleutians when the war ended, William Chesney wrote that the twenty whites aboard were assigned to upper cabins while the much-more-numerous Blacks were below decks. However, Chesney made it possible for three top-level Black sergeants to come up and get cabins, too.

Army weatherman Robert Rhoades was based on Shemya as the war drew to a close. "Must have been 5,000 of us running the air base," he said. "[Also, there were at] least 5,000 Blacks doing all the other dirty work [on the island because of] discrimination … and separation."

Blacks also found the islands forbidding. As found in the Garfield archive, a Black cook on Kiska said, "Ain't nothin' but miles and miles of miles and miles."

A college thesis by Christopher Roe while at the University of Anchorage revealed that Fort Glenn near Dutch Harbor had an engineering battalion of African American soldiers during the war. Their "negro" area was isolated from other areas of the base, and had its own PX and clinic. Roe concluded that this policy of segregation was standard military practice.

The Black 93rd Engineering Regiment in the Aleutians organized a baseball team, which eventually played against white teams. The unit's GIs were given USO shows for Blacks only, or if the shows only offered one performance, the seating was segregated.

As in the lower forty-eight states, there were opportunities for bringing the races together in live performances. In 1943 on Kiska, a Black chorus of army men entertained white troops. "[They have] sung over the radio on several occasions," said the island's *Overseas Chatter* newspaper. "This will be something different for us."

The bartender at an Adak officer's club in 1943. *National Archives in Seattle*

Sailor Dale Standley, who served on the destroyer USS *Hatfield*, said:

A colored person couldn't be anything but a steward's mate. There wasn't no choice for 'em except [that job]. If any part of 'em were colored, they were classified as steward's mates; that was their duty … They were the ones that did all the servin' [of] food for the officers and took care of the officers' quarters, ironed their clothes, [polished] their shoes, cooked their meals … They accepted what they had, you know, at that time … They had a chief steward's mate, which was the officer's head cook, that was really well-respected aboard ship and he was a regular Joe Louis. He'd get in all these [boxing matches] and he'd take on everybody. He was a good man.[1]

Only once in a while did Black men work alongside whites, as in 1943 when some Black heavy equipment operators worked with white engineer units on Adak.

Dashiell Hammett's army newspaper crew on Adak included Black journalists—one of the few permanently integrated work teams.

USO visitor and famed boxer Joe Lewis in an Attu mess hall, probably signing autographs. *National Archives at Seattle*

Racial relations could be rocky. At the National Archives in Seattle is the record of a navy court-martial on Adak in 1943 that involved a "colored boy" accused of being drunk, failing to come to attention in front of a lieutenant, and telling him to "go fuck himself." Apparently, this took place in a tent where some Black mess orderlies were playing craps. The man was harshly punished with solitary confinement on bread and water for twenty days with a solid meal every three days, followed by cleaning duties for two months and a fine of $75. He was judged by a panel of lieutenants.

In another case found in the National Archives, a Black man was convicted of stealing a pistol and wristwatch from officers.

I have only one story of considerable length about a Black/white relationship, written by navy officer Charles Fitzpatrick in his book *From Then 'Til Now, My Journal*:

I met the colored steward … who cared for our Quonset hut. He came in to work the hut; my cubicle was first. I was working on a model railroad box car. Being curious, he looked over my shoulder, asking questions. He was pleasant and small talk ensued. It seemed only natural to ask, "What's your home town?"

"Baltimore, sir."

"I'm from Baltimore too. What's your name?"

"John, sir." Here again it seemed only natural for me to stand and offer my hand in greeting. He extended his, we shook, and in addition [he gave me] the biggest white-tooth smile I'd seen in a long time.

"Where in Baltimore do you live, John?"

"On Pennsylvania Avenue, sir, few blocks below North Avenue."

"I know where that is, John." Again, more small talk. He knew generally where I lived, remarking he had friends who did gardening "out there." Something one of us said brought up the Harlem Theater on Pennsylvania Avenue. Casually, I mentioned [my] dad worked there checking theater attendance. Then [I added], for the lack of anything else to say, "Do you know Buddy the bouncer at the Harlem?"

"Yes, sir. How do you know him, sir?"

"I don't but my father does. I believe my father and he are on good terms. My father is a short fellow and I'm sure Buddy kind of looks out for him."

"Ain't that something. Well, Mr. Fitz, that kind of makes us friends."

Commodore Gehres would have died at [hearing that], as would a good number of my fellow senior officers. John mentioned he also worked at the officer's mess in the kitchen. He seemed content to talk, so once again not knowing for sure what to say, I asked, "John, what happens to all that fresh fruit I hear about but don't see?"

"If you like fruit I'll sees you gets some. I'll put it right here," he said, pointing to my dresser. "I has to take care of a citizen friend from Baltimore." Thus the next few days I found an apple or orange on my dresser. It was sparse but fresh fruit, no less. The conniving part of me began to give thought of how I might increase production by several pieces each week at the minimum. Knowing enlisted men were allowed only 3.2 [percent] beer and alcohol was taboo, I waited for John one day and when he arrived asked him if he would on occasion like a little drink.

"Oh! My, Mr. Fitz, what jus' a little one would do."

I explained to John if I were to find an additional apple or orange in my drawer, and showed him where, he might find on occasion a drink or two. However, the subject had to be kept a strict secret. My fruit ratio increased a bit. John said a close watch was being kept on it and besides it was difficult to carry out unnoticed.

We had a good thing going. I got more fresh fruit and he made a few dollars selling a few shots of bourbon.

A month later I was advised John's tour of duty was up and he returned to the States. I didn't dare commence a fruit deal with a perfect stranger. After all, John and I did have certain ties. Though doubtful at best. I'd have to admit my fruit and booze deal was wrong to begin with.[2]

In the book *Radioman*, navy man Ray Daves talked about some integration that took place on Alaska's Kodiak Island, admittedly not one of the Aleutian Islands, but indicative of general attitudes. "[My CO] said we were getting a new radioman," related Daves, "and he was colored … [He] wanted to know if I had a problem with that. I was shocked … I couldn't think what I had ever said or done that would cause my commanding officer to ask me such a question.

"As far as I know," said Daves, "the newest member of the radio gang at Kodiak was the first and only African American on the whole base, and I was the first to meet with him … He seemed a little nervous … I told him not to worry."

In the National Archives in Seattle is recorded the story of a Black man, James Ward, who, while on liberty at Dutch Harbor, had been drinking and had been in a restaurant. The official account read: "On reaching the ferry slip, he broke away and ran off the dock … Evidence fails to disclose any motive for suicide or suicidal intent." The body was never found.

President Truman finally desegregated the armed forces in 1948.

Another minority looked upon with sometimes jaundiced eyes was the Jews.

George Sinclair, a sonar man on the seaplane tender ship *Casco*, recorded these conflicting views:

[I was] standing watch with Smalken, twenty-one-year-old L.A. Jew. College graduate; journalist … [He's] new on ship [and] off on wrong foot … I can't figure him out … Am rather disgusted with him … I hate him. I have a secret dislike for Smalken and I'm trying to get him off the sound gear. [He's] writing radical politics on watch; very good journalist. Stupid in several ways. A genius in others.

Later, Sinclair wrote, "Smalken improving slowly by continuous teaching. Lent him $5.00 to buy shoes."

Eliot Asinof, a lieutenant in the army air force on Adak, wrote he had been verbally denigrated as a Jew by his colonel.

During the war, there were claims that Jews had either avoided the draft or had secured rear-echelon, noncombat jobs for themselves. After the war, an accounting disclosed the names of 11,000 Jewish Americans who were killed, 24,000 who were wounded, and 36,000 who were decorated during the war.

To a lesser degree, Hispanic Americans were often seen as different. Ramon Rivas, with a pencil-thin mustache, was the only Spanish-speaking man in his Dutch Harbor-area unit. He looked forward to being able to pick up a Texas radio station broadcasting in Spanish late at night so he could maintain his Spanish-speaking ability. From time to time, others (trying to be humorous or not) would call him a "spic."

Chapter 21
Finding Things to Do

That night, for over an hour, Yehudi Menuhin treated twenty men to an impromptu violin concert. He played some pieces with his eyes closed and went from one selection to the next without saying anything.

There were some men, early in the war and on newly occupied islands, whose day consisted mostly of working, eating, defecating, and sleeping—with no days off. They must have begun to feel like machines.

As time went on, GIs' standard of living tended to improve. Housing was often upgraded. They ate in mess halls. Most had warm showers. Enough new men arrived so work schedules could allow some free time. What GIs did with this free time varied. Some were just bored and didn't go beyond playing cards, shooting the bull, and going to movies. Others needed more recreation—planned or impromptu—to ease work pressures and the feeling of being confined.

Occasionally, someone would gamely try to plant a tree on the treeless terrain. Navy navigator Charles Fitzpatrick on Attu, the furthest-out island, said, "Some enterprising navy officer brought a tree up in his plane from Whidbey Island [near Seattle] and planted it. It lived, well, sort of, you might say." A more serious attempt was the planting of 2,000 spruce trees on Adak in 1943. Six survived. A more careful planting in 1944 resulted in a 90 percent survival rate. They were a symbol of GIs' desire to make their environment a little more like home.

Some of the men took up photography as a hobby. Lt. Herman Miller on Amchitka wrote: "Some of us took photographs and developed them ourselves with supplies available from the PX … [However,] during the war, Kodak film was … only occasionally available in PXs."

In addition, censorship prevented many photos from being mailed home.

Before the age of television and the internet, print publications, radio, and movies ruled the day. Robert Rhoades wrote about serving on Shemya: "There was a big … dresser-type fixture in the barracks loaded with paperback books. I suppose I read fifty of them or more. Ones I remember [were] by Erskine Caldwell. Anything by him was pretty risqué, and boy that made the rounds real quick."

My father wrote to his parents that "I have finished quite a few novels so far. I never knew I could take so much enjoyment out of reading."

Army air force pilot John Pletcher told about "one enterprising GI [who] had gone out to one of the ships that had come in with supplies. He had gathered up magazines … like *Life* and *Time* … and *Readers' Digest* … And he had a tent set up and he was selling these a nickel apiece. Well, I'll tell you what, a lot of those magazines got thoroughly read by many people. It didn't matter if it was six months old; it was something to do."

Military newspapers were seen as a way to raise morale, and the best in the Aleutians was *The Adakian*, on Adak Island. Early on, it was run by forty-eight-year-old Dashiell Hammett, famous author of *The Maltese Falcon* and *The Thin Man*, and a person accustomed to high-society life in New York City and Hollywood. Not being in good health, and having Russian and communist sympathies, he had surprised many by volunteering for the army at his advanced age.

His group of nine men, using a simple mimeograph machine, put out a four-page, 5,000-copy newspaper every day of the week. Their newspaper aimed to give Aleutian GIs an accurate snapshot of progress in the campaigns against the Japanese and nazis. The most popular feature was the well-drawn, true-to-life cartoons (many of which are reproduced in this book) drawn by three staff artists. The cartoons copied the popular style used by the *New Yorker* magazine, with one-liner captions. Lore has it that Hammett wrote many of them.

The Adakian was willing to occasionally publish negative news, such as mentioning in 1945 that fifty-two American submarines had been lost in the war. There was more mundane information too, about bowling scores and touch football, along with a schedule of radio shows.

A GI working closely with Hammett was Bill Glackin, later an entertainment editor for the *Sacramento Bee*, who wrote that "we were all a little in awe of Hammett …"

Hammett's staff didn't quite know how to converse with him at length, and he could be distant, but they enjoyed his intellect and humor, and didn't mind hearing stories about his celebrity friends.

Hammett's duty on Adak was one of the happier times of his life because he stayed away from alcohol and was around regular people who looked up to him. According to Sgt. Frank Carnes, movie stars in traveling USO shows would drop by to visit him. However, when Hammett was reassigned to Anchorage for writing and PR duties, he returned to drinking, and his thumbing of military conventions made his bosses uneasy. He left the army as a sergeant.

As an aside, it's been said that while Hammett was in the army, the FBI doggedly tried tracking him down because an informant had told them about his communist sympathies.

GIs set up some ostensibly illegal, low-power radio stations on the islands. At Cold Bay, on the easternmost end of the islands, some bored radio men—with their base commander's approval—pieced together an impromptu radio station and created their own programming. While perusing military archives, I only saw one instance of someone court-martialed for operating such a station. Kiska eventually was alloted radio station WXLT and Adak had WXLB, which, according to Dix Fetzer, was the responsibility of Hammett. In 1945, WXLB had scheduled programs featuring news, big band music, radio drama, a radio classroom, and programs called *The Supper Club* and *Breakfast Melodies*. Sprinkled in between were sports news briefs.

Enlisted men often had radios in their tents and barracks in the Aleutians. If their radio picked up shortwave stations, they might listen to broadcasts from KGEI in San Francisco, and if atmospheric conditions were favorable at night, commercial AM stations in the United States could be heard. For example, GIs from Arkansas based at Dutch Harbor were sometimes able to listen to KTHS in Hot Springs, Arkansas. William Chesney was able to receive a Salt Lake City AM station some nights.

Tokyo Rose—actually several different women broadcasting at different times—competed with the island radio stations. Broadcasting from Radio Tokyo, "she" offered propaganda and the latest American music. Often, GIs learned more about what was happening in and around their islands from Tokyo than from their own tight-lipped news services.

Hale Burge of the Army Air Force said Toyko Rose mentioned their asphalt plant being built on Shemya, and that the Japanese would bomb it. They never did.

According to Dix Fetzer, Tokyo Rose would mention particular GIs on particular islands by name. Bill Hutcherson recalled, "On my first day on Attu Island, I heard my name on the radio, given by Tokyo Rose. She had our squadron members' [names] right … as well as the names of our home towns."

Cpl. John Haverstick wrote in *Yank* newspaper that "Rose's stories furnish free entertainment to the island-isolated GIs. There is one yarn about the general who flew to the mainland on [temporary duty]. This general's house caught fire shortly after he left and his plane picked up a radio report describing the fire and telling him he'd better get back. The report, of course, came from Tokyo Rose."

According to one of Rose's stories, a Japanese sub's photographer took pictures of an Aleutian island one night and printed his pictures in the island airbase's photo lab.

Army man Wilkins Dixon on Umnak said his buddies learned from Radio Tokyo that their PX was on fire, so they went outside to watch.

Navy radio man James Doyle told me: "I never heard Tokyo Rose talk about Adak, but she would typically say that 'You boys could be home right now—after all, there are other boyfriends going out with your girlfriends now.' [She'd] try to make us feel bad."

Of course, Tokyo Rose and Radio Tokyo were not about to detail the hardships the Japanese home population was increasingly enduring.

To this day, the ability of Radio Tokyo to obtain details about individual American GIs, their units, or the movement of those units hasn't been explained. Perhaps a lot of it came from radio intercepts.

Even though they were off the beaten path, the Aleutian Islands were visited by movie stars and other entertainers and performers—for both patriotic and publicity reasons—and even by President Franklin Roosevelt. The entertainers gamely put up with Aleutian weather, inconveniences, and distances to bring a little of the outside world (especially women) to the isolated GIs. Compared to the men's ubiquitous pinups, the USO women were amazingly alive—and they smiled back!

The most popular Aleutian USO visitor, according to several GIs, was not a woman, but actor and comedian Joe E. Brown. An equally famous actor—Errol Flynn—received mixed reviews. Army pilot Thomas Erickson met him in a latrine, where Flynn confessed he was having his "first good shit … in three days."

Most of the men in the Aleutians had never heard of classical violinist Yehudi Menuhin, but he, too, was talked into touring the islands. Paul Carrigan wrote about Menuhin's surprise visit:

World-famous concert violinist Yehudi Menuhin walked into our air operations hut. He was scheduled to give a concert … at Attu but weather had prevented [that]. Menuhin would have to spend at least the night [at our location] on Shemya.

Mr. Menuhin, his small entourage, and the flight crew clustered around the warmth of our stove … By this time the group … had grown to perhaps twenty people. Having pictured Menuhin as being a man in his sixties, I was surprised at

At a Christmas Party at Attu's firehouse, lucky enlisted men dance with visiting USO women. *National Archives at Seattle*

his youth and boyish charm … I had also expected a concert violinist to be somber and quiet but Menuhin talked and laughed with the small group.

Our stove had been turned up and … Menuhin flexed his fingers over the stove for a while and then removed his violin from its velvet-lined case … That night, for over an hour, Yehudi Menuhin treated twenty men to an impromptu violin concert. He played some pieces with his eyes closed and went from one selection to the next without saying anything. Spellbound, we listened. I was shocked with the realization that classical music devotees might not be crazy after all.

During all the time that I spent in the Aleutians, Yehudi Menuhin was the only celebrity entertainer or personality … I saw, and this was by accident. I'm certain that if I had been [on] Attu I would not have taken the trouble to get bundled up and struggle through miles of mud to sit through a two-hour violin concert.[1]

Famous African American boxer Joe Louis was another unlikely visitor. Of Louis's visit, Lt. Eliot Asinof, whose responsibility was GI entertainment and recreation, wrote:

He wasn't happy to be here. Apparently the army didn't know what to do with him when he was drafted, so they sent him on tour. He was embarrassed to be put in this position. I arranged one exhibition bout with a heavyweight amateur … We set up a ring in the mess hall … Men came to see it but nothing excited them. By the second round they were bored.

In the end, I took him around to visit men in their huts. Just walk in, after supper, sit on a cot and gab. He actually liked doing that, and the men loved it. Eight or nine huts. It made for good entries in letters home.[2]

A USO tap dancer entertaining the troops. *Alaska State Library, ASL-P545-31*

The Adakian military newspaper ran a blurb in 1944 for a USO show on Adak: "The current USO variety show has what … audiences want, and that's three very comely lasses present in these flavors: blonde, brunette, and redtop … The wolf-whistle-getting blonde is Lucille Burnett, a femme magician, and good." There were some guys in the show as well—a magician, an accordion player, and a Sally Rand impersonator.

Lt. Asinof described a USO show in progress that got a little out of hand:

Then, finally, came the blonde beauty, in a sexy gown [singing] *"Embraceable You."* … The men were enchanted [as] … she moved off stage, needing to get closer to them all …

She was moving from one to another, her lovely body making seductive moves.

Then she stopped, having found the receptacle for her passion. It was Private Walter Wayne, small and wiry, definitely comedic. She took his hand, drew him to his feet, kissed his mostly bald head. The audience began to yell … The song was taking on a whole other context, luring the men … My throat locked in one of those this-is-not-good sensations. I knew Walter well enough to sense his insecurities. For another, you don't play sensual games with sex-starved GIs on Adak.

The soldier was grinning at his sudden fame but I could see he wasn't happy about it. [As she continued singing] she took his hands and drew them around her back … There they were locked belly to belly like lovers in foreplay. The men began foot stamping, whistling, practically drowning out the singing. They shouted Walter's name in rhythmic cries, demanding that he do for them what he'd been chosen to do. So he began to clasp her buttocks, buried his mouth into her neck, stifling her … She tried to pull away, but he wouldn't let her go. The crowd was out of control, cheering every move he made. He needed her. His pelvis was pumping her, magnifying the screaming. The anticipation of raw sex on that stage was all that mattered.

[A musician named] Eddie left his giant accordion on stage and went to pull the soldier from her. The string-bean tap dancer struck Walter on the back with his guitar. Walter didn't care. Suddenly blessed with super strength, he pulled the singer to the floor and the audience roared, "Go, Walter, go!" and he pumped away in sync with their cries.

I stood watching, nervous as hell at what was happening. There was no way it could end favorably nor could I do anything to stop it … This was a USO show I had introduced and I had become its victim.

Then, suddenly without warning, a gunshot! It stopped everything … The men backed away from the stage. Walter was attacked by three MPs who pulled him away from the girl. The colonel stood there on the stage, his gun raised to the ceiling as if to lend dignity to the shot. Eddie and the tap dancer led the girl off the floor … The colonel hollered at the MPs to take the soldier to the guardhouse. I heard him say the words "court-martial" to Captain Franklin, his adjutant. Two words. Everybody heard. It was as if Walter had betrayed his country.

When I went to see him in the guardhouse that night, he was a mess. Angry at the girl, furious at himself, [saying] "I just wanted her to love me."[3]

A rather dour view of such entertainment came from an army psychiatrist: "The selection of USO shows for the Aleutians was poor. Most shows had inferior performers and too often included homosexuals and prostitutes."

There's a photograph of actress Ingrid Bergman having a meal with GI officers and enlisted men in Alaska. She's broadly smiling, and there's a Christmas tree in the background.

Eliot Asinof wrote about an unnamed Hollywood starlet visiting Adak:

The biggest question that faced us: What to do with her? She can't sing or dance. She can talk but what can she say?

She said she wanted to be with the soldiers. She would cheer them up. It was why she had come.

So be it. We would take her to a mess hall [and] have her eat lunch with the men. Perhaps she could cheer them up. Maybe even captivate them. Or, more likely, they would think she was somehow out of her mind.

After lunch, one of the [men] told me what had happened: "Nothing. She didn't know what to say to us, and we didn't know what to say to her. It was unreal!"

So much for the lunch idea. What else could we try to do? I thought of something: a photo binge. Let them take pictures of her with them, one soldier at a time. All men who had cameras would gather at the rec hall.[4]

This time around, the starlet and the men clicked.

Ray Galloway wrote that the only women he ever saw in the Aleutians were singer Francis Langford, four USO dancers, and four navy nurses.

An article in *Air Force Magazine* told about a pilot named Mullins who knew a visiting USO performer and invited the entire female troupe over to his hut after the show. "The boys cleaned the hut up for the first time in months; they were shaved and slicked up—only to have the girls telephone at the last minute and say the general had asked them over so they couldn't come." Later, Mullins was envied by the other pilots when he had two dates with [the] friend of his in the show.

Pvt. Edward Thomas wasn't very impressed with a traveling USO show, writing, "A couple of days ago, I saw a USO show … It consisted of one fairly good-looking dancer, one fat off-key swing singer, one small middle-aged blond female who was the comedian, one male accordion player, and a tall, lanky master of ceremonies … The actors did their best but they were handicapped by [trying] to revive cheap old-fashioned vaudeville under the pretense of mocking it."

The highest-profile visitor of all was President Franklin Roosevelt, who stopped by Adak during a three-week journey to Pacific bases. This was despite his poor health—he died seven months later.

Despite GIs' complaints that important visitors only saw good weather, a williwaw hit while the President's ship was anchored at Adak.

A total of 160 men from the various military services were chosen by lot to have lunch with the President, who ate from an aluminum tray just like them.

After lunch, the paraplegic president spoke, getting guffaws by saying he liked their food and climate. He said the war had accelerated progress in Alaska. Roosevelt had been assistant secretary of the navy and enjoyed travel by ship, so on the way home he arranged for a voyage down the inside passage of the Alaskan panhandle.

On built-up islands, movie theaters were a welcome diversion from boredom and bad weather. Adak eventually sported five: There were the Village, Tundra, Huskie, Ripcord, and Castle theaters.

Navy air navigator Charles Fitzpatrick in his book *From Then 'Til Now, My Journal* wrote about their moving-picture experience on Attu:

Movies were fine and we had quite a nice variety for being at the end of the Aleutian chain … When you first got into the so-called theater, everyone felt delightfully warm. [But] by the middle of the movie your ankles were nearly numb [from cold], your eyes burned from cigarette smoke, non-smokers' clothes stunk, and you wondered how long it would be before you'd get emphysema. Jackets and many times hats were worn in the movie.

In the Attu Theater … whistling, catcalls, and booing were not uncommon. Nevertheless, there was hardly a soul who ever missed a movie.[5]

A document in the National Archives in Seattle disclosed that in an unnamed theater on one of the islands, "the tendency to make unnecessary noise and loud comment has been noted in a small group of the men attending the shows … Ninety percent of the spectators are uninterested in personal wisecracks."

The cost to attend a movie at the Roxy theater on Kiska was ten cents. The theater also hosted classical music listening sessions.

In April 1945, at Dutch Harbor, the navy theater was screening *Blonde Fever*, starring Mary Astor, while the Seabee Theater was showing *Bahama Passage*, starring Madeleine Carroll. *Keys of My Kingdom* with Gregory Peck and Thomas Mitchell (with no female lead) was at the Sub Base Theater.

Ships would swap movies with each other, according to Ernest Maloney on the USS *Phelps*.

Some of the films shown had wartime connections: In *The Clock*, Judy Garland and Robert Walker starred as wartime young lovers in New York City. *Brewster's Millions* (the 1945 version) was a farce about a returning GI who must spend a million dollars in order to inherit eight million. A reviewer in *The Adakian* newspaper called it "mostly silly."

As testimony to the amount of money the military eventually put into the Aleutians to keep the men happy, at least one of the islands had a bowling alley—as though the military planned to stay forever. There was also a basketball court or two within large Quonset huts. In the summertime, baseball was played outside.

Card games (also mentioned in the chapter about gambling) filled in the time for a lot of men. Walter Stohler, in an oral history interview, remembered playing cards a lot, especially cribbage. "That's where I learned to smoke cigarettes and got hooked on 'em. Drank lots of coffee and played cards," he said.

Tommy Olsson of the army air force on Unimak recalled "playing hearts till the lights went out and then we lit candles and continued playing till [the] wee hours of the morning"—and also spending an "evening playing cards during which the gang brought out a bottle of hooch so the evening ended not so quietly."

Other men played chess.

Fish could be plentiful in Aleutian waters and creeks. Aviation machinist mate Robert Buchanan, who served on Attu and Amchitka, mentioned during an oral interview: "Oh yeah! I did go fishing. [We'd] catch halibut out in the bay … You'd go down and you could check out a rod and reel … and get a life raft and take it out and go out and fish … I remember when the salmon [were] going up to spawn in those hills, there was a little [creek] right there close to our Quonset huts. It wasn't very deep because we'd walk through it … That [creek] was just full of salmon … I couldn't believe it. I never thought I'd ever see that many fish. They were so thick they were just one on top of another."

GIs would bring some back to their barracks to fry.

My father, Harry Paul Jr., wrote his parents: "Am going fishing in the morning. Still trying to catch some trout. You can catch codfish most any place but they are wormy now. I'd like to try for some halibut and big salmon sometime in the Bering Sea. We haven't had the salmon run yet but it shouldn't be long."

An officer and two enlisted men giving fishing a try at Dutch Harbor. *National Archives at Seattle*

In an oral history interview, army air force veteran Jim Schroeder said, "We liked to fish ... We had enough [fishing] line and ... we pounded up pennies for spinners to catch fish on. And get chunks of meat and go down to the docks down there, and catch pretty good-size codfish and bring 'em home."

When the winter ended and wildflowers bloomed on the muskeg in profusion, men were attracted. My father wrote that he "got off at four and went for a two-hour walk along the bay. Found some new flowers and put them in a book to press. I understand that there are two varieties of orchids that grow up here. Not very pretty ones however. We do have some nice pretty [other flowers], however. I found ten different kinds that one day. All colors: red, pink, blue, purple, yellow, white. The narcissus that came out so thick at first have now almost all gone."

Another time, he wrote about "some pretty Monkshood ... [and some flowers] that are the same as at home—for instance, purple violets."

"D'YA S'POSE IT'D BE ALL RIGHT IF I TOOK MY TIE OFF?"

GIs with time off sometimes climbed the heights for the views. Here, they appear to be observing Sweeper Cove on Adak. *Artist: Oliver Pedigo*

Not exactly under the heading of recreation but definitely a part of Aleutian life were religious services for Protestant, Catholic, and Jewish GIs. A good example is in the forty-five-minute-long Aleutian documentary film *Report from the Aleutians*, with scenes showing a burial in grasslands of what appears to be an airman, and an outdoors church service. The weather in both, not surprisingly, appears to be breezy and cool.

Miscellaneous other activities on some of the islands were gun and archery target practice, volleyball, pool and ping-pong, woodworking (where my dad made my brother and I a toy power shovel), and skiing. One of the islands even offered a tanning room.

Joe Baldeschi told about being on a boxing team. "They brought in some kid, I forget from what island. They said, 'Hey Baldeschi, you're in trouble. That guy's got fifteen knockouts in the first round.' I said, 'I'll take care of him.' I got in that ring with the guy, the bell rang and … about twenty seconds later I didn't know where I was. He just let me have it and I was down on the deck and listening to the birds sing … He put out my lights in a hurry."

Andy Anderson remembered improvising a winter activity on Attu:

One time, a piece of plywood came in on the beach. There was snow on the ground then, and we thought we could make a toboggan out of that thing … That night … the moon came out and the mountain was beautiful. So we … went up there … [and] jumped on this thing and started going down. We were going 100 miles an hour. The thing tipped over … and we looked back; we couldn't see [one of the riders].

We went back up there and he says, "I think my leg's broken." [A] corpsman looks at him and he says, "Your leg's not broken. We're gonna tie you to the plywood board and get you down the mountain." We tied him on and we got down.[6]

At the National Archives in Seattle is a letter from "Lou" telling about a GI who took a couple days off during a good weather spell to make an overnight trip to a trapper's cabin about 10 miles from his post. After informing his superiors, he set out with all the provisions and clothing he'd need. During the morning of his expected return,

someone takes it into his head that Dietz must be suffering untold miseries out there on the cold, desolate tundra. After all, he's … a mere 24 years old. So people just off their night watches are roused from their sacks, sleepy-eyed … and the snow Jeep is filled to overflowing … So off across the tundra we went … We'd no sooner got a couple miles from camp when whom should we see, in the best of condition, shuffling leisurely on his skis … the object of our search.[7]

Others were drawn to the sea in their spare time. Navy radioman James Doyle and friends found an abandoned coast guard lifeboat at Clam Lagoon on Adak and started taking it out on afternoon rowing trips. Elsewhere on Adak, two men borrowed a boat to go fishing but they went too far out and when the water got rough, one drowned when the boat sank. Wilkins Dixon on Umnak and some other guys bought a boat from natives and worked after hours to rehabilitate it, later using it for fishing.

In the Brian Garfield archive, there's a note about a gravel pit where an excavator and bulldozer had uncovered ivory tusks, which the men would gather and saw into pieces, to later carve into heart shapes. However, taking the tusks was soon prohibited—"disappointing news to men who are half crazy with boredom." Evidently, Alaskan natives themselves carved ivory. My dad wrote to his parents, "Have been able to buy some ivory things. A paper weight with a carved-out whale on top, and a letter opener. I'm giving them to [my wife] for our anniversary."

Military bands were present in the Aleutians and provided some entertainment. Bill Maris, a seaplane crewmember at Dutch Harbor, said some band members "lived in our wing of the barracks, so every afternoon or evening they would gather and play requests for us as they practiced their regular music. Most of these men were former pros from named bands so they were good."

However, band member Robert Johnson said they were given the unenviable duty of marching near various barracks at Dutch Harbor early in the morning, playing loud music to wake up GIs. They also went down to the docks and played when troop ships came in, and played hymns at the chapel. They had a vocalist or two for variety.

Tame and wild animals provided a different sort of diversion. Joe Baldeschi described finding four tiny native foxes and bringing them into his hut to raise. At another location, Frederick Rust noted that blue foxes were tame enough to eat out of his hand, and they would wait for handouts.

Sometimes guys liked to chase semitame foxes. B-25 pilot Joe Jeffers said he and some buddies "saw two foxes and shot at them with our Colt .45 pistols, acting [like] little kids throwing rocks."

Army radar officer Robert Dougal on Kiska told about a red fox which became frozen overnight to some kitchen garbage it was trying to eat: "When the cooks came in the morning they found him. And they [wrapped] him in a burlap bag and [took] him into the kitchen and put him near the stove to thaw out ... And after a while he became a pet ... We always had something for him to eat."

Some garbage-eating foxes on Attu, according to Walter Anderson, got friendly enough to go into their hut, but "you had to be careful. If you frightened them, they'd start to urinate and that smelled up the whole place."

Some GIs flouted the rules and kept pet dogs. Navy radioman James Doyle remembered an enlisted man had to hide his during inspections. Lt. Herman Miller remembered dogs abandoned on Amchitka when their owners returned to the States, "so there were packs of hungry dogs running around. We were told to [isolate] the dogs we wanted to keep, for a day, while the military police went around and shot all the loose dogs."

Harry Bailey, an army barge man on Agattu, mentioned a GI trying to provoke a reaction from some sea birds sitting on a cliff with the use of a .50-caliber machine gun on his ship. "Little did we know," wrote Bailey, "that this was a nesting place and as the shot exploded on the cliff, hundreds of birds took to their wings. For all the noise and confusion, I doubt we did little damage, and they quietly settled back into their nesting routine." He also mentioned a GI who shot and killed a curious eagle. "It seemed nothing at that time, but we were contributing to the near-extinction of the eagle in the western Aleutians."

Paul Carrigan and a friend, Don, were intensely interested in a nearby family of eagles. Wrote Carrigan: "Many hours were spent awaiting ... eggs to hatch ... We sweated out this event like nervous fathers outside a hospital maternity room. Two eagle chicks cracked their shells and emerged. Our quiet, close presence as we looked down upon the nest [from the top of a cliff] did not seem to frighten the parents. Momma and papa began bringing home small fish and chunks of large fish for their young."

Carrigan ignored rules against enlisted men owning cameras and obtained one via the GI underground. It was a simple Kodak Brownie, so Carrigan decided to make his way down the cliff to get close enough for decent photos. The going became increasingly perilous, but he came within 15 feet of the nest.

"Look out!" Don shouted.

"The full-grown eagle gave a shrill squeaky cry," wrote Carrigan, "before I turned and saw it. With powerful feathered legs ending in sharp talons spread wide and thrust forward, the fierce-eyed eagle came at me. I threw one arm up to cover my face as a taloned claw raked the shoulder of my foul-weather jacket. Thrashing wings beat at me for a second before the eagle dove off to one side, lost altitude and flapped majestically away."

Don returned with help and a coil of rope, which Carrigan managed to tie to himself. The eagle returned for a second dive. "There was a rapid whooshing sound as great wings beat the air close to my head. At the same time I received a jarring thump on my back."

After Carrigan retreated and was helped back up the cliff, they spent a few days anxiously awaiting the return of photographs from a processor in Anchorage. Unfortunately, none of the pictures turned out.

Carrigan was able to foster a better relationship with an eagle later. This time he and a pal found a distressed young eagle along the Shemya shoreline after a powerful storm. Bringing it back to their hut and nursing it to health, Carrigan allowed his hut mates to name it Butch. It was content with spending most of its time on a high-up perch, and avidly ate virtually any kind of meat.

Wrote Carrigan:

The eagle became a celebrity. Officers and enlisted men, both army and navy, frequently dropped in to "see that eagle." There was only one person that Butch at first did not like, and then quickly began to hate. This guy was the leading chief boatswain's mate of the naval facility. He began teasing the eagle, and the chief and I almost came to blows over it. From the beginning, the chief seemed to be jealous of the bird.

I found out … that the chief had stopped by our hut several times during daylight and teased the eagle while I was [out]. My hut mates had not told me this because they were afraid of what I might do.

I was sound asleep in my sack one night. The chief was back with Butch playing a … game. All hell suddenly broke loose and the chief ran through the hut and out the door. The slamming door stopped Butch because he was right on the chief's tail. I woke up at this commotion and asked what had happened … [I learned the chief had aggressively teased the eagle] and Butch attacked him.

During the next few nights the chief came to our hut … to check and see if Butch were still there. As soon as the chief opened the door, Butch uttered a high-pitched screeking sound and rocketed from his perch and attacked. He wouldn't let the chief in the hut. Then a really spooky thing happened that I hope some bird expert will explain to me someday. This occurred three times.

That evening we were all sitting or lying around when Butch started to raise hell. "The chief's coming," said a hut mate. "How do you know that?" I asked.

"I don't but Butch does," he replied.

My mind wrestled with what my ears had heard. "That's impossible," I said.

"Impossible or not, Butch knows. Wait and see."

Sure enough, several seconds later the chief tried to enter the hut. Right on cue and on target, the eagle flashed across the room from his perch. The chief swore, backed out, and slammed the door as Butch crashed into it. The eagle then stood facing the door with his wings arched in a very aggressive manner as he made a hissing noise.

[A few days later] I turned Butch loose. He didn't want to leave at first … [but] his flights became longer and returns fewer. On about the third day he flew toward Attu and never came back. I'm sure he knew where his home was.[8]

Carrigan had one more bird story to tell. In a land of many unusual and sometimes exotic-looking migratory birds, a newly arrived weatherman would be easily convinced that a veteran weatherman had just seen the winter arrival of a rare bird:

"Well," [a veteran] would announce, "the kee birds are back. I just heard one cry out." Other old-timers would perk up immediately.

"Why do they stop here in the winter at all and why so late?" one would ask. "Why don't they keep flying south to sunny California or South America like other birds do?"

"Because they're such incredibly dumb birds," a man would reply.

At this point the neophyte Aleutianite, his curiosity about to burst, would invariably ask, "What kind of a noise do they make?"

"KEEEEEEEEEERRiiiST! IT'S CUCK-CUCK-CUCK-COOOOOOOOLD!" we'd all chorus.

Realizing he'd been conned, the newcomer would cuss us out … [as] one more select member had been initiated into the Aleutian Kee Bird Club.[9]

Thinking they were helping raise GIs' morale, according to Bernard Mehren on Shemya, stateside organizations and individuals donated cigarettes. Also, a few cigarettes were provided with every K-ration package. The use of cigarettes peaked during the war years.

Even the most stalwart and blasé of the Aleutian veterans could get emotional and nostalgic around Christmastime, which was something to look forward to. Thomas Needham, a Seabee, recalled in an oral interview that he and his buddies built a Christmas tree out of pipe fittings, added packing-material tinsel, and then had a big Christmas dinner and party. But there were no presents and no Santa Claus.

On the other hand, some higher-ups were only ready to dampen that joy, because printed on the back of a Christmas meal menu my father saved from Adak (shortly after the end of the war in 1945) was this admonition:

This is the first Christmas in five years that the world has been at peace … The departure … of many of our shipmates at Adak places a heavy burden upon those of us who remain. Paralleling this is the necessity of returning to standards maintained in the naval service during times of peace. Many regulations and age-old customs have been held in abeyance … [but now] it is incumbent upon each member of this command to readjust his personal habits and military conduct accordingly."

[signed] Robert R. DeWolfe, Captain, USN[10]

My father had written below the paragraph, "Xmas greetings?"

While the winds of an approaching storm howled and wet snow fell on his hut, weather officer Bernard Mehren on Shemya displayed a literary bent as he wrote this Christmas story:

The machines of war have been rolled out of Hanger #1 and in their place is a sea of faces. Several thousand men have come to pay homage to the Prince of Peace at a solemn high midnight mass. Against the center wall a simple altar has been built, flanked by Christmas trees flown in from the mainland … Civilian workers, soldiers, sailors—their voices made up the choir [singing] … the saintly music of "*Silent Night*" … I knew it was silent and peaceful in Phoenix tonight and I longed to be there. And then suddenly I closed my eyes and this cold hangar on a lonely island became a great and warm cathedral and my family and friends stood next to me singing the beautiful words … I didn't have to look to see them; I knew they were there.[11]

Pvt. Edward Thomas said he woke at 11:30 Christmas morning and went to the mess hall for his turkey dinner, where he wasn't much impressed by "two scrawny Christmas trees at one end of the mess hall." The night before, he had checked out some ice skates and skated in a high wind. All he had to do was stretch his arms out and scoot along the ice with the wind. On Christmas day, he went skating again.

Navy seaplane crewman Bill Maris on Dutch Harbor enjoyed a beer party on Christmas Eve, noting that most "hands came home with a glorious feeling." However, "a couple of the guys didn't [make it home,] so we went looking for them and found them asleep in a snow bank along [the] side of the road."

In a token gesture on Amchitka, "the air base officers did KP for Christmas dinner," said Lieutenant Herman Miller.

Chapter 22
After the A-Bomb, a Hurry to Leave

Through these months some of us had built up a fellowship akin to brotherhood which continues to this day.

GIs on Attu celebrating Japan's surrender. The prospect of returning home was tantalizing. *Photograph by David Tewes*

News of the end of the war reached Aleutian GIs in various ways. Garvin Germany Jr. and other navy men on Shemya first learned of it from a Russian radio station. Whiskey was forbidden to them during the war, but a bottle was brought out by officers to toast the victory (hopefully shared with the enlisted men). Their navy commander, Germany said, climbed a flagpole while another officer tried to chop it down.

James Havron, later an army lieutenant colonel, feared trouble from higher-ups when told to immediately report to his headquarters. He was relieved to find a large number of officers present. Even though Japan had surrendered, a general read a radiogram which stated something like: "Japanese task force ... headed north. Lost in the fog. Believed to be an attack on our Aleutian Islands. This is for your information. Signed, [Admiral] Nimitz."

Havron got in his Jeep and drove around his island, looking for smoke on the horizon. Later, he learned the task force was Russian, attacking the Japanese Kurile Islands.

Army airman Robert Brown then flew a reconnaissance sortie over those islands:

[We were told not to] fire unless fired upon. And so when we got over there … a Russian fighter … came up to check us over, but no harm done. We went over to the island which we had been constantly bombing and the Russian landing craft were going in there. And we were just a little pushed out of shape on that because we've been doing all the work and then they just go on in with their boats and take over.[1]

Army sergeant Delbert Morley, who coded and decoded military messages, said he was seeing radio traffic at the end of the war that made him think war with Russia was possible.

Even mowing a lawn was looked forward to. *Artist: Oliver Pedigo*

GIs had endured long tours in the Aleutians. Finally seeing the light at the end of the tunnel, they were impatient to return home. Unfortunately, days spent waiting could drag on into weeks, and weeks could drag on into months.

My navy lieutenant father, Harry Paul Jr., was chomping at the bit to return, as expressed in letters:

The commanding officer can hold me three more months … if he can prove there is a military necessity … It makes me pretty disgusted because of some things that go on here. They can get along without me if they wanted to … The regular navy doesn't care if we ever get out or not. They want to keep us around as long as possible to make it easier for them.

[And, in another letter:] Things are tough here and morale is zero … I'm in hope Admiral Nimitz may rectify some of the bad parts of the navy system and speed up demobilization a little. We have over 1,000 men here waiting to get out—Attu is closing …

[And, in yet another letter:] Some men are getting out and it appears to be stepping up a little. The biggest trouble is to get transportation back but most of them get out within a month after they are eligible. The army shipped out over 2,000 men on one ship about two weeks ago.[2]

There was often resentment about who got to return home first. Army airman Harry Dickey was angry because, he said, draftees returned home before he, an enlistee, was allowed to.

On the other hand, if someone eligible to return home didn't want to, it was a cause for concern. Lt. Herman Miller wrote: "In October 1945, the detachment commander had enough points to go home, but he planned to go back to college, and [fall was a bad] time to start college. He told squadron headquarters he would like to remain on Amchitka for a while. Headquarters thought there must be something funny going on if he wanted to stay, so the personnel officer was sent to investigate."

Military orders to return to the States would typically specify "by the first available government transportation." For navy radioman James Doyle, who had to wait three months after the end of the war to leave, that meant a troopship. Officers, he said, got to leave by plane. "As my boat was leaving the harbor, everybody was on the guardrail with [their middle] finger up, if you know what I mean," said Doyle.

A common refrain upon leaving, as spelled out in a poem by Marine Fred Ellis, was that "we served our hitch in Hell." In another poem, he hoped to never see another island without a tree.

"Mac" McGalliard wrote that his outfit was billeted in a holding area before shipping out:

One day going to chow two guys began to argue. Why, I don't know. One was Jason Grey, if I can recollect properly. They got to scuffling and rolling in the dirt and rolled to a mud puddle. By this time Jason was on top and had his friend by the ears and was holding him face down in the mud puddle. Along come our flight surgeon and another officer. They looked at the situation and said, "Be careful, Jason" and walked on. Jason was so stunned by the officer's comment that he just got up and walked to the chow hall in silence. We were all ready to go home.

[While waiting,] I got a letter from my mom one day and for some unknown reason, I couldn't stop crying.[3]

A mirage? A GI back home ponders the sudden appearance of women. Ravens, common in the Aleutians, appeared in several other cartoons in *The Adakian* as a sidekick. *Artist: Donald Miller*

Flier Billy Wheeler headed back to the States on a crowded Liberty ship with terrible food. Upon reaching the distant shores again, he exclaimed, "Home again. How strange it seems to see trees—and women!"

Floyd Erickson said he subsisted on candy bars on his troopship bound for home from Kiska, adding, "Somebody said there's waves out there 50 feet [high], and I believed it. I just stayed in my bunk as long as I could. We landed at Fort Lawton, Washington. And there were German prisoners serving in the mess halls. I couldn't believe it."

When Roy Dover's twenty months in Alaska came to an end, he wanted to bring back a Japanese .25-caliber pistol as a souvenir. Hearing it would be confiscated, he sold it to another soldier for $15. "It turned out that everyone was packing guns and helmets and things in their baggage," he said, "and no one was stopping them. So that was a mistake."

GIs wait for their ship home and take in a promising new horizon—with a sun. *Artist: Donald Miller*

Elmer Rafiner, who later became a lieutenant colonel, was "tickled to death" to return home. However, when he flew into Minneapolis, his plane was met by fifty MPs who wouldn't let him and the other men go into town, saying, according to Rafiner, "We've had people from Alaska down here and they go crazy when they get back to civilization."

Navy airman Garvin Germany Jr. said he paid a yeoman in Kodiak $25 to be able to fly to Washington state instead of waiting along with 900 other GIs to take a ship which was only set up to accommodate 300.

Besides unneeded GIs after the war, there was a lot of excess materiel. Lieutenant Herman Miller remembered excess "ammunition being exploded, and some supplies and equipment ... dumped off a high cliff into deep water because they were not worth shipping back to the mainland."

Jake Cogan similarly described pushing vehicles including earthmoving equipment off a cliff.

P-40 fighter planes were destroyed en masse at a scrapyard in Anchorage.

The speedy withdrawal of GIs and their units left debris and pollution that littered some of the Aleutian Islands. The Japanese also left debris. Twenty-eight sites were once listed as needing cleanup. For many years, live ammunition could still be found.

Upon returning to the lower forty-eight states, some war veterans made the effort to keep in touch with buddies or other vets. Bill Maris was inducted into a Veterans of Foreign Wars post in Anacortes, Washington. Army sergeant Paul Plesha attended five reunions with his Aleutian outfit before the get-togethers petered out. He was also one of the few who later returned to visit Attu Island, and when he did, the sun was out!

In 2014, former army engineer Clint Goodwin said, "We did our reunions every year and [when] we started out, we had almost 100 guys. Then it goes down to 70, 60, 40, 30. And now, outside of myself [and two others], I think that's all I know of. That's it."

Jim Schroeder, who served on Shemya, said that fellow vets finally located him in 1990, so he began attending reunions. "They had reunions every year," said Schroeder. "But they kept getting further and further [apart] ... [Now] there's only four of us actually left."

Ghosts of the war still turn up in the news from time to time. A volunteer wildlife biologist visiting uninhabited Buldir island, not far from Attu, came upon the remains of a soldier in 1988. She found the GI's skeleton, a military pocket watch, a wrist watch, a 1940s quarter, a comb, empty ammunition clips, an M-1 rifle, a sheath knife, a pocket knife, and a wallet in very good condition. The remains had waited forty-three years to be discovered.

The skeleton was conclusively identified later by the army's Central Identification Lab in Hawaii as that of Cpl. Carl Houston, age twenty-one, from Manitowoc, Wisconsin. After having received arctic survival training, he had readily volunteered to serve at the remote weather station on the island along with four others, writing home that "Lady Luck" helped him win that duty. The post only had mail service twice a year. Called "a good all-American fun-loving kid" by a relative, he was engaged to marry his girlfriend back home.

Houston had gone for a walk in March 1945 (which the GIs did to avoid cabin fever) and never returned. Various attempts by land and air to locate him failed, and some thought he'd been buried in a landslide. His mother feared he'd been captured by the Japanese. The death site was not far from the island's volcano, Mount Eccentric.

His remains were eventually shipped to his sister in Wisconsin for burial. The military presence on the island ended after Japan's surrender.

Earlier, this book covered the limited types of food served to men in the Aleutians. When returning home, they wasted no time enjoying the foods they'd missed. In an interview, Earl Long said: "There was something I had hungered for ... for nearly a year ... No sooner had I gotten squared away [in the lower forty-eight states] than I ... was treated to the most mouth-watering delicacy: a lettuce and tomato sandwich."

James Doyle looked forward to apple pie and ice cream.

Roald Forseth made up for lost time:

I wound up in Fort Lewis near Seattle … I was a corporal by then, and awaiting assignment to officer candidate school, … [I] applied for a job in the officers' mess and worked as a waiter. There was no money in it, but I got all the food I wanted. I ate better than the officers did.

After serving breakfast, I would eat six eggs if I was hungry enough, and at dinner I would eat as much as I could stomach. I blew up like a balloon … I didn't care. After the Aleutians, I never wanted to be hungry again. When I'd get some time off, I would go into Seattle to eat. I wanted vegetables so bad. I'd order a big salad and gobble it down.[3]

Men returned to their old occupations or found new ones. My father returned to his job as a rural letter carrier, where he was pretty much his own boss. He too looked forward to eating salads. He bought a war-surplus Jeep, built a plywood cab over it, and used it on his mail route. It was also our family car for a while. Because of his work with navy radio operations, he introduced my brother and I to ham radio, and later opened the best radio and TV repair shop in the county. However, I think he missed some aspects of military discipline and the perks of being an officer.

Another GI, David Dennison, said that military duty made him more philosophical about problems: "I don't think there was anything that got me upset [once back home] … There was never anything I went through that could compare with the problems we had in the army. I [had] lived in a sleeping bag for four years."

After wartime merchant marine service in the Aleutians, James Jolly later found work on a tugboat in the Atlantic Ocean and the Caribbean Sea.

Kenneth Skinner, a seaplane crew member, said in an interview: "After the war, I wound up shoveling coal for a while—jobs were a little hard to get. I sold insurance on the side and real estate, and I wound up going to work for the power company … [retiring] as a power engineer in 1982."

After the war, Roy Dover built Hudson cars on an assembly line before returning to farming. He met Willie Myree Porter at a church musical event and married her in 1947. He jammed with country and bluegrass groups for many years, playing fiddle and guitar.

Battle memories followed some GIs home. Naomi Robinson of Arizona wrote about her returning fiancé: "I was nineteen years old [when I] watched my fiancé leave by train in … 1943. I did not see him again for two years, when he finally returned on leave from the terrible battle [on Attu]. On the leave … we married and I realized that my husband's life had been damaged. His nerves were severely affected by the trauma of war."

If anyone was likely to put positive spin on Aleutian wartime duty, it would be an officer. Col. Samuel Dows, quoted in the Brian Garfield archive, said: "I believe I could give you quite a roster of people who found the service there very challenging and who have many pleasant memories."

Army air force mechanic Mac McGalliard had good things to say: "We had a good time together—just like kids—19, 20, 21—thrown together from all sides of the US of A—different sizes, personalities, color, religions—but we came to be 'one.' We made lasting friendships. Until I die, I will be unable to forget my brothers who served with me for a short time from one end of the Aleutian chain to the other."

Harry Bailey wrote: "Through these months some of us had built up a fellowship akin to brotherhood which continues to this day."

Some Aleutian veterans held on to their dislike or hatred of the Japanese after the war. In an interview, Dean Galles described visiting Hawaii many years after the war where he ran into Japanese American residents or visitors from Japan: "The Japanese people really got to me there. And [my wife] says, 'What's wrong with you?' And I couldn't tell her."

James Jolly, having heard stories of Japanese pilots machine gunning American lifeboats and of Japanese treating prisoners badly, didn't want anything to do with Japanese individuals or companies after the war. Some GIs categorically refused to buy anything made in Japan.

Perhaps the proper way to end this chapter is an excerpt from an interview with Earl Long, a navy Seabee:

What we experienced turned many … young [boys into] young men. Over the years since, I have known the love of a good and caring woman … I have watched my three sons grow to manhood and been thankful that they have been spared the ordeal of fire my generation was tested under.

I have owned my own business and prospered. I have a lifetime of memories, the good ones far outweighing bad. I have enjoyed a long life, years that for many of my generation were cut short … Those years [in the Aleutians], now so long a part of my past … remain to a large degree one of the high-water marks of my life. For only those who have experienced war know the strength of the ties that forever binds you to the event.[4]

Chapter 23
The Aleutians Today: Bullets for Caribou

Abandoned bunkers, whole suburban streets of empty military housing.

At the height of the war, thousands of GIs were stationed in the Aleutians. Airfields, housing, roads, and harbors were built. Millions were spent to make living tolerable. Then, after the islands of Attu and Kiska had been recaptured, military activity in the islands slowly began to wind down.

Soon after Japan surrendered, most military men left. A few Aleutian bases were kept in operation, often with new missions because of the Cold War with Russia. But over time, even those operations closed. For a brief period, underground atomic bomb tests were conducted on Amchitka Island. The only remaining military facility in the outer islands known to the author is the air base on Shemya Island.

Rusting Japanese 75 mm anti-aircraft guns on Kiska remain in place today, stripped of parts by souvenir hunters. *By Lisa Hupp, US Fish and Wildlife Service*

A veteran of the battle for Attu, Bill Jones, returned to that island with four other vets as part of the filming of the documentary *Red, White, Black and Blue* in 2003. He stood alone on the beach at Massacre Bay where they landed, and immersed in his vivid memories, he cried. He and other vets have protested the titanium Japanese monument on Attu honoring all the military men killed in the North Pacific during the war.

A much more modest, privately financed memorial embedded in a boulder on Attu commemorates the American dead. The inscription, written by Bill Jones, partly reads:

This plaque [is] inscribed and placed here … to honor the boys-men who prematurely gave their lives during the Battle of Attu and in remembrance of the mothers, fathers, wives, children and sweethearts whose lives were forever changed due to their loss.[1]

The Peace Memorial memorializing Japanese and Allied war dead in the northern Pacific, paid for by the Japanese government and erected on Attu in 1987. *US Coast Guard*

Where once thousands of GIs were stationed on Adak Island, now only a small civilian city of about a hundred souls remains, along with an airfield with regular service to Anchorage.

Governance over the islands and nearby waters was passed on to the indigenous natives of the Aleut Corporation in 1972. Also, some portions of the islands are now wildlife refuges.

Today, tourism and fishing are the main Aleutian industries. Birdwatchers visit the islands to add to their lifetime species-count numbers. There are a number of species best seen in the Aleutians.

Caribou were introduced on Adak Island during the 1950s to give military personnel something to hunt and as a source of emergency food. As the caribou population expanded, nonmilitary hunters were attracted.

Stefan Milkowski, writing in the *Fairbanks News-Miner*, found hunting caribou on Adak difficult:

In good weather, the island looked merely strange—abandoned bunkers, whole suburban streets of empty military housing … One afternoon, when the wind and rain made hunting futile, we explored the northern end of the island. A whole series of concrete buildings, abandoned. A playground by the ocean, abandoned.

A privately financed monument on Attu honoring Americans war dead. *Photo by Lisa Hupp, US Fish and Wildlife Service*

Birdwatchers visit the Aleutians today to view a great variety of birds such as this tufted puffin. *By Lisa Hupp of the US Fish and Wildlife Service*

We struggled to stand in the wind … Honestly, we weren't having much fun. The weather was often miserable, and just getting around was hard work. In all the hours we spent hunting, we'd seen two animals.

The next morning we climbed toward Husky Pass … From the pass, we spotted some animals on a distant hillside … A dozen [caribou] were grazing heads-down. When they wandered out of view, we grabbed our rifles and hurried closer. We crept up the side of the ridge, trying to see them before they saw us. We were silent. The wind was right. Ian's eyes lit up. There they were, still grazing at close range.[2]

The hunters' aim was good.

From time to time, volcanoes along the windswept chain still erupt and earthquakes rattle windows. On a regular basis, comfortable passenger jets flying the great circle route to China and Japan from the United States pass high overhead. The Aleutian Islands have settled back into their former, much quieter existence. It takes a special kind of person to want to live there.

A special thanks to Paul Carrigan, on right, the navy weatherman whose memoir contributed so many flavorful and well-written stories to this book. Walter Andersen is at left. *Image courtesy of Walter Andersen via National Park Service*

Afterword

In researching this book, I came upon some often-repeated stories that fit the category of legends or myths. Maybe they contained some small basis of fact, but upon being retold and retold, they attained a life of their own.

The most often-repeated tale was about a Japanese soldier who survived the Battle of Attu and hid out until hunger overcame his fear of Americans. He was said to have been found dressed in American gear, standing in a chow line, eager for food.

Ralph Bartholomew wrote in the *Americans Home from Siberia* newsletter that "five months after the battle on Attu, [an American flight crew was] awarded an unusual passenger for the trip back to Anchorage. The only remaining Japanese survivor of the battle had been living in the caves on the north side of the island and was discovered just that morning in the early chow line."

Bill Hutchison said, "I missed being a real hero when I didn't recognize an ill-clad Japanese rummaging in our garbage barrel as I was on my way to duty armed with a .45-caliber pistol. The Jap had come down from the mountain in search of food."

Another version, from an interview with Kenneth Skinner, related that "the army saw … what appeared to be a Japanese in their chow line and the fellow's clothes didn't fit him too well. So one of the sergeants grabbed the guy and started questioning [him] … And, of course, the guy's answers weren't right. So the sergeant hauled him into headquarters … and they found out he was a Japanese soldier who got hungry and stole some American uniforms."

Still another version, related by Wilkins Dixon, was that the Japanese soldier was found *serving* food.

The mythical George Washington cherry tree story is a great example of the desire to embroider and embellish the past. Mythmaking also was in play when many Americans began to color World War II veterans uniformly as heroes. The term "Greatest Generation" has been applied to them. Certainly, after the war, many GIs' families thought of them as heroes, and that's natural. However, I don't think most Aleutian vets thought of themselves as heroic. In fact, two-thirds of American soldiers and sailors had been drafted in World War II.

Instead, they were regular Joes with all sorts of personalities and backgrounds who pulled together to get the job done with pluck, grousing, and humor. Many risked their lives. They knew they were contributing to a greater good and that the American public was behind them. More than anything else, they simply wanted to return home to apple pie, regular jobs, and families.

Following such a massive, catastrophic, world-wide war, there was again hope—epitomized by the formation of the United Nations—that future wars would be avoided. Unfortunately, conflicts in Korea, Vietnam, Iraq, and Afghanistan followed. They didn't offer the same sense of closure that World War II did, and the American public was often divided about supporting them. Times have changed.

Endnotes

Note: Misspellings and punctuation errors may be seen in some of the following internet addresses, but they are the actual URLs.

Chapter 2

1. Mark Forseth (quoting his father, Roald Forseth). "World War II Memories That Will Never Be Forgotten," *Baltimore Post-Examiner* (online edition), May 28, 2012, accessed 2017, https://baltimorepostexaminer.com/world-war-ii-memories-that-never-will-be-forgotten/2012/05/28.

2. Mac Eads (transcript from interview of June 16, 2008), "Bob and Mac Eads Interview," *Aleutian World War II National Historic Area Oral History Program*, National Park Service, accessed 2017, https://www.nps.gov/aleu /learn/photos-multimedia/upload/Eads-Transcript-508.pdf.

3. Mac McGalliard, "Mac McGalliard's War Stories," *Aleutian World War II National Historic Area*, National Park Service, accessed 2017, https://www.nps.gov/articles/000/mac-mcgalliard-stories.htm.

4. Wylie Hunt, *Aleutian World War II National Historic Area 2015 calendar* (Aug. page), National Park Service, https://www.nps.gov/aleu/upload/2-Aleutian-WWII-Calendar-2015-508.pdf.

5. Charles House (in a letter to Commander Neil F. O'Connor), "Charles House and the Invasion of Kiska," *Aleutian World War II National Historic Area*; National Park Service; accessed 2017; https://www.nps.gov/articles /charles-house-letter.htm.

6. House, "Charles House and the Invasion of Kiska."

7. House, "Charles House and the Invasion of Kiska."

8. House, "Charles House and the Invasion of Kiska."

9. House, "Charles House and the Invasion of Kiska."

10. House, "Charles House and the Invasion of Kiska."

Chapter 3

1. Paul Carrigan, memoir provided by program manager, Aleutian World War II National Historical Area, National Park Service, Anchorage, AK.

2. Carrigan; memoir.

3. Frederick Rust, *18th Engineers Regimental Diary*; from Brian Garfield archive, Special Collections and University Archives, Univ. of Oregon, Eugene.

Chapter 4

1. Billy Wheeler, *"History of the 36th Bombardment Squadron (H),"* records group 342, National Archives, Washington, DC.

2. Hale Burge (transcript from recorded memoir), "Hale Burge Interview," *Aleutian World War II National Historic Area*; National Park Service, accessed 2017, https://www.nps.gov/aleu/learn/photosmultimedia/upload/Hale-Burge-Clip-7-508.pdf.

3. Excerpt from "Ode to Spam"; *Cheechako Don in Alaska and Aleutians: Collections of a GI*, Anchorage, AK, Alaskan Publishing, 1945, Anchorage, p. 25.

4. John W. Pletcher (transcript from interview of Aug. 24, 2006), "Interview with John W. Pletcher," *World War II Unalaska Oral History Project,* National Park Service, accessed 2017, https://www.nps.gov/aleu/learn/photosmultimedia/upload/John-Pletcher-Clip-28-t-508.pdf.

Chapter 5

1. Floyd Erickson (transcript from recorded memoir of Mar. 7, 2009), "Floyd Harry Erickson," *The Veterans' History Project*, Library of Congress, accessed 2017, https://memory.loc.gov/diglib/vhp/story/loc.natlib.afc2001001.66422/transcript?ID=sr0001.
2. Billy Wheeler, *"History of the 36th Bombardment Squadron (H),"* records group 342, National Archives; Washington, DC.
3. Mack Collings (transcript from recorded memoir of Mar. 28, 2012), "Interview with Mack Collings," *Aleutian World War II National Historic Area Oral History Program*, National Park Service, accessed 2017, https://www.nps.gov/aleu/learn/photosmultimedia/upload/Collings-Transcript.pdf.
4. Paul Carrigan, memoir provided by program manager, Aleutian World War II National Historical Area, National Park Service, Anchorage, AK.
5. Frank Carnes, "Frank Carnes," *Aleutian World War II National Historic Area*, National Park Service, accessed 2017, https://www.nps.gov/aleu/learn/photosmultimedia /upload/Aleutians-Carnes-all-508.pdf.
6. Charles Fitzpatrick, "VPB-136 History," *From Then until Now; My Journal; US Navy Patrol Squadrons,* accessed 2017, https://www.vpnavy.com/fitzpatrick.html.
7. Bernard Mehren, "Shemya scrapbooks—Bernard Walsh Mehren—1944-1945+," *Shemya, Aleutian Islands, AK*, accessed 2017, http://shemya.hlswilliwaw.com/index_htm_files/Memoirs_of_Bernard_W_Mehren_WWII..pdf.
8. Frank Davis, from Brian Garfield archive, AX 294, Special Collections and University Archives, Univ. of Oregon Libraries, Eugene, OR.
9. John Pletcher (transcript from interview), "John Pletcher," *Aleutian World War II National Historic Area*, National Park Service, accessed 2017, https://www.nps.gov/people/john-pletcher.htm.
10. James Havron (transcript from interview of Sept. 16, 2002), "Interview with James C. Havron," *The Veteran's History Project*, Library of Congress, accessed 2017, http://memory.loc.gov /diglib/vhp/story/loc.natlib.afc2001001.09552/transcript?ID=sr000.
11. Mark Forseth (quoting his father Roald Forseth), "World War II Memories That Will Never Be Forgotten," *Baltimore Post-Examiner* (online edition), May 28, 2012, accessed 2017, https://baltimorepostexaminer.com/world-war-ii-memories- that-never-will-be-forgotten/2012/05/28.

Chapter 6

1. Probable author: Lewis "Pat" Patteson, from unidentified publication in Special Collections and Archives, University of Oregon Library, Eugene, accessed 2017.
2. "The Rambling Wreck"; *Air Force Magazine*, 1943, December issue, Air Force Assn., Arlington, VA, accessed 2017, p. 26, https://www.airforcemag.com.
3. Brian Garfield, from Garfield archive, AX 294, Special Collections and University Archives; University of Oregon Libraries, Eugene, OR, accessed 2017.

4. Bernard Mehren, "Shemya Scrapbooks—Bernard Walsh Mehren—1944-1945+," *Shemya, Aleutian Islands, AK,* accessed 2017, http://shemya.hlswilliwaw.com/index_htm_files/Memoirs_of_Bernard_W_Mehren_WWII..pdf.

5. Harry Bailey, "Harry Bailey Interview"; *Aleutian World War II National Historic Area,* National Park Service, accessed 2017, https://www.nps.gov/articles/000/harry-bailey-interview.htm.

6. Garfield, from the Garfield archive.

7. L. O. Gardner, "Baptism of Fire," *Air Force Magazine,* Service Journal of the US Army Air Forces, 1943, Feb. issue, pp. 17–24, accessed 2017, https://media.defense.gov/2011/Apr/25/2001330205/-1/-1/0/AFD-110425-054.pdf.

8. Bill Thies, "*Lt. William Thies—VP42—Fleet Air Wing 4—The Aleutians 1941–1942,*" revised Aug. 27, 2007, accessed 2017, https://www.angelfire.com/wa/wathies/billthies1.html.

9. Ray Galloway, *"A Year in the Aleutian Islands, July 1942–1943,"* Special Collections (SFM 231), Univ. of Oregon Libraries, Eugene, OR.

10. Murray Hanson, "The Aleuts: Flying PBYs with VP-61 in the Aleutians," *Military Journal Online,* Issue #1, Merriam Press, accessed 2017; https://www.merriam-press.com/ww2ejour/articles/iss_001/is001_08.htm.

11. Charles Fitzpatrick, "VPB-136 History," *From Then until Now; My Journal; US Navy Patrol Squadrons,* accessed 2017, https://www.vpnavy.com/fitzpatrick.html.

12. Firzpatrick; "VPB-136 History."

13. Bernard Mehren, "Memoirs of Bernard Walsh Mehren WX Observer, Shemya, Alaska WWII," *Shemya, Aleutian Islands, AK,* accessed 2017, http://shemya.hls-williwaw.com/index_htm_files/Memoirs_of_Bernard_W_Mehren_WWII..pdf.

14. Royal Sorensen, Brian Garfield archive, AX 294, Special Collections and University Archives, University of Oregon Libraries, Eugene, OR, accessed 2017.

15. Fitzpatrick, "VPB-136 History."

16. Bill Maris, "Flight Log of VP-43," *Bill Maris Stories,* Aleutian World War II National Historic Area, National Park Service, accessed 2017, https://www.nps.gov/aleu/learn/photosmultimedia/upload/maris-flight-log-508.pdf.

Chapter 7

1. Bill Thies, transcript from interview of September 15, 2010; *"Interview with William Nouris Thies,"* Aleutian World War II Historical Area Oral History Project, National Park Service, accessed 2017, https://www.nps.gov/aleu/learn/photosmultimedia/upload/Thies-Transcript-508.pdf.

2. Roger Vance, from letter home, SSFM 229 collection, University of Oregon Libraries, Eugene, OR, accessed 2017.

3. James Beardsley, excerpt from poem, "Kiska Mission," *Air Force Magazine*; 1943, Oct. issue, Air Force Association, Arlington, VA, p. 16.

4. Irving Waddlington; "Surprise Raid on Kiska," *Air Force Magazine,* 1943, Air Force Association, Arlington, VA, p. 19.

5. Herbert Ringold, Brian Garfield archive, AX 294, Special Collections and University Archives; University of Oregon Libraries, Eugene, OR, accessed 2017.

6. Billy Wheeler, *"History of the 36th Bombardment Squadron (H),"* records group 342, National Archives, Washington, DC.

7. Ira Wintermute, "War in the Fog," *Windemuth Family News Letter,* Jan. 2013, accessed 2017, www.windemuth.org/adobe/january-2013.pdf.

8. John Stavinoh, transcript from interview of Nov. 12, 2011, "Interview with John Stavinoha," *Experiencing War—Stories from the Veterans' History Project*, Library of Congress, accessed 2017, https://memory.loc.gov/diglib/vhp-stories/loc.natlib. afc2001001.87592/transcript?ID=sr0001.

9. Lawrence Reineke, excerpt from his poetry, SFM 234 archive, Special Collections and University Archives, University of Oregon, Eugene, OR, accessed 2017.

10. "As Others See Us," *The Adakian*, vol. 1, number 19, 1944, January 29 (probable), US Army; Adak Island.

Chapter 8

1. Paul Carrigan, memoir provided by program manager, Aleutian World War II National Historical Area, National Park Service, Anchorage, AK.

2. Harry Bailey, "Harry Bailey's WWII Service on a Power Barge," *Aleutian World War II Historical Area Oral History Project,* National Park Service, accessed 2017, https://www.nps.gov/articles/aleu-memoir-bailey.htm.

Chapter 9

1. Earl Long, transcript from interview of May 17, 1999, "Interview with Earl W. Long," *Experiencing War—Stories from the Veterans' History Project,* Library of Congress, accessed 2017, https://memory.loc.gov/diglib/vhp-stories/loc.natlib. afc2001001.02316/transcript?ID=sr0001.

2. Bill Thies, *"Lt. William Thies—VP42—Fleet Air Wing 4—The Aleutians 1941–1942,"* revised August 27, 2007, https://www.angelfire.com/wa/wathies/billthies1.html.

3. Joe Baldeschi, "Joseph Baldeschi Interview," *Aleutian World War II Historical Area*; National Park Service, accessed 2017, https://www.nps.gov/articles/joseph-baldeschi.htm.

4. Paul Carrigan, memoir provided by program manager, Aleutian World War II National Historical Area, National Park Service, Anchorage, AK.

5. Carrigan; memoir.

6. Royal Sorensen, Brian Garfield archive, AX 294, Special Collections and University Archives; University of Oregon Libraries, Eugene, OR, accessed 2017.

7. Carrigan, memoir.

8. Carrigan, memoir.

9. Carrigan, memoir.

10. Mac McGalliard, "Mac McGalliard's War Stories," *Aleutian World War II National Historic Area,* National Park Service, accessed 2017, https://www.nps.gov/articles/000/mac-mcgalliard-stories.htm.

11. Billy Wheeler, *"History of the 36th Bombardment Squadron (H),"* records group 342, National Archives, Washington, DC.

12. Carrigan, memoir.

13. Charles Fitzpatrick, "VPB-136 History," *From Then until Now; My Journal*; US Navy Patrol Squadrons, accessed 2017, https://www.vpnavy.com/fitzpatrick.html.

Chapter 10

1. Earl Long, "Interview with Earl W. Long," *Experiencing War-Stories from the Veterans' History Project,* Library of Congress, accessed 2017, https://memory.loc.gov/diglib/vhp-stories/loc.natlib.afc2001001.02316/transcript?ID=sr0001.
2. Mack Collings, "Interview with Mack Collings," *Aleutian World War II National Historical Area Oral History Program,* National Park Service, accessed 2017; https://www.nps.gov/aleu/learn/photosmultimedia/upload/Collings-Transcript.pdf.
3. Harry Bailey, "Harry Bailey's WWII Service on a Power Barge," *Aleutian World War II Historical Area Oral History Project,* National Park Service, accessed 2017, https://www.nps.gov/articles/aleu-memoir-bailey.htm.

Chapter 11

1. Brian Garfield quoting poem by William Eareckson, *"The Thousand-Mile War: World War II in Alaska and the Aleutians,* 1982, January, Bantam Books, New York, NY, p. 211.
2. Dean Galles, "Interview with Dean E. Galles," *Experiencing War-Stories from the Veterans' History Project*, Library of Congress, accessed 2017, https://memory.loc.gov/diglib/vhp-stories/loc.natlib.afc2001001.76663/transcript?ID=mv0001.
3. William Jones; *American Veterans' Center*; accessed 2017; https://www.american-veteranscenter.org/avc-media/magazine/wwiichronicles/wwii-chron-issue-1-page-test/the-battle-of-attu.
4. H. D. Long, *Aleutian Magazine,* 1943, July, accessed in Brian Garfield archive, AX 294, Special Collections and University Archives, University of Oregon Libraries, Eugene, OR.
5. Galles, "Interview with Dean E. Galles."
6. Long, *Aleutian Magazine.*
7. Paul Carrigan, memoir provided by Program Manager, Aleutian World War II National Historical Area, National Park Service, Anchorage, AK, chapter XXII, pp. 32–33.
8. "The Attack on Clevesy Pass—2," *The Capture of Attu: As Told by the Men Who Fought There,* 1944, October, The Infantry Journal, Washington, DC, pp. 70–71.
9. Theodore Miller, *The Capture of Attu,* p. 147.
10. *The Capture of Attu,* p. 162.
11. Darwin Krystall, *The Capture of Attu,* pp.135–136.
12. Paul Nobuo Tatsuguchi (translated), "Diary of Nebu Tatsuguri," *The Aleutians,* accessed 2017, http://aleutians.hlswilliwaw.com/Attu/html/attu-diary_of_nebu_tat-suguri.htm.
13. *The Capture of Attu,* p. 164.
14. Galles, "Interview with Dean E. Galles."
15. *The Capture of Attu,* pp. 164–165.
16. Lawrence Kelley, *The Capture of Attu,* pp. 167–168.
17. George Buehler, *The Capture of Attu,* pp. 171–174.

18. Paul Carrigan, memoir provided by program manager, Aleutian World War II National Historical Area, National Park Service, Anchorage, AK, chapter XXII, pp. 68–69.

Chapter 12

1. Nate White, "Officers' Clubs and Men's Morale," *Mifflinburg Telegraph,* 1946, Jan. 3, Mifflinburg, PA, accessed 2017.
2. Mac McGalliard, "Mac McGalliard's War Stories—Part Two," *Aleutian World War II National Historic Area,* National Park Service, accessed 2017, https://www.nps.gov/articles/aleu-memoir-mcgalliard-2.htm.
3. Oliver Glenn, "On Thin Ice: A Memoir of the Aleutian Campaign," *Foundation Magazine,* Naval Aviation Museum Foundation, Pensacola, FL, Fall 2013, http://www.navalaviationfoundation.org/namf/documents/oliver-glenn-foundation-magazine.pdf.
4. Mac McGalliard, "Mac McGalliard's War Stories—Part Two."
5. Eliot Asinof, unpublished memoir, "My War on Adak and Elsewhere," provided by family.
6. Asinof, "My War on Adak."
7. Paul Carrigan, memoir provided by program manager, Aleutian World War II National Historical Area, National Park Service, Anchorage, AK, accessed 2017, chapter XX, pp. 96–97.
8. Carrigan, memoir, chapter XXI, p. 41.
9. Asinof, "My War on Adak."
10. Henry Lesa, "Interview with Henry Lesa," *Experiencing War-Stories from the Veterans' History Project,* Library of Congress, accessed 2017, https://memory.loc.gov/diglib/vhp-stories/loc.natlib.afc2001001.02547/transcript?ID=mv0001.
11. McGalliard, "Mac McGalliard's War Stories—Part Five."
12. Bill Maris, "Bill Maris Stories—Keeping Up Morale," *Aleutian World War II National Historic Area,* National Park Service, accessed 2017, https://www.nps.gov/aleu/learn/photosmultimedia/upload/maris-Morale-508.pdf.
13. Excerpts from court-martial record, USS *Challenge,* National Archives, Seattle, accessed 2017.
14. Harry B. Paul Jr., letter to parents in Wisconsin, 1945, author's collection.
15. Murray Hanson, "The Aleuts: Flying PBYs with VP-61 in the Aleutians," *Military Journal Online #1,* accessed 2017, https://www.merriam-press.com/ww2ejour/articles/iss_001/is001_08.htm.
16. Charles Fitzpatrick, "VPB-136 History," *From Then until Now; My Journal,* US Navy Patrol Squadrons, accessed 2017; https://www.vpnavy.com/fitzpatrick.html.
17. Fitzpatrick, "VPB-136 History."

Chapter 13

1. Earl Long, "Interview with Earl W. Long," *Experiencing War—the Veterans' History Project,* Library of Congress, 1999, May 17, accessed 2017, https://memory.loc.gov/diglib/vhp-stories/loc.natlib.afc2001001.02316/transcript?ID=sr0001.
2. *Battle Stations!* magazine, 1996, Fall edition, Canoga Park, CA, p. 22.

3. Gerald E. Doescher (as told to John Howsden), "My Service on the USS *Pasco*," Columbia College, accessed 2017, https://www.gocolumbia.edu/library/stories/doescher/doescher.php.
4. Charles Fitzpatrick, "VPB-136 History," *From Then until Now; My Journal*, U.S. Navy Patrol Squadrons, accessed 2017, https://www.vpnavy.com/fitzpatrick.html.
5. Mac McGalliard, "Mac McGalliard's War Stories—Part Six," *Aleutian World War II National Historic Area*, National Park Service, accessed 2017, https://www.nps.gov/articles/aleu-memoir-mcgalliard-6.htm.
6. Harry B. Paul Jr., letter to parents, 1946, author's collection.
7. Ottis Littlejohn, "Interview with Ottis Littlejohn," *Aleutian World War II National Historic Area Oral History Program*, National Park Service, https://www.nps.gov/aleu/learn/photosmultimedia/upload/Littlejohn-Transcript-508.pdfript-508.pdf.
8. Paul Carrigan, memoir provided by program manager, Aleutian World War II National Historical Area, National Park Service, Anchorage, AK, accessed 2017, chapter XXIII, p. 13.
9. Carrigan, memoir, chapter XXIII, p. 34.
10. Carrigan, memoir, chapter XXIII, pp. 39–40.
11. Carrigan, memoir, chapter XXIII, pp. 48–50
12. Doescher, "My Service on the USS *Pasco*."
13. Doescher, "My Service on the USS *Pasco*."

Chapter 14

1. "Laying the Groundwork," *Air Force Magazine*, 1943, Oct. issue, Air Force Association, Arlington, VA, 2017, pp. 14–15, https://www.airforcemag.com.
2. Paul Carrigan, memoir provided by Program Manager, Aleutian World War II National Historical Area, National Park Service, Anchorage, AK, chapter XX, p. 7.

Chapter 15

1. Charles Fitzpatrick, "VPB-136 History," *From Then until Now; My Journal*, U.S. Navy Patrol Squadrons, accessed 2017, https://www.vpnavy.com/fitzpatrick.html.
2. Walter Kellog, *"World War II in Alaska: Reminiscences,"* accessed 2017, https://walterkellogg.wordpress.com/reminiscences.
3. Samuel McKay, "Samuel 'Mack' McKay Letters Home," *Aleutian World War II National Historic Area*, National Park Service, accessed 2017, https://www.nps.gov/media/photo/gallery.htm?pg=6508759&id=ECAEC5FE-1DD8-B71B-0B99ED92C777EC06.
4. "Mail," *Air Force Magazine*, 1943, Dec. issue, Air Force Association, Arlington, VA, 2017, p. 26, https://www.airforcemag.com.
5. Eliot Asinof, unpublished memoir, "My War on Adak and Elsewhere," provided by family.
6. Jerry Dubuque, "Shemya Scrapbooks, Jerry Dubuque—1943–1946," *Shemya, Aleutian Islands, AK*, accessed 2017, https://www.hlswilliwaw.com/Shemya/shemya_scrapbook_jerry_dubuque.htm.
7. Robert Glassburn, "The Sad Saga of Pvt. McFudd," *Cheechako Don in Alaska and Aleutians: Collections of a G.I.*; 1945, Alaskan Publishing, Anchorage, p. 21.

Chapter 16

1. Harry Paul Jr., letter to parents, 1945, author's collection.
2. Brian Garfield archive, AX 294, Special Collections and University Archives, Univ. of Oregon Libraries, Eugene, OR, http://archiveswest.orbiscascade.org/ark:/80444/xv11126.
3. Earl Long, "Interview with Earl W. Long," *Experiencing War—Stories from the Veterans' History Project,* Library of Congress, accessed 2017, https://memory.loc.gov/diglib/vhp-stories/loc.natlib.afc2001001.02316/transcript?ID=sr0001.
4. Frank Carnes, "Frank Carnes," *Aleutian World War II National Historic Area,* National Park Service, accessed 2017, https://www.nps.gov/aleu/learn/photosmultimedia /upload/Aleutians-Carnes-all-508.pdf.

Chapter 17

1. Milt Zack, "Milt's Military Memoirs: Part III—Overseas," accessed 2017, archived website, http://www.oocities.org/tempelhof.geo/warstories.html.
2. Charles Fitzpatrick, "VPB-136 History," *From Then until Now; My Journal,* US Navy Patrol Squadrons, accessed 2017, https://www.vpnavy.com/fitzpatrick.html.
3. Fitzpatrick, "VPB-136 History."
4. Fitzpatrick, "VPB-136 History."
5. Fitzpatrick, "VPB-136 History."
6. Ray Duncan, "Stairway to the Kuriles," *Yank* magazine, 1945, August 31, US Army, Seattle, WA, pp. 2–4.
7. Joe Baldeschi, "Interview with Joe Baldeschi," *Aleutian World War II National Historic Area Oral History Program,* National Park Service, accessed 2017, https://www.nps.gov/aleu/learn/photosmultimedia/upload/Joe-Baldeschi-transcript-508.pdf.
8. "Kuriles Photo Missions and Nishizawa's Lost Battle," *North Pacific Skies—People and Machines,* accessed 2017, https://www.norpacwar.com/kurile-photo-missions.
9. Louis Blau and Frank Gash, "Bombs for Paramushiru," *Air Force Magazine,* 1943, Nov., Air Force Association, Arlington, VA; 2017, p. 26.
10. Zack; "Milt's Military Memoirs: Part III—Overseas."
11. Thomas Erickson, "Thomas Erickson, World War II Co-pilot in the Aleutians," *Aleutian World War II National Historic Area,* National Park Service, accessed 2017, https://www.nps.gov/articles/aleu-memoir-erickson.htm.
12. Baldeschi, "Interview with Joe Baldeschi."
13. Fitzpatrick, "VPB-136 History."

Chapter 18

1. Allan Berube, *Coming Out under Fire: The History of Gay Men and Women in World War Two,* 1990, Free Press, division of Simon and Schuster, New York, p. 48.
2. Paul Carrigan, memoir provided by program manager, Aleutian World War II National Historical Area, National Park Service, Anchorage, AK, accessed 2017, chapter XXII, p. 63.
3. Carrigan, memoir, chapter XXII, pp. 63–65.
4. Berube, *Coming Out under Fire,* p. 37.
5. Berube, *Coming Out under Fire,* p. 181.

6. Paul Carrigan, memoir, chapter XXI, pp. 42–43.
7. Thomas Erickson, "Thomas Erickson, World War II Co-pilot in the Aleutians," *Aleutian World War II National Historic Area,* National Park Service, accessed 2017, https://www.nps.gov/articles/aleu-memoir-erickson.htm.
8. Carrigan, memoir, chapter XXV, p. 28.
9. "A Taking Girl," *Overseas Chatter,* navy newsletter on Kiska, Mar. 1944, National Archives, Seattle.
10. James McCrary, *Overseas Chatter,* Oct. 1943; National Archives, Seattle.

Chapter 19

1. Van Vechten, AX 294, Special Collections and University Archives, Univ. of Oregon Libraries, Eugene, OR.
2. Fred Ellis, excerpt from "Aleutian Blues," *Aleutian Poetry by Fred Ellis,* accessed 2017, http://aleutians.hlswilliwaw.com/Aleutians/html/aleutians-poems.htm.
3. Vechten, AX 294, Special Collections.
4. Paul Carrigan, memoir provided by program manager, Aleutian World War II National Historical Area, National Park Service, Anchorage, AK, accessed 2017, chapter XXV, pp. 21–24.
5. Murray Hanson, "The Aleuts: Flying PBYs with VP-61 in the Aleutians," *Military Journal Online Issue #1,* Merriam Press, accessed 2017, https://www.merriam-press.com/ww2ejour/articles/iss_001/is001_08.htm.
6. Eliot Asinof, unpublished memoir, "My War on Adak and Elsewhere," provided by family.
7. Mark Forseth quoting his father, Roald Forseth, "World War II Memories That Will Never Be Forgotten," *Baltimore Post-Examiner* (online edition), 2012, May 28, accessed 2017, https://baltimorepostexaminer.com/world-war-ii-memories-that-never-will-be-forgotten/2012/05/28.
8. Earl Long, "Interview with Earl W. Long," *Experiencing War—Stories from the Veterans' History Project,* Library of Congress, May 17, 1999, accessed 2017, https://memory.loc.gov/diglib/vhp-stories/loc.natlib.afc2001001.02316/transcript?ID=sr0001.
9. Bill Grigsby and Gene Fox, *Grigs! A Beauuutiful Life,* 2004, August 1, Sports Publishing, Champaign, IL.

Chapter 20

1. Dale Standley, "The U.S. Navy during World War II: One Man's Experience," Tacoma Community History Project, Univ. of Washington/Tacoma library, accessed 2017, https://digitalcollections.lib.washington.edu/digital/collection/tacomacomm/id/380/rec/5.
2. Charles Fitzpatrick, "VPB-136 History," *From Then until Now; My Journal,* US Navy Patrol Squadrons, accessed 2017, https://www.vpnavy.com/fitzpatrick.html.
3. George Sinclair, "Navy War Diary—Aleutian Front," *Scott Nelson Art,* accessed 2017, http://scottnelsonart.com/navy-war-diary-aleutian-front.

Chapter 21

1. Paul Carrigan, memoir provided by program manager, Aleutian World War II National Historical Area, National Park Service, Anchorage, AK, accessed 2017, chapter XXVI, pp. 11–12.

2. Eliot Asinof, unpublished memoir, "My War on Adak and Elsewhere," provided by family.

3. Asinof, unpublished memoir.

4. Asinof, unpublished memoir.

5. Charles Fitzpatrick, "VPB-136 History," *From Then until Now; My Journal,* US Navy Patrol Squadrons, accessed 2017, https://www.vpnavy.com/fitzpatrick.html.

6. Andy Anderson, "Walter 'Andy' Anderson," *Aleutian World War II National Historic Area;* National Park Service, accessed 2017, https://www.nps.gov/people/andy-anderson.htm.

7. Letter home from "Lou," National Archives at Seattle, written Jan. 23, 1945.

8. Paul Carrigan, memoir, chapter XXVI, pp. 13–20.

9. Paul Carrigan, memoir, chapter XXI, pp. 24–26.

10. Robert DeWolfe, from 1945 Christmas menu, USN, Adak, in author's collection.

11. Bernard Mehren, "Shemya scrapbooks—Bernard Walsh Mehren—1944–1945+," *Shemya, Aleutian Islands, AK,* written Dec. 25, 1944, accessed 2017, http://shemya.hlswilliwaw.com/index_htm_files/Memoirs_of_Bernard_W_Mehren_WWII..pdf.

Chapter 22

1. Robert Brown, "Interview with Col. Robert Brown," *Aleutian World War II National Historic Area Oral History Program,* National Park Service, accessed 2017, https://www.nps.gov/aleu/learn/photosmultimedia/upload/Lt-Col-Robert-Brown-508.pdf.

2. Harry Paul Jr., letter home to parents, 1946, author's collection.

3. Mac McGalliard, "Mac McGalliard's War Stories—Part Five," *Aleutian World War II National Historic Area,* National Park Service, accessed 2017, https://www.nps.gov/articles/aleu-memoir-mcgalliard-5.htm.

4. Mark Forseth quoting his father, Roald Forseth, "World War II Memories That Will Never Be Forgotten," *Baltimore Post-Examiner* (online edition), 2012, May 28, accessed 2017, https://baltimorepostexaminer.com/world-war-ii-memories-that-never-will-be-forgotten/2012/05/28.

5. Earl Long, "Interview with Earl W. Long," *Experiencing War—Stories from the Veterans' History Project,* Library of Congress, May 17, 1999, accessed 2017, https://memory.loc.gov/diglib/vhp-stories/loc.natlib.afc2001001.02316/transcript?ID=sr0001.

Chapter 23

1. Bill Jones, inscription on plaque on Attu Island.

2. Stefan Milkowski, "Trip to Adak Island Makes for Interesting, and Successful Caribou Hunt," *Fairbanks Daily News Miner* (online edition), Apr. 18, 2014, Fairbanks, AK, accessed 2017, https://www.newsminer.com/features/outdoors/trip-to-adak-island-makes-for-interesting-and-successful-caribou/article_d29b7336-c6a5-11e3-b9e5-001a4bcf6878.html.

Bibliography

Books

Chandonnet, Fern. *Alaska at War: The Forgotten War Remembered 1941–1945*. Fairbanks: Univ. of Alaska Press, 2008.

Cloe, John Haile. *Attu: The Forgotten Battle*. National Park Service and the Government Printing Office.

Cohen, Stan. *The Forgotten War: A Pictorial History of World War II in Alaska and Northwestern Canada*. Missoula, MT: Pictorial Histories, 1981.

Cook, Linda. *World War II in the Aleutians*. Anchorage, AK: US Dept. of the Interior, 1992.

Daves, Ray, and Carol Edgemon Hipperson. *Radioman: An Eyewitness Account of Pearl Harbor and World War II in the Pacific*. New York: St. Martin's, 2008.

Fitzpatrick, Charles. *From Then until Now; My Journal*. Self-published.

Ford, Corey. *Short Cut to Tokyo: The Battle for the Aleutians*. New York: Charles Scribner's Sons, 1943. Contains Ford's earlier articles for *Collier's* magazine.

Fussell, Paul. *The Great War and Modern Memory*. New York: Oxford Univ. Press, 1975.

Garfield, Brian. *The Thousand-Mile War: World War II in Alaska and the Aleutians*. New York: Doubleday, 1982.

Goldstein, Donald, and Katherine Dillon. *The Williwaw War: The Arkansas National Guard in the Aleutians in World War II*. Fayetteville: Univ. of Arkansas Press, 1992.

Grigsby, Bill, and Gene Fox. *Grigs! A Beauuutiful Life*. Champaign, IL: Sports Publishing, 2004.

Hammett, Dashiell, and Robert Colodny. *The Battle for the Aleutians: A Graphic History 1942–1943*. Army publication, 1944.

Jeffers, Joe. *My World War II Air Combat: Learning the Facts of Life by Trial and Error*. Victoria, BC: Univ. of Akron Martin B-26 Archives Advisory Council, 2003.

Jones, John Bush. *The Songs That Fought the War: Popular Music and the Home Front, 1939–1945*. Waltham, MA: Brandeis Univ. Press, 2006.

Meredith, William. *Love Letter from an Impossible Land*. New Haven, CT: Yale Univ. Press, 1944.

Page, Martin. *The Bawdy Songs and Ballads of Word War II*. Bungay, UK: Granada, 1982.

Perras, Galen Roger. *Stepping Stones to Nowhere—the Aleutian Islands, Alaska, and American Military Strategy, 1867–1945*. Vancouver, BC: UBC Press, Univ. of British Columbia, 2003.

Smith, Donald. *Cheechako Don in Alaska and Aleutians: Collections of a G.I.* Anchorage, AK: Alaskan Publishing.

War Department. *The Capture of Attu: As Told by the Men Who Fought There*. Washington, DC: Infantry Journal, 1944.

War Psychiatry. Office of Surgeon General (US). TMM Series, 1995.

Periodicals

Air Force Magazine. WWII issues. Archives of Air Force Association, Arlington, VA.

"Aleutian Attack: U.S. Armada Occupies Andreanofs." *LIFE* magazine, Oct. 19, 1942, p. 38–39.

Burns, George Creswell. Neuropsychiatric Problems at an Aleutian Post. *American Journal of Psychiatry*, Sept. 1945, p. 207.

Forseth, Mark. World War II Memories That Will Never Be Forgotten. *Baltimore Post-Examiner* (online edition), Baltimore, MD; May 28, 2012.

Porco, Peter. Dashing Dashiell Hammett's Adak Newspaper for the Troops (Jan. 18, 2015) and When the President Came to Dinner: FDR in Alaska (September 11, 2014). *Anchorage Daily News*, Anchorage, AK.

The Adakian. US Army's WWII newspaper on Adak Island. Several (plus many separated cartoons) are in author's collection. Some are in the collection of the Beinecke Rare Book and Manuscript Library, Univ. of Connecticut, Hartford, CT. Others are in the National Archives in Seattle.

White, Nate. Officers' Clubs and Men's Morale. *Mifflinburg Telegraph*, Mifflinburg, PA. 1946.

Yank. WWII magazine published by War Department, New York. All issues available (in 2021) at https://onlinebooks.library.upenn.edu/webbin/serial?id=yank1942.

Archives

Beinecke Rare Book and Manuscript Library, Univ. of Connecticut, Hartford, CT.

Brian Garfield archive. Research notes and materials for his book *The Thousand-Mile War*. Special Collections and University Archives, Univ. of Oregon Library, Eugene, OR.

Collections and University Archives, SFM 234 and SSFM 229 collections, Univ. of Oregon Library, Eugene, OR.

National Archives, records group 342, Washington, DC.

National Archives, Alaska Collection, Seattle, WA.

Online

Doescher, Gerald E. "My Service on the USS Pasco." Columbia College, accessed 2017, https://www.gocolumbia.edu/library/stories/doescher/doescher.php.

Dubuque, Jerry. "Shemya Scrapbooks, Jerry Dubuque—1943–1946; Shemya, Aleutian Islands, AK." accessed 2017, https://www.hlswilliwaw.com/Shemya/shemya_scrapbook_jerry_dubuque.htm.

Hanson, Murray. "The Aleuts: Flying PBYs with VP-61 in the Aleutians." Military Journal Online Issue #1, accessed 2021, https://www.merriam-press.com/ww2ejour/articles/iss_001/is001_08.htm.

Kellog, Walter. "World War II in Alaska: Reminiscences." Accessed 2017, https://walterkellogg.wordpress.com/reminiscences.

Library of Congress. "The Aleutian Islands: WWII's Unknown Campaign." Experiencing War: Stories from the Veterans' History Project, accessed 2017, https://www.loc.gov/vets/stories/ex-war-aleutians.html.

National Park Service (Alaska) WWII web sites with numerous Aleutian interviews, memoirs and photographs:

Veterans of the Marines. www.nps.gov/aleu/learnculture/marines.htm

Veterans of the US Navy. www.nps.gov/aleu/learn/historyculture/navy.htm

Veterans of the US Army and the Army Air Corps. www.nps.gov/aleu/historyculture/navy.htm

Veterans of the US Coast Guard. www.nps/gov/aleu/learn/historyculture/army.htm

Veterans of the Canadian Armed Forces. www.nps.gov/aleu/learn/historyculture.canadian-forces.htm

Aerographers. www.nps.gov/articles/000/aerographers.htm

Aleutian Servicemen. www.nps.gov/learn/historyculture/aleutian-servicemen.htm

The Invasion of Kiska. www.jps.gov/articles/the-invasion-of-kiska.htm

Oral Histories. www.nps.gov/subjects/worldwarii/oralhistories.htm

Women in World War II. www.nps.gov/subjects/worldwarii/women.htm

Series: World War II Military Unit Histories [Aleutian]. www.nps.gov/articles/series.htm?id=C434C5FB-C68A-00B2-E531EDFB1A5418F8.

Thies, William. "Lt. William Thies—VP442—Fleet Air Wing 4—The Aleutians 1941–1942." Accessed 2017, https://www.angelfire.com/wa/wathies/billthies1.html.

Wintermute, Ira. "War in the Fog." Windermuth Family News Letter, January 2013, accessed 2017, www.windermuth.org/adobe/january-2013/pdf.

Zack, Milt. "Milt's Military Memoirs: Part III—Overseas." Accessed 2017, archived website, http://www.oocities.org/tempelhof.geo/warstories.html.

Index